CASSIODORUS

James J. O'Donnell

CASSIODORUS

University of California Press
Berkeley · Los Angeles · London

University of California Press
Berkeley and Los Angeles, California

University of California Press, Ltd.
London, England

ISBN 0-520-03646-8
Library of Congress Catalog Card Number: 77-93470
Printed in the United States of America

1 2 3 4 5 6 7 8 9

Dedicated to
My Mother
In Memory of My Father

Contents

Preface

THREE centuries have passed since the last thoroughgoing scholarly study of the life and works of Cassiodorus saw the light of day in the prolegomena to Garet's 1679 edition of the complete works. The time has come, it seems to me, to take a fresh look at the primary sources, review the accumulated scholarship, and attempt a new survey. Much remains to be done, both on Cassiodorus and on his age; I hope this volume will at least facilitate that work.

To make Cassiodorus accessible to all who might be curious, I have quoted his own words liberally in translations of my own. Some of the renderings verge on paraphrase, not out of ineptitude or intention to deceive, but out of sympathy for the reader. Cassiodorus' prose is wooden and artificial enough in Latin; literally translated into English, it would generally induce deep stupor.

I have incurred a long list of debts in the course of my researches, with no hope of repaying them adequately: to teachers at Princeton (where this book began in the form of several undergraduate papers—most of them never actually written—in 1970–1972), at University College, Dublin (1972–1973), and at Yale (where a dissertation based on an earlier version of chapters 1–3 of what follows was accepted for the doctorate in 1975, supervised by Dean Jaroslav J. Pelikan and examined by Lowry Nelson, Jr., and Gordon Williams); to publishers' readers and others since, whose comments have been never less than useful and often indispensable (some were anonymous, but I know I can thank James W. Halporn and T. D. Barnes); to attentive and critical audiences who heard some of my arguments at Bryn Mawr College (February 1975), the 107th Annual Meeting of the American Philological Association (December 1975), and Colorado College (February 1976); to Bryn Mawr College and to Cornell University for financial assistance in preparing the typescript; to August Frugé of the University of California Press at Berkeley for his sponsorship, encouragement, and criticism (and to the editorial staff there for their meticulous attentions); and to many other friends and colleagues, unwilling victims who have heard a great deal more about Cassiodorus than they cared to these past eight years.

Cassiodorus himself—a little more than sinner, a little less than saint—has been a constant source of inspiration. It is with reluctance that I put the final touches on a work that has served to keep my eyes riveted on so instructive and admonitory an example of what the Christian scholar can and must be. I cannot imagine how I could have employed my time more pleasurably or more profitably than with Cassiodorus as my companion.

J. J. O'D.

Ithaca, New York
February 26, 1978

Abbreviations

I. WORKS BY CASSIODORUS

Quotations from Cassiodorus' writings are always made from the editions cited below and identified in the ways indicated. In addition to the editions listed below, all of Cassiodorus' works are available in volumes 69 and 70 of *Patrologia Latina,* for the most part in the edition of the Maurist J. Garet (1679).

Chron.   *Chronica.* Entries cited by year (in the Dionysian reckoning B.C./A.D.) after the edition of Theodor Mommsen, *Abhandlungen der phil.-hist. Classe der kön. sächischen Gesellschaft der Wissenschaften,* 8 (1861), 547–596; reprinted with a shorter preface in *MGH.AA.*XI (Chron. Min. II), 1894. The full preface is in Mommsen, *Gesammelte Schriften,* 7(1909), 668–690.

Comp.   *Complexiones in Epistulas.* Cited by column and section from *PL* 70.1309–1422, which is a reprint of the edition of Scipio Maffei (Florence, 1721).

De an.   *De anima.* Cited by chapter and line numbers from the edition of J. W. Halporn, *CCSL* 96 (1973), which reprints Halporn's text published in *Traditio,* 16 (1960) 39–109; but the line numbers are not the same in both editions. Halporn's chapter divisions differ from all previous editions.

De orth.   *De orthographia.* Cited by page and line from the edition of H. Keil, *Grammatici Latini* (1880), 7.143–210.

Ex. Ps.   *Expositio Psalmorum.* Cited by Psalm (or, for the preface, by "Praef." and sometimes the chapter thereof) and line numbers from the edition of M. Adriaen, *CCSL* 97–98 (1958).

Get.   *Getica.* Jordanes' abridgment, titled by him *De origine actibusque getarum,* cited from Mommsen's edition, *MGH.AA.*V (1882), using the chapter and section numbers given there. When I wish to refer to Cassiodorus' original work in twelve books, I call it the *Gothic History.*

Hist. trip.	*Historia ecclesiastica tripartita.* Cited by book, chapter, and section, from the edition of W. Jacob and R. Hanslik, *CSEL* 71 (1952).
Inst.	*Institutiones.* Cited by book, chapter, and section, from the edition of R. A. B. Mynors (1937).
Ordo gen.	*Ordo generis Cassiodororum,* also known as the *Anecdoton Holderi.* Cited by line numbers from the edition given in Appendix I, below.
Var.	*Variae.* Cited by book, letter, and section, from the edition of A. J. Fridh, *CCSL* 96 (1973). These references are equally valid for Mommsen's edition, *MGH.AA.*XII (1894).

II. OTHER WORKS

AJP	*American Journal of Philology.*
ALMA	*Archivum Latinitatis Medii Aevi (Bulletin Du Cange).*
Anon. Vales.	Anonymus Valesianus.
BARB	*Bulletin de la classe des lettres et des sciences morales et politiques de l'académie royale du Belgique.*
CCSL	*Corpus Christianorum, Series Latina* (Turnhout).
CIG	*Corpus Inscriptionum Graecarum.*
CIL	*Corpus Inscriptionum Latinarum.*
CJ	*Codex Justinianus.*
Courcelle, *LLW*	P. Courcelle, *Late Latin Writers and Their Greek Sources* (1969).
CSEL	*Corpus Scriptorum Ecclesiasticorum Latinorum* (Vienna).
DA	*Dissertation Abstracts* (Ann Arbor).
DACL	*Dictionnaire d'archéologie chrétienne et de liturgie.*
DHGE	*Dictionnaire d'histoire et de géographie ecclésiastiques.*
Fliche et Martin	A. Fliche et V. Martin, eds., *Histoire de l'église.*
HSCP	*Harvard Studies in Classical Philology.*
IG	*Inscriptiones Graecae.*
Jones, *LRE*	A. H. M. Jones, *The Later Roman Empire, 284–602* (1964), using pagination of the American edition to refer to the notes.
JRS	*Journal of Roman Studies.*
JThS	*Journal of Theological Studies.*
Lowe, *CLA*	E. A. Lowe, *Codices Latini Antiquiores* (1934–1971).

Mansi	J. D. Mansi, *Sacrorum Conciliorum Nova et Amplissima Collectio* (1759–1798).
MEFR	*Mélanges d'archéologie et d'histoire de l'École Française de Rome.*
MGH	*Monumenta Germaniae Historica. (AA = Auctores Antiquissimi.)*
PBA	*Proceedings of the British Academy.*
PG	*Patrologia Graeca.*
PL	*Patrologia Latina. (PLS = Patrologiae Latinae Supplementum* [ed. A. Hamman].)
PLRE	*Prospography of the Later Roman Empire* (ed. Jones, Martindale, and Morris).
Reg. Ben.	*Regula Benedicti.*
Rev. Ben.	*Revue Bénédictine.*
RTAM	*Recherches de théologie ancienne et médiévale.*
SC	*Sources Chrétiennes.*
SE	*Sacris Erudiri.*
Settimane	*Settimane di Studio del Centro Italiano di Studi sull'Alto Medioevo* (Spoleto).
SMRL	*Studies in Medieval and Renaissance Latin Language and Literature* (The Catholic University of America).

Chronology

These dates embody the conclusions of this study, but do not always fully reflect uncertainties inherent in those conclusions.

476	Deposition of Romulus Augustulus by Odovacer.
484–490	Cassiodorus born. (His father at this time governing first Sicily, then Lucania et Bruttii.)
493	Theoderic becomes sole ruler of Italy.
c. 503–507	Cassiodorus' father praetorian prefect, Cassiodorus his aide.
507–511	Cassiodorus quaestor.
514	Cassiodorus consul ordinarius.
519	Cassiodorus writes *Chronica, Gothic History*. Eutharic and Justin share the consulship.
523–527	Cassiodorus *magister officiorum*.
526	Theoderic dies.
527	Justinian accedes to eastern throne.
533	Cassiodorus becomes praetorian prefect.
534	Death of Athalaric.
535	Death of Amalasuintha. Gothic war begins. Agapetus becomes pope.
536	Deaths of Theodahad and Pope Agapetus. Cassiodorus delivers oration on the marriage of Witigis and Mathesuentha.
538	Compilation of *Variae*. *De anima* written.
540	Belisarius captures Ravenna. Cassiodorus to Constantinople.
c. 540–548	Writing of *Expositio Psalmorum*.
550	Cassiodorus at Constantinople (Vigilius' testimony).
551	Cassiodorus at Constantinople (Jordanes' testimony). *Getica* published.
553	End of Gothic war. Second Council of Constantinople.

Prologue

Cassiodorus and the Sixth Century

THE sixth century after the birth of Christ must unquestionably but regrettably be assigned to the "Dark Ages." This is not the result of any intrinsic deficiency of illumination so much as of the dimness in which historians, prisoners of the evidence which happenstance caused to survive or perish in the ensuing centuries, are compelled to view it. So ill-attested an age has often been spurned as an illegitimate child by both ancient and medieval historians.[1]

The sixth century is poorly known to us chiefly because it was a fragmented age, following upon the most homogeneous centuries that ancient civilization ever knew. The world was growing more complex again in defiance of the age-long tendency towards centralization and assimilation under the Roman empire. Insofar as modern students attend to the events of this epoch, they usually confine themselves to one or another fragment or cluster of fragments; it is an age in which the specializations of the modern historian begin to replace the more comprehensive approach of the classicist. And yet it is possible, perhaps necessary, to lament this tendency to lose sight of the broader picture. Taken together, all the fragments compose a mosaic of unusual richness and variety.

It is the political fragmentation of Europe that is most obvious to historians accustomed to the extensive pattern of

---

1. The best connected narratives of the period are still T. Hodgkin, *Italy and Her Invaders* (1885), volumes 3 and 4; and J. B. Bury, *History of the Later Roman Empire from the Death of Theodosius I to the Death of Justinian I* (reprint, 1958). But the history of the Ostrogothic kingdom in particular needs to be rewritten.

hegemony exercised by Roman emperors from the first century B.C. onwards. The Roman empire as such had withdrawn for all practical purposes into the eastern Mediterranean world. A rejuvenated Persian force had finally ended Roman claims to be a land power in Asia and regained control of Mesopotamia. What was left of the once-vast realms that had responded to the commands of Roman emperors was now limited to the Greek-speaking eastern shores of the Mediterranean: Asia Minor, the Levant, Egypt, and present day Greece. Territorial claims over the Balkans grew progressively more fantastic when emperors found that they could only rule in those lands through the intermediacy of barbarian chieftains.

A theoretical claim to sovereignty, at least, was maintained over much of the western Mediterranean world as well; but here, too, the real power was in the hands of barbarian tribes that settled in the Latin west during the fifth century. Great Britain was divided between Anglo-Saxons and warring Celts, North Africa acknowledged Vandal control, Visigoths ruled the Iberian peninsula and southern Gaul, much of the rest of Gaul was Frankish, and Italy and much of the northern Balkans as far as modern Hungary answered to the Ostrogoths. Lesser powers controlled smaller stretches of territory, of which the most notable was the Burgundian kingdom, a kind of buffer state between Franks, Visigoths, and Ostrogoths.

This political disintegration was further emphasized by an ensuing cultural fragmentation. Where once an official Roman culture had exercised a measure of domination over the entire Mediterranean world, at least four principal groupings of increasingly independent and mutually hostile character had arisen, complicated by religious differences. The eastern realms still held by the Constantinopolitan emperors were Greek-speaking; Latin remained as a dying language of official documents through the sixth century in the capital itself, but it is legitimate to see in the Greek-speaking Roman empire of the fifth and sixth centuries the foundation of the completely Greek Byzantine empire, which would survive until 1453. Byzantine theological tendencies were generally Monophysite (despite noisy exceptions), tending to hold that the human nature of Christ was at least subordinated to his divine nature, if not entirely subsumed by it—this in contradiction of the teachings of the fourth great ecumenical council of the ancient church at Chalcedon in 451.

In the western lands, Latin continued as the spoken and literary language of the native inhabitants. It was not until the early ninth century that the local dialectization of Latin produced a recognized difference between those "Romance" dialects and "Latin" as a literary language, but the decline of centralized Roman government in the west left room for that slow process of individuation to take place. The Latin west adhered to the doctrines of Chalcedon (over which Pope Leo the Great had exercised considerable influence by remote control), and came increasingly under the spiritual governance of the bishops of Rome in a curious kind of translation of authority from the political to the spiritual realm. The west still looked to Rome for guidance, but for guidance of a different sort.

But the real political power in western Europe lay in the hands of Germanic peoples. Most of the first wave of invaders (including Vandals, Franks, and both of the Gothic tribes) had lived on the fringes of the Roman world long enough to know and appreciate the benefits of Roman culture; their royal families sometimes studied the language of their subjects and seemed to enjoy being praised in Ciceronian periods. But the German peoples were divided among themselves along lines not only national but also religious. The bulk of the eastern Germanic tribes (including Vandals and Goths) had been evangelized in the fourth century by a mission beginning with the Arian bishop Ulfilas, whose translation of scripture into Gothic is the earliest monument of that language. Thus at the period of which we speak, the circle of lands around the western Mediterranean coast was held by Arian invaders living with their orthodox Catholic subjects in greater and lesser degrees of mutual toleration (greater perhaps in Italy, lesser in Vandal North Africa).

But the Franks, whose control of Gaul and neighboring territory would expand slowly but inexorably until reaching its greatest extent in the Carolingian empire, chose to embrace orthodox Catholicism—and thus achieved a greater degree of mutual admiration and respect with their Roman subjects than did the other Germanic tribes. The conversion of Clovis to orthodox Christianity in A.D. 496 is rightly regarded as a landmark of European history.

Not only is the sixth century an age of fragmentation: it was an age in which fragmentation was perceived and regretted. The ambitious emperor Justinian (who reigned at Constantinople from 527 until 565) bestirred himself to do more than bemoan the disorder into which the Roman world had fallen; he set out to rectify it. In an ambitious pattern of conquest, chronicled well and faithfully by his official historian Procopius, he turned his attention successively to the Persians, the Vandals, the Ostrogoths, and the Visigoths. Between the 530's and the 550's, on four fronts at the remotest corners of the old Roman world, he sought to reestablish the Roman empire in all its former glory. His success was at best mixed.

For while the Vandal kingdom in North Africa fell as swiftly as a house of cards, the Ostrogoths proved more tenacious, tying up the Byzantine forces in a seventeen-year war of attrition up and down the Italian peninsula. Justinian was in the end, by his own lights, successful; but in fact he contributed more to the shattering of his world by attempting to restore it than he would have by tolerating what he found. For his successors were unable to maintain his conquests with the resources and vigor that they required; as a result, the Latin west (and to a lesser extent the eastern front with Persia) was left a prey to a second wave of barbarian invasions. These invaders were on the whole less familiar with the benefits of Roman civilization and less conciliatory in their relations with their conquered subjects. In Italy particularly, the political disorder left in the wake of Justinian's reconquest and ensuing invasions may not unfancifully be observed to have lasted at least into the nineteenth century.

Three years after Justinian's death, the first of this new wave of barbarians came down out of central Europe: the Lombards. Not many years later, political power in Italy was uneasily divided among various factions of the Lombards, the Byzantine exarchs at Ravenna, and the popes at Rome. The seventh century saw the entry into Mediterranean consciousness of the forces of Islam, which drove Byzantine forces to retreat from Africa almost as swiftly as they had come and then proceeded to make mincemeat of the Visigoths in Spain. The last blows to the post-imperial order that we perceive in the west in the sixth century came with the eighth-century arrival of the Vikings from the north.

Culturally these successive waves of invasion left eventual chaos. After the first waves, the survival of traditional Latin culture seemed temporarily assured. The ancient schools continued to impart ponderous erudition and precious rhetorical training. The authors of this period show a surprising fidelity to classical norms of language and style; Boethius, Ennodius, and Avitus are ancient, not medieval, in their literary ambitions and achievements. But the second wave of invasions finally demolished the ancient forms of intellectual life, and from the sixth to the eighth centuries intellectual culture became something of a cottage industry, as often as not a utilitarian business directly in the service of the church.

But in the first decades of the sixth century it was possible to be more optimistic than events proved was justified. In the ways just described, the Latin west at this time was a mass of fragments compared to what it had once been; but these fragments were for the most part rationally constituted and governed and were generally at peace with one another. After the turbulence of the fifth century's invasions, a calm had settled back over Europe; even if it was in fact only the calm at the eye of the storm, at the time it gave promise of enduring. It is in this world that the career of our subject began; hence it repays our closer attention.

The Ostrogothic kingdom of Italy at this epoch was in many ways a looking-glass world with a logic all its own. The legal pretense accepted by rulers and subjects alike was that the

German kings held authority—in ways that were usually left carefully undefined—as viceroys for the Roman emperors at Constantinople. The civil government of Italy, in particular, was left in the hands of the large, sometimes suffocatingly efficient bureaucracy that had grown up over generations of imperial rule. The highest offices in this civil government continued to be parceled out to the overeducated representatives of the ancient senatorial aristocracy who looked upon them as their hereditary prerogative. Military power was completely in Gothic hands, but there is little evidence that the native Romans felt threatened by this arrangement. Quite the contrary: the Gothic troops were settled on the land (mostly in the plains of northern Italy) and became part of what they had conquered. In that way they must have seemed to many natives a welcome addition to a peaceful society. For now, instead of relying for defense against wave after wave of invaders on cynical and brutal conscripts in the service of a distant emperor, the natives of Italy could look to their Gothic neighbors as a kind of local militia with a vested interest in defending their own homes as much as those of their Latin-speaking neighbors. The mildly prosperous classes must have felt that at least one's taxes now went to support a military establishment that was a little more likely to be of some real benefit to the taxpayers than what had been the case in the recent past.

For the fifth century had not been a settled time in Italy. Through most of the century, some kind of pretence of imperial rule was kept up from the new capital at Ravenna (to which a cowardly court had fled in 402, seeking comfort in the surrounding marshes as a natural defense against invasion—and finding them in the end a source of malaria). In practice, ever since the regency exercised in the name of Theodosius' sons by Stilicho at the turn of the fifth century, the real power was held by a succession of generals themselves German in origin, commanding armies comprising a motley variety of mostly German troops. More than once it would have been difficult for a stray observer on the field of battle to tell which side was attacking and which defending the Roman empire.

The pretext of government by resident emperors was finally abolished in 476 (the traditional date in old history textbooks for the "Fall of the Roman Empire") in a tawdry sequence of intrigues. The barbarian general Odovacer first created a puppet emperor named Romulus Augustulus (the bitter parody of the names of the first and second founders of Rome went not unnoticed), who was in fact not recognized by the emperor at Constantinople. (Official recognition remained with a prince named Julius Nepos, who did not show his face again in Italy and died in 480.) Odovacer then deposed his puppet and sent the imperial insignia back to Constantinople with the protestation that he would henceforth be firmly loyal to the eastern emperors. In practice, he absolved himself of all possibility of local interference in return for pledging an allegiance that was never more than lip service.

This state of affairs persisted for two hostile and uneasy decades. It was during this time that an open rift (the so-called Acacian schism) occurred between the Roman and Constantinopolitan churches over the Christological dogmas of Chalcedon. For the next three decades, orthodox Catholic Romans would not be in communion with their eastern counterparts and would find it relatively easy to coexist with the tolerant (if rather fundamentalist) German Arians of Italy.

Meanwhile, the eastern emperors were under intermittent pressure from marauding barbarian forces in the Balkans. After a confused period of divided leadership, these forces came to owe their allegiance mostly to a dynamic young Gothic general, Theoderic. The emperor Zeno finally hit upon the strategem of dispatching Theoderic to Italy as his deputy to reclaim the rebellious province to allegiance to the eastern throne. It is probable that Zeno hoped merely to simplify his problems by playing two of his enemies off against each other and in either case to confine his enemies to distant Italy, away from the threatening proximity of the Balkans.

Theoderic responded to the challenge with a will and succeeded in a few short campaigns in making himself master of Italy and in executing Odovacer with his own hands, relying on a little discreet treachery to achieve his ends. Theoderic then ruled in Italy from 493 until his death in 526; it is particularly the first two decades of this period that appear in our sources as something of a golden age of peace and prosperity under an enlightened ruler. Even sources later hostile to Theoderic admit that his rule at this time was beneficent and just.

What possibility there was for religious dissension between Arians and Catholics was minimized by schism in the Catholic community itself, arising out of a disputed election for the papacy in 499 and lasting for fifteen years. Theoderic contrived to throw his support to the faction of the Catholic community that eventually prevailed in this struggle. All this was not unrelated to the continuing split with the east: the defeated Catholic faction, broadly speaking, favored conciliation with Constantinople, while the prevailing party was unyielding on dogmatic points. Theoderic could count, for the moment at least, on support from powerful Catholic aristocrats who would be grateful for his backing.

The year 519 marked a turning point. On the surface, it was a year of great joy for partisans of the Ostrogothic kingdom. The new eastern emperor had made concessions that brought about peace between eastern and western churches and had at the same time extended friendly overtures to the Goths themselves. The heir to the Gothic throne was actually allowed to share the consulship of that year with the new emperor, Justin I himself. But the remaining years of Theoderic's life unexpectedly became a time of increasing uneasiness. He suspected his Catholic subjects of collaborating with imperial authorities (with whom they were now back in religious communion) to the detriment of his rule—and his suspicions may have been justified. Only the relatively sudden death of Theoderic in 526 seems to have averted an outright persecution of orthodox Catholicism in Italy in revenge for steps Justin had taken against Arians resident in Constantinople. Of the Roman aristocracy, Boethius and Symmachus were executed by Theoderic, sacrificial victims to his suspicions.

Theoderic's successors (his daughter at first exercised a regency for his grandson, then chose another Gothic prince as her consort when the child died in 534) pursued a milder policy than he had been threatening.[2] For a few years all seemed well as the new eastern emperor Justinian was busy on his eastern front with the Persians. Once he turned his attentions to the west, however, it was only a matter of time before terrible warfare, breaking out in the mid-530's, put an end to whatever hopes there had been of maintaining Ostrogothic Italy as a haven of enlightened coexistence between Goths and Romans. The war lasted almost twenty years, dragging to a brutal end that saw the theological subjection of the pope to an eastern ecumenical council and the utter subjugation of the Gothic kingdom to Byzantine forces. As we shall see, Cassiodorus' second career began in Italy, almost fifty years after his first, in this era of destruction and despair. His first career had entertained hopes of a political order in a time of peace, but his second career transferred those hopes to the spiritual realm, the only place where there seemed much hope at all at this dark hour.

The Ostrogothic kingdom, for its turbulent half century of existence, was a microcosm of the fragmentations that beset western society at this time. No scholarly study has yet made completely coherent sense out of the welter of peoples and parties that competed under Theoderic; the realities of the situation may simply have been too complex to be grasped accurately at this distance.

At the top of society, at least in terms of political and military power, was the court of Theoderic, itself a hybrid and fragmented affair. The king was surrounded by a Gothic nobility that had some occasional pretensions of culture (one princeling affected a knowledge of Platonic doctrines), but which contained rough military types as well. The same court also boasted a shifting coterie of Romans, mostly of the upper classes, involved in one way or another in the business of gov-

---

2. For the royal connections of the Goths in this period, see the genealogical chart in Appendix III, below.

ernment. Here, if at no other layer of society, there must have been fairly constant and close contact between nationalities. Some of the Romans who accepted high office in the civil government adopted a hostile attitude and attempted to show the Goths a little of what Roman discipline and culture could accomplish. Other Romans, perhaps mostly the less wellborn and wealthy among them, were more compliant servants of the throne. The conflicts that were possible came out in 534, when a delegation was sent to Constantinople to explain the death of Theoderic's daughter, the queen Amalasuintha. One faction in the delegation stuck by the mild official version of her death put out by the ruling faction of the Goths; but an elderly and distinguished patrician, Liberius by name (who had served over forty years in public life already and would still be seen leading a flotilla of warships twenty years later), insisted on revealing the truth of the queen's murder to Justinian.

The most visible segments of the population were the Ostrogothic settlers (for their military vigor and their presumed influence with the Gothic monarch) and the senatorial aristocracy: the first families of Rome, so to speak. While the Ostrogoths were largely settled in northern Italy on relatively good terms with their neighbors, the aristocracy, powerful in places like Campania and Sicily, was always touchier: now grateful to Theoderic for support in an ecclesiastical dispute, now scheming behind his back in indignation over imagined insults. Behind this division in society lay, of course, the division of the two churches (Arian and Catholic), a division often marked by striking mutual toleration (made possible by discreet segregation: it is possible to chart the pattern of residence of Goths and natives in Rome itself by the location of their respective churches), but always carrying the potential of violent disagreement.

Somewhere behind all these great social forces, of course, lay the bulk of the Italian population, still Latin-speaking, increasingly restricted in its freedom of motion and economic opportunity. Both in the power of the great aristocrats over their vast estates and in the development of Germanic patterns of kingship and subordinate authority, one can begin to see the beginnings of feudal society and to see in the striking docility of the agricultural population at large a foreshadowing of the subjugation that will be at the foundation of medieval society. The one escape from oppression that lay open to the population at large is itself a recognizable foreshadowing of the medieval pattern: the monasteries that began to grow in discipline and influence through the sixth century.

The world in which Cassiodorus lived, then, was in many ways new and confusing. In an age when education still centered, for the wealthy native population, on the classics of Roman literature and their images of empire, the world was a puzzling and shattered place. The interest in Cassiodorus for the student of this period lies in the ways in which he reflected the world around him. He was a man of many fragments. The range of his experiences over space and time is difficult to conceive, so kaleidoscopic was its variety. It is unfortunate that his life is represented to us by evidence so forbiddingly pedestrian and impersonal; the scholar must resist the temptation to import melodrama to the narrative, but the temptation is strong.

At the very least, one must begin such a study with some appreciation of the enthusiasm, the energy, and the constant willingness to start over and accept changed circumstances that characterized the life of Cassiodorus. He began life as the scion of a family that had (perhaps only two generations earlier) eagerly embraced the traditional culture and life of the Roman aristocracy, fitting into a pattern that had not changed significantly for centuries. Cassiodorus' progress in public life, in a peaceable and harmonious kingdom, was rapid and distinguished.

But after a thirty-years' progress to the summit of public life as he and his ancestors had known it, Cassiodorus saw his world stood on its ear. After a lifetime in a closed society whose ways he had mastered, he was whisked away to a gaudy foreign capital where he could not even speak the language. He spent fifteen more years there, a period unfortunately almost hidden from our view. When he emerged from that interlude, however, he changed his plumage once again.

For now the man who had spent all his adult life in great cities and political capitals—Ravenna, Rome, Constantinople—went to the opposite extreme. He settled in a tiny monastery on an isolated seacoast with a reputation for shipwreck and piracy, forsook all thought of political affairs, and became a monk, a teacher, and a theologian. Incredibly, this last career very nearly equaled in length his first one; he spent another thirty years of active life at the Vivarium. He wrote his last book at the nearly unbelievable age of ninety-two.

Thus, despite the frustrations inherent in dealing with the limitations and obscurities of the surviving evidence, close scrutiny of the life and works of Cassiodorus can show with some clarity the variety of the man's talents and the resilience of his spirit. He is a study in indefatigability. If in seeing the way he moved through the patchwork world in which he lived we learn more about that world itself, it is only an added benefit of such a study.

I

Backgrounds and Some Dates

WE possess no certain information for the dates of Cassiodorus' birth and death. Plausible dates can be suggested for both events and more demonstrable ones for other epochs in his life, but certainty is most elusive. We cannot tell if he ever married or sired children, though his silence on this point may mean that he did not.

Here as elsewhere the limitations of our knowledge are those of the sources. Apart from the works of Cassiodorus himself and incidental documents dated to his consulship, there are only three mentions of any of his family in the documents of late Roman history, namely in letters of popes Gelasius, John II, and Vigilius; on the other hand, the list of authors by whom one fails to see Cassiodorus mentioned is impressive: Ennodius, Procopius, the "Anonymus Valesianus," and especially Boethius, to cite only the most obvious. It will be helpful to bear in mind that Cassiodorus may not have been so conspicuous in the politics of sixth-century Italy to his contemporaries as he is to us.

But all of Cassiodorus' own works betray at least some hint of the circumstances in which they were composed, and biographical data are not altogether impossible to come by on their pages. In this chapter we will summarize what we know and what we do not know about the public life of Cassiodorus. For our purposes there are two chief sources.

First is the fragment published as the *Anecdoton Holderi* a little over a century ago.[1] This short text, apparently excerpted

---

1. Properly, *Ordo generis Cassiodororum*. I give a text with notes in Appendix I, below.

from some larger catalogue, provides indispensable information for the biographers of Boethius, his father-in-law Symmachus, and Cassiodorus himself. There is no question of the fundamental authenticity of this document; but there is no agreement on its date of composition. Furthermore, there are two textual cruces that obscure important information about both Cassiodorus and the nature of the fragment itself.

The dates suggested for the *Ordo generis* vary widely. The test is addressed explicitly to one Rufius Petronius Nichomachus, who is the same Flavius Rufius Petronius Nichomachus Cethegus who was ordinary consul in 504, later *magister officiorum,* and *princeps senatus* during the worst years of the Byzantine reconquest; he last appears in Sicily in 558. Significantly, he was mentioned in the same breath as Cassiodorus as present in Constantinople on the fringes of the party of Pope Vigilius in 550.[2] In Appendix I, below, I present a circumstantial case for assigning the work to some time between the last years of Cassiodorus' service as *magister officiorum* and his appointment as praetorian prefect (hence, 527–533); but it has been dated as early as 522 and as late as 538. The state of the text does not permit confident resolution of the issue.

The text's transmission to us raises perplexing questions as well. One must first attempt to deduce what sort of treatise these lines were taken from: perhaps a letter not much longer than the surviving fragment. The three entries are tersely worded and exhibit clear parallels of verbal construction among themselves; in longer notices the demands of elegant literary variation would have required the original author to diversify his technique precisely where the format of a catalogue of short notices encourages formal order. The appendix below also indicates the points that lead one to suspect that the excerptor was an associate or subordinate from the period of Cassiodorus' monastic career, provided we accept Cassiodorus' original responsibility and impute some further originality to the ex-

2. For the evidence on Cethegus, see J. Sundwall, *Abhandlungen zur Geschichte des ausgehenden Römertums* (1919), 107–109.

cerptor.[3] But the truth may very well be even more complex than that; we have no way of knowing.

More information than the *Ordo generis* provides has always been available in our second source, the *Variae*. Apart from the whole work's function as a record of the public acts of the Ostrogothic kingdom in which Cassiodorus was involved, several of the letters included directly concern the family of the Cassiodori.[4] Letters of appointment in the *Variae* frequently mention the ancestry, living relatives, and earlier career of the individual involved. In the case of other families, these documents help to establish a reliable prosopography of the senatorial class in sixth-century Italy.[5] In the case of the Cassiodori, this information is obviously privileged and vital to our study.[6]

The most complete catalogue of the family's past appears in the letter that notified the senate of the elevation of the father of our subject to the patriciate. Theoderic, in a script drafted by Cassiodorus, noted the *fama* of the foregoing generations and added that the name Cassiodorus "really belongs to this particular family, even if it is heard of in others."[7] Theoderic then listed the achievements of the father and grandfather of the man he was honoring; thus there are four known generations of Cassiodori, spanning a century of the history of Italy. After the mention of direct ancestors comes the clearest statement of the origins of the entire family in the eastern half of the empire: "We ourselves [sc. Theoderic] saw at Constantinople one Heliodorus, a blood relative of the Cassiodori, during his eigh-

3. Cf. Appendix I.

4. *Var.* 1.3, 1.4, 3.28, 9.24, 9.25. The letters in Cassiodorus' own name announcing his appointment as praetorian prefect to various dignitaries (*Var.* 11.1–3) are also helpful.

5. Sundwall, *Abhandlungen,* 84–177, covers the whole Ostrogothic period and its leading lights.

6. The other two published works of the public career, the *Chronica* and the *Getica,* furnish scanty but still indispensable data.

7. *Var.* 1.4.9. The same passage includes a characterization of the family that includes the only physical description of them: "Antiqua proles, laudata prosapies, cum togatis clari, inter viros fortes eximii, quando et valetudine membrorum et corporis proceritate floruerunt."

teen years as prefect. This is a family illustrious in both realms"
(*Var.* 1.4.15). The mention of Heliodorus alludes to Theoderic's
time in Constantinople as a hostage (c. 461–471). At that time
the *Codex Justinianus* records a *comes sacrarum largitionum* named
Heliodorus who may very well be the relative mentioned here
(*CJ* 10.23.3–4). The natural and perhaps correct assumption is
that the division of the family into eastern and western
branches was a comparatively recent one; this would explain
why the catalogue of illustrious Cassiodori of Italy goes back
only four generations. Further evidence for an eastern origin of
the family is in the very name; for the only other testimonies to
its use come from Greek inscriptions, and its etymology refers
to a deity honored near Antioch as late as the sixth century.[8]

The passage quoted above on this family's special right to
the name Cassiodorus implies that all the members of the family of whom we know bore that name; explicit testimony is
given for the first, third, and fourth members of the line of
generation. The fullest version of the name of our own Cassiodorus was Flavius Magnus Aurelius Cassiodorus Senator.
(The first two names are largely decorative, and they appear
only occasionally.) Despite the confusion caused by an abundance of Cassiodori, modern scholars have always used that
name, usually alone, for the author of the works we are studying; his contemporaries knew him simply as Senator. He so
appears in the consular list of his own *Chronica* for the year 514,
and he is thus named in the superscriptions and texts of the
letters addressed to and mentioning him in the *Variae;* finally,
the pontifical letters that mention him refer to him only as
Senator.[9] His works are all transmitted with at least the last two
elements (and works of his political career generally with more
of the initial decorations); Bede and Paul the Deacon were the
first writers to refer to our subject only as Cassiodorus.

If the Cassiodori were originally Syrian, they must have

8. See Appendix II, below, on the origins and history of the name Cassiodorus.

9. E.g., Mansi, 8.228; Cassiodorus allows himself a very mild pun on the
name in *Var.* 11.1.1.

been Greek-speakers.[10] It is thus at least a coincidence that they were always associated with that part of Italy traditionally known as Magna Graecia.[11] The family estates at Squillace, later the site of Cassiodorus' monastic foundation, were a powerful magnet to which every generation of the family was drawn. In the Mediterranean itinerary of Aeneas, Squillace had a reputation for danger, and its modern situation, however striking, has little of the earthly paradise about it.[12] For Cassiodorus, however, the situation was altogether different.

Situated on the Ionian Sea just at the base of the toe of Italy's boot, Squillace (Cassiodorus says) looks toward the rising sun coming up out of the sea (*Var.* 12.15).[13] The situation of the city on a hill reminds him of a hanging cluster of grapes; its temperate climate features sunny winters and cool summers. Without walls, the city has a charming air of rusticity, situated in country that produces all three of antiquity's staples: grain, grapes, and olives.[14]

10. It has been suggested that the family, probably in the person of our subject's great-grandfather, came west with Placidia and Valentinian III in 423; this is only speculation (J. J. van den Besselaar, *Cassiodorus Senator, Leven en Weerken* [1950], 32).

11. The actual level of Greek proficiency possessed by the provincials of this area is a riddle with no solution; I summarize the issues in Chapter 6, below.

12. *Aeneid,* 3.551–553:

> hinc sinus Herculei (si vera est fama) Tarenti
> cernitur, attollit se diva Lacinia contra,
> Caulonisque arces et navifragum Scylaceum.

13. Cf. T. Hodgkin, *The Letters of Cassiodorus* (1886), 503–505.

14. As new men, the Cassiodori may have been conscious that theirs was not the best address for a villa in Italy, and some of this chamber-of-commerce puffery may exaggerate. Perhaps this bustling metropolis, whose absence of walls added a rustic flavor, was in truth only a farming town with delusions of grandeur; similarly the descriptions of the lush surroundings may have been inflated for the benefit of the local real-estate industry. The present state of that countryside is not known to me, though the strikingly comprehensive collection of photographs published in the volume *Basilicata—Calabria* published by the Touring Club Italiano (1968) shows a country grown nearly barren, yet still visually striking.

All four of the Cassiodori whom we know are clearly connected with Squillace. The first of the four, the great-grandfather of our subject, flourished early in the fifth century and was remembered by Theoderic for defending Sicily and Calabria from the Vandals under Genseric around 440 (*Var.* 1.4.14). At the time of those attacks, this Cassiodorus had already reached the rank of *illustris,* the highest civil rank in the Empire.

The second Cassiodorus, son of the defender of Sicily and grandfather of our subject, is described at greater length in the *Variae.* He was a tribune and notary under Valentinian III and seems to have befriended the powerful patrician Aetius (*Var.* 1.4.10–13). In company with Aetius' son Carpilio, this Cassiodorus undertook a sort of embassy to the court of Attila. He is reported to have been offered all manner of high rank as a reward for his services, but he turned them down to retire to Squillace.

The third Cassiodorus was our subject's father. He must have been born not much later than the middle of the fifth century and would have been well along in years by the time of the letters addressed to him in the *Variae* (*Var.* 1.3–4, 3.28). Of his career we are reasonably well-informed.

His rise was not precipitous, but rather a gradual and measured process (*Var.* 1.4.3). Nevertheless, his first position in government was that of *comes rerum privatarum,* in charge of the imperial lands; he soon moved to the post of *comes sacrarum largitionum* (concerned with the strictly monetary fiscal matters of the realm), where "the further he advanced in rank, the more he was praised for the decency of his character" (*Var.* 1.4.4). He moved on then to what are referred to as provincial governorships without specification of place or date; this summary concludes with the note that "he came to our court tested in the service of our predecessor [Odovacer] and found worthy of well-earned praise" (*Var.* 1.4.6). From there the story can be traced in another letter of appointment, where it appears that he held the governorship of Sicily at the time of Theoderic's entry into Italy (c. 490–493). "In the first days of our reign, when the provinces were in turmoil with the state of affairs and the new-ness of our rule was an excuse to sneer at an untried monarch, this faithful servant diverted the distrustful Sicilians from precipitous resistance to us, saving them from blame and sparing us the necessity of punishing them" (*Var.* 1.3.3–4). Governor Cassiodorus had picked the winner of the Odovacer-Theoderic contest quickly and soon accommodated himself to the new power in Italy. While this enunciation of the flexible governor's virtues does not fail to mention the remarkable absence of personal avarice with which the office was performed, what is unstated here as elsewhere is the facility of all the Cassiodori for accommodating themselves to the party in power. The first Cassiodorus opposed an invader when it was politic to do so, the second was on close personal terms with the power behind the throne, while the third sided with another invader when that course seemed (and was) the most fruitful. The later career of the fourth Cassiodorus through the Symplegades that Ostrogothic politics became will give further testimony to this aptitude for compromise with power.

At any rate, in reward for staunch service in Sicily the third Cassiodorus was granted the governorship of his home province (*Var.* 1.3.5). In recalling these honors and the proficiency with which the public offices were performed, Theoderic makes the transition into what he claims is the pleasant recollection of the deeds of the third Cassiodorus as praetorian prefect. The earliest possible date for this appointment as prefect is approximately 501: the candidate seems to be out of office at the time his son becomes quaestor (for none of the letters of the *Variae* are addressed to him in his role as prefect), but not too long out of office (for it was as his father's *consiliarius* that our subject made the impression on Theoderic that won him advancement).[15] The third Cassiodorus held no official position

15. Anon. Vales. 68 reports the retirement of Liberius from the prefecture in 500 on the occasion of Theoderic's visit to Rome and gives his successor as Flavius Theodorus. Son of the consul of 480, this Theodorus himself took the consulship in 505, giving a *terminus ante quem* for his putting off the prefecture. See the *Ordo generis,* lines 27–31, for the rise of the fourth Cassiodorus during

after 507, and his elevation to the patriciate came as he brought his career to a close and returned to Squillace.

For the last of the Cassiodori, there is no surer evidence for the dates of his birth and death than for his ancestors. There is, however, a great amount of indirect, circumstantial, and allusive evidence to weigh. It is best to begin with the dates from his career that are to some extent certain.

The central unshakable Cassiodorian date is 514, the year of his consulship. The evidence for this is clear, both in his own *fasti* in the *Chronica* and in all the other records that survive as well. The entry in the *Chronica* records the most significant event of that year, the end of the Laurentian schism upon the election of Pope Hormisdas: "During my consulship it was to the credit of the Gothic rulers that longed-for concord returned to the reunited clergy and people of the Roman church" (*Chron.*, s.a. 514 A.D.). Cassiodorus was the only consul for this year, for reasons that are not known. The honor may have been achieved accidentally; while there is no explicit evidence to explain the lack of an eastern nominee, the disruptions caused at that time by the insurrection of Vitalian may well have caused the omission of the ritual appointment.[16] The consul's duties were to give his name to the year and to stage the most spectacular of the annual games; one reason for the occasional appointment of two men from one half of the empire was to enable the nominees to pool the expenses. But the games were not an irreplaceable element of the annual calendar, since appointment of two consuls from one half of the empire meant the omission of the games in the other half; thus incipient civil war is an easily adequate justification for omitting the appointment.

---

his father's prefecture. 507 is the accepted date for both the father's retirement and the son's appointment as quaestor, and it is convenient to assume that there was no significant gap between the two events, especially since the son was already in office to draft the letters granting the father the patriciate.

16. This cause was suggested by Hodgkin, *The Letters of Cassiodorus* (1886), 25.

Appointment to the consulship does not itself give presumptive evidence for the age of the holder. There was a tendency in the late empire for the consulship to be a young man's privilege, usually funded by proud fathers. Thus the distinguished prefect Liberius saw his son, still of *tenera aetas,* consul in 507, while a *primaevus* was consul in 509; Boethius was told by Philosophia that he had had in his adolescence honors often denied to old men, and his own sons followed him in the consulship by only twelve years, apparently even more remarkably young than he had been.[17]

We know, however, that the consulship was not the young Cassiodorus' first post in public life. "He was still a very young man [*adeo iuvenis*] when he became *consiliarius* to his father, the praetorian prefect and patrician Cassiodorus, and delivered a highly eloquent oration in praise of Theoderic, king of the Goths; he was made quaestor by the king, then patrician and consul, and afterwards *magister officiorum*" (*Ordo gen.*, lines 27–32). This is partially confirmed by the letter of Athalaric naming Cassiodorus praetorian prefect in 533; Theoderic "took him on as quaestor while still a *primaevus* but soon found him conscientious and learned in the law" (*Var.* 9.24.3). In both cases the remarkable youth of the new quaestor was singled out. The two terms used to describe the young Cassiodorus *(iuvenis, primaevus)* are fatally vague for the biographer's purpose; the only direct evidence to enable us to judge their import in this place is the use by Cassiodorus, writing in the name of Theoderic's daughter Amalasuintha, of the term *primaevus* to describe Athalaric at the time of his death.[18] Athalaric's parents

17. On Liberius' son Venantius in 507, *Var.* 2.15.1; for Inportunus in 509, *Var.* 3.5.6; for Boethius, *Consolatio philosophiae*, 2, prosa 3. By *Var.* 1.10 and 1.45 Boethius seems to have been *patricius* before he was thirty. Inportunus was elevated to the patriciate upon leaving the consulship while still not yet *maturus* (*Var.* 3.5).

18. Perhaps significant of an upper range for the term, note that the apostate Julian is said (by a man who saw him within a few months of the event) to have been *primaevus* upon his elevation to the rank of Caesar at age twenty-three (A.D. 355): Ammianus 15.8.12, 16.1.5. That Inportunus was called *primaevus* at

were married in 515, and his birth took place in 516 (according to Jordanes) or in 518 (according to Procopius), making him something between fifteen and eighteen at the time of his death.[19]

It would be difficult to accept that Cassiodorus could have been as young as fifteen when he became quaestor, having already served some time as *consiliarius* to his father (though it is to be noted that such a job might very well have been the source of much of the legal knowledge for which Athalaric later praised him) and having received an education equal to the performance manifested from the first page of the *Variae*. Nevertheless, the use of the term *primaevus* in referring to the adolescent Athalaric and the *iuvenis* Cassiodorus cannot be completely without meaning; even a society unobsessed with birth dates would make some broad discriminations between young men of various ages, although the terminology would not be precise—and all these terms were actually written down and transmitted to us by the pen of one man, Cassiodorus himself. It is difficult to believe in the face of this evidence that Cassiodorus could have been older than twenty-three at the time of entering his quaestorship, and he was very possibly not over twenty-one.[20]

---

the time of his consulship in 509 (*Var.* 3.5.6) is no help, since we have no other dates for fixing his age; his father, Caecina Decius Maximus Basilius the younger, had been consul in 480, twenty-nine years before his son. Senarius was appointed *comes privatarum* in 509 while still *primaevus* (*Var.* 4.4.5: "... primaevis introeuntibus ..."); his talents seem to be considerable, and several more letters are addressed to him. Other *primaevi* appointed to high office include a quaestor in 527/528 (*Var.* 8.18.2) and an urban prefect c. 527 (*Var.* 9.7.4–5); see also Rutilius Namatianus, *De reditu suo,* 1.172, who says of a friend that "primaevus meruit principis ore loqui." —For Athalaric, see *Var.* 10.3.1.

19. *Getica* 59; Procopius, *De bello gothico* 1.2. He is already described as *adulescens* in 526 (*Var.* 8.1.3, 8.2.2), while only eight to ten years old.

20. It must be admitted that every year taken off Cassiodorus' age at this crucial point is another year added to his career in later life, giving more latitude for dating later activities. It is thus difficult to avoid overemphasizing the youth and precocity of Cassiodorus the quaestor; at best the numbers are educated guesses.

Happily the date of accession to the quaestorship can be fixed with fair accuracy by an examination of the contents of the *Variae*. The letters of the first four books (and the last two letters in Book V, out of place for literary reasons discussed in Chapter 3, below) contain the literary remains of Cassiodorus' term as quaestor. The bulk of the letters are undatable, or datable only very loosely, and the limits within which they can be presumed to fall are determined by the letters which, by explicit mention of the date or by obvious connection with otherwise datable historical events, admit of narrower dating. Mommsen established dates of from 507 to 511 for the first four books, and they have not been convincingly shaken.[21] With this information in hand, we can make our closest approximation of Cassiodorus' date of birth. Recalling our earlier remarks about the significance of *iuvenis* and *primaevus*, subtracting the highest possibility from the earliest date, we arrive at a birth date of 484; but if the precocity of the young *eruditus* was truly astonishing and his age at appointment closer to Athalaric's at death, his birth could have been as late as 490. At any rate, the range 484–490 is close to certain and usable in later calculations.[22]

One important conclusion can be drawn from this calculation of the date of Cassiodorus' birth. We have already seen that his father was functioning as governor of Sicily at the time of Theoderic's entry into Italy and that he accepted the governorship of Calabria (then technically the province of "Lucania et Bruttii") not long after. Since his appointment to the prefecture was no earlier than 501 or 503, there is every likelihood that the family spent the years from the late 480's on through our Cassiodorus' childhood without straying far from native

21. Mommsen argued the dates in the preface to his edition of the *Variae* (*MGH.AA*.XII) and printed them at the head of each letter; his conclusions have been followed in Fridh's edition. Some well-advised minor modifications appear in L. Ruggini, *Economia e società nell' "Italia Annonaria"* (1961), 554–557.

22. We know from the preface to the *De orthographia* that Cassiodorus lived into his ninety-third year (i.e., to at least age 92) and we may keep in mind a probable date of death no earlier than 576 and perhaps several years into the 580's; see further Chapter 7, below.

Squillace. Since the family's political (and presumably financial) standing at this time was a happy one, such a childhood in a family well enough knit to inspire Cassiodorus' later obvious loyalty, on luxurious estates overlooking the Ionian Sea, could well have been the period when the young Cassiodorus learned for himself to love the native soil that so attracted him in later life.

Beyond this pleasant speculation, however, we know nothing of Cassiodorus' early life. The question of his proficiency in the Greek language will occupy us in Chapter 6, but it is worth noting that he does not seem to have the facility of a Boethius (who probably studied for a time in the east) and that there is no evidence that he ever left Italy for any of his education; indeed, if he began acting as his father's *consiliarius* by his mid- or late teens, he scarcely would have had time for such formal advancement of his education. He speaks fondly in later life of Dionysius Exiguus, to whom he devotes a substantial half-chapter of the *Institutiones* (*Inst.* 1.23.2–4).[23] His praise of Dionysius is full and effuse, emphasizing his remarkable proficiency in Greek and Latin (he was able, Cassiodorus says, to read off a translation into either language merely by glancing at a text written in the other), his literary achievements, and his virtues. Dionysius seems to have been active in Rome between 498 and 526, and it has been speculated prudently that he may have been one of Cassiodorus' teachers.[24]

With these dates so far established, we can now suggest that Cassiodorus was in his mid- to late twenties when he served as consul in 514. The consulship is the one securely dated event in a decade of obscurity in Cassiodorus' life; there is no evidence that he held public office apart from the consulship between 511 and 523, just during the years when he was reaching what

23. "Fuit enim nostris temporibus et Dionisius monachus, Scytha natione sed moribus omnino Romanus."

24. This suggestion was made by J. Chapman, *Saint Benedict and the Sixth Century* (1929), 37, based on the ambiguous phrase (*Inst.* 1.23.2), "qui mecum dialecticam legit."

moderns would call maturity.[25] The *Chronica,* discussed at length in the next chapter, was published in 519, specifically in honor of the consulship of Eutharic, Theoderic's son-in-law; but we can only speculate whether this was the product of an author-in-residence at court or of an ambitious young man hoping to get back into office by calling attention to himself in this way. For this, as for the next, period of obscurity in Cassiodorus' life, two possible centers of activity are probable, though the amount of time distributed between them is impossible to define: Rome and Squillace. First, Dionysius Exiguus was still in Rome, and Cassiodorus may have made or remade his acquaintance at this time. Since the consulship was still associated with the city of Rome itself, it seems likely that at least that one year was spent in the city. Furthermore, later mention of a library once held at Rome by Cassiodorus implies that at some period of his adult life he resided there normally and was surrounding himself with books (*Inst.* 2.5.10). But Squillace was also home to him, and as we shall see later on, there is reason to suspect that he was active there during his years out of office as well.

It is difficult to know, therefore, how much to make of this period of apparent rustication. It was in fact unusual for senatorial figures to spend as much time in public life at this time as did Cassiodorus. It was not unusual for scions of wealthy families to content themselves with the consulship and a year or two as an *illustris;* lower offices did not appeal to them at all.[26] Thus it is difficult to say whether the eleven years that Cas-

---

25. The following passage from *Var.* 11.39.5 was long thought to indicate that Cassiodorus held the governorship of his home province at some time during the gaps in his public career: "Nam licet et alias provincias studuerim reficere, nihil tamen in illis actum est quod voluerim vindicare. Senserunt me iudicem suum et quibus privatus ab avis atavisque profui, vivacius nisus sum in meis fascibus adiuvare, ut me agnoscerent retinere affectum patriae, quos in meis provectibus sentiebam propensa exultatione gaudere." Besselaar, *Cassiodorus Senator en zijn Variae* (1945), 24, was the first to point out that this passage implies no such thing.

26. Jones, *LRE,* 557–559.

siodorus spent in office over three decades seemed to him at the time to be much or little.

Whatever the significance of the interlude out of office, it clearly comes to an end in the 520's. From the dates of the letters in Books V, VIII, and IX of the *Variae,* broad limits for his activity at court at this time of roughly 523–527 can be established; note, for example, that the earliest firmly datable letters in this series make appointments for the third indiction (A.D. 524–525) and therefore were written sometime around 1 September 524 (*Var.* 5.3–4, 5.40–41). We can also conclude that the bulk of his activity at this time was in the post of *magister officiorum;* this is attested to not only by the ordering of titles in the *Ordo generis* and other works, but by the explicit testimony of Athalaric's letters from 533 appointing Cassiodorus praetorian prefect (*Var.* 9.24–25). There we learn that he was originally appointed to the office of *magister* and that he was still in office when Theoderic died on 30 August 526 (*Var.* 9.24.6, 9.25.8). Thus he was involved in the transition of power from the old king to the regency exercised in the name of the young one.

Both of these sources make a further reference to Cassiodorus' activities at this period. The first mentions the service as *magister* and adds that "in office you were always available to the quaestors; for whenever they needed some specially polished prose, the matter was forthwith entrusted to your talents" (*Var.* 9.24.6). The second begins by noting that Athalaric came to the throne to find Cassiodorus already *magister,* "but he served us in the post of quaestor as well."[27] It would be easy to make light of these references, but the repetition seems to indicate that Cassiodorus really was filling two offices at this time. This is the solution to the infrequently posed problem of the origins of the letters contained in the *Variae* after the fourth book. For there is not a significant change in the content of the

27. *Var.* 9.25.8; see also *Var.,* Praef. 7, where Cassiodorus' friends are made to say, obviously referring to the term as prefect, "Addimus etiam, quod frequenter quaesturae vicibus ingravato otii tempus adimit crebra cogitatio, et velut mediocribus fascibus insudanti illa tibi de aliis honoribus principes videntur imponere, quae proprii iudices nequeunt explicare."

letters from the period of the official quaestorship to the later terms as *magister* and prefect. The clear import of Athalaric's words is that the literary talents of Cassiodorus were so remarkable in the Ostrogothic court that whenever he was in service in Ravenna some significant public documents were entrusted to him for drafting, no matter who technically exercised the office of quaestor. This further explains the presence in the *Variae* of the sixth and seventh books, the collections of *formulae* for letters of appointment. There are no clearly datable references in these *formulae,* and, while Mommsen suggested that they came from 511, the collection could have been put together at any time before 534 (when the consulship, for which a *formula* is provided in Book VI, was last filled in the west). However, given the respect in which Cassiodorus' quaestorial products were held by the court, an earlier date would have preference over a later; the occasion of compilation might well have been the termination of either of his first two periods of service when, as he was preparing to leave Ravenna, his associates implored him to prepare the collection so that they would have something a little special for the bulk of the routine letters of appointment it fell on them to compose each year.

Two other aspects of Cassiodorus' activities at court in the 520's are attested by the sources. First, Athalaric tells us that during his time as *magister* under Theoderic, Cassiodorus was a favored companion of the king. "To the monarch you were a friendly judge and an honored intimate. For when he got free of his offical cares he looked to your conversation for the precepts of the sages, that he might make himself a worthy equal to the great men of old. Ever curious, he wanted to hear about the courses of the stars, the tides of the sea, and legendary fountains, that his earnest study of natural science might make him seem to be a veritable philosopher in the purple" (*Var.* 9.24.8). A vignette of king and courtier passing the hours in learned discourse also appears in the preface at the beginning of the *Variae,* where mention is made of Cassiodorus' familiarity with the "exalted colloquies of kings" (*Var.*, Praef. 8).

As if to confirm the indispensability of Cassiodorus to the

royal court, Athalaric's announcement of the prefectorial appointment to the senate went on to laud Cassiodorus' activities
in the first troubled days of the young monarch's own reign.
"How earnestly did he not labor in the first days of our rule,
when the newness of our reign required that much be set in
order? He was the one man who was everywhere, issuing proclamations, assisting at our councils; what labor he undertook
was spared to us. . . . He assisted the first steps of our rule with
both sword and pen. For when we were troubled over coastal
defense, he shot out of his literary sanctuary and assumed military command [*ducatus*] no less intrepidly than did his ancestors; he found no enemy to fight, yet triumphed by his
courageous behavior" (*Var.* 9.25.7–9). This military action may
have been a response to fears of assault from Vandal or Byzantine forces interested in influencing the succession and government. The danger passed, Athalaric makes clear a little further
on, when the onset of winter made the seas an unlikely source
of peril. There is no evidence that Cassiodorus held any regular
military command at this time, and there is specific evidence
that he returned to his official chores as *magister* after the military alarm was over (*Var.* 9.25.10). It seems obvious that he
was simply acting as events demanded without color of formal
appointment.

Here our special knowledge of Cassiodorus' employment at
court in the 520's comes to an end. What is remarkable about
the evidence is not how much it says, but how much it does
not say. It is precisely this reticence that most inflames suspicions that there was something not altogether honorable about
the circumstances of Cassiodorus' return to office.

For it is almost indisputable that he accepted advancement in
523 as the immediate successor of Boethius, who was then fall-
ing from grace after less than a year as *magister officiorum,* and
who was sent to prison and later executed. In addition, Boethius' father-in-law (and step-father) Symmachus, by this time a
distinguished elder statesman, followed Boethius to the block
within a year. All this was a result of the worsening split between the ancient senatorial aristocracy centered in Rome and

the adherents of Gothic rule at Ravenna. But to read Cassiodorus' *Variae* one would never suspect such goings-on.

For both Boethius and his accusers fare equally well in the treatment accorded them by successive kings in the letters Cassiodorus selected to preserve. The only letters to Boethius date, of course, from Cassiodorus' first years as quaestor. They include one directive to look into charges that the Gothic troops were being cheated on their pay and two requests to provide presents (in one case a water clock and a sundial, and in the other a musician) for the warring kings in Gaul, Gundobad, and Clovis (*Var.* 1.10, 1.45, 2.40). Symmachus, furthermore, received three letters, two on ordinary administrative matters and one full of praise, a directive to undertake the rebuilding of a theater (*Var.* 2.14, 4.10, 4.51).[28] Three of the four books of letters from the period 507–511 end with letters or pairs of letters involving Boethius or Symmachus; as we shall see below in Chapter 3, the first and last positions in each book of the *Variae* were places of honor for special letters.

None of this is surprising to readers of the *Ordo generis,* especially if that document is interpreted to mean that Cassiodorus was claiming Boethius and Symmachus as relatives of his. But it has long aroused curiosity that no mention is made there of their deaths.[29]

Against the retention, in a collection published more than a decade after the events in question, of favorable mentions of executed politicians, there must also be weighed the favorable

28. He appears in passing as a juror in a case of two senators (with the august names Basilius and Praetextatus) charged with practicing *magici artes* (*Var.* 4.22.3); the defendant was found guilty and burned at the stake (Gregory the Great, *Dialogi* 1.4). Cf. C. H. Coster, *The Iudicium Quinquevirale* (1935), esp. 37–39; with amendments in his *Late Roman Studies* (1968), 22–45.

29. The omission of any mention of their deaths was decisive in leading Hermann Usener to date the *Ordo generis* to 522, after Boethius' appointment as *magister officiorum* but before his death. It is also notable that the other victim of the intrigue that defeated Boethius, Albinus, also has two letters in Books I and IV addressed to him (*Var.* 1.20, 4.30), in one case appointing him to the supervision of one of the circus factions in Rome, and in the other directing him to undertake a rebuilding project.

attention paid to Cyprian, the chief opponent of Boethius, and his whole rather distasteful family. Both Cyprian and his brother Opilio appear in the books of the *Variae* dating from the time of Cassiodorus' service as *magister officiorum,* appointed to high offices with praise neither more nor less enthusiastic than that for all of the other figures who are seen receiving promotions on the pages of the *Variae* (e.g., *Var.* 8.21).

There is no interpretation of Cassiodorus' actions that fully exonerates him from all suspicion of having participated in the downfall of Boethius, if only by profiting personally from promotion in Boethius' stead. And Theoderic in his last years, as best we can gather from other sources, was not the benign patron of religious toleration that he had seemed earlier in his reign; indeed, his death cut short what could well have developed into a major persecution of Catholic churches in retaliation for measures taken by Justin in Constantinople against Arians there. Sadly for Cassiodorus' reputation, it is precisely at this period that the letters quoted earlier make the most of his frequent, friendly discourses with the king; together with the utter lack of evidence for any concrete actions that Cassiodorus may have taken against the increasing harshness of Theoderic's policies, the positive evidence does Cassiodorus little credit.

The atmosphere of the court seems to have improved in the first years after Theoderic. While Theoderic's grandson Athalaric held the throne, it was the boy's mother Amalasuintha who held the power; she knew the benefits of Roman education and was determined to pass them on to her son. In this relatively happy and enlightened court, Cassiodorus seems to have completed the last year of his service as *magister officiorum.* It is ominous, however, that one of his immediate successors in that post was the very Cyprian who had accused Boethius. The more uncompromising faction within the Gothic camp (and their adherents among the Romans of the upper classes) was in the ascendancy once again in the early 530's, culminating in the murder of further alleged conspirators against the throne.

This last storm seems to have passed, however, when Cassiodorus returned to court for his last and most distinguished appointment, as praetorian prefect for Italy. This post was effectively the prime ministership of the Ostrogothic civil government and an honored culmination for any career. Among Cassiodorus' first activities when he arrived back in Ravenna was the writing up of his own appointment and that of the consul for 534. Athalaric died shortly afterwards in early 534, and the remainder of Cassiodorus' public career fell under storm clouds of Byzantine reconquest and dynastic intrigue among the Ostrogoths.

It is to this period that we can provisionally date Cassiodorus' activities in connection with Pope Agapetus to establish a school of Christian higher learning in Rome (*Inst.* 1, praef. 1). Thus our image of Cassiodorus during his prefecture is a picture divided between the complaisant courtier doing his master's bidding and the private man increasingly concerned with the affairs of the church. Perhaps his concern for Christian studies specifically at Rome is evidence that he had spent some of the period between his tours of duty in Ravenna back at Rome associated with the religious and intellectual life of that city. At any rate, it is on this note that the public career of Cassiodorus disappears from our view. The last letters in the *Variae* that admit of secure dating are from late 537 or early 538.[30] Moreover, the last letters written in the name of Witigis, the last of the Gothic kings whom Cassiodorus served, cannot be put much beyond the end of 536 (*Var.* 10.33–34). Neither of the two prefaces that Cassiodorus inserted in the *Variae* makes any mention of the conclusion of the author's term of office; they are open to the interpretation that they were written and the *Variae* published while Cassiodorus still held office as prefect. This would also indicate that the treatise *De anima* (mentioned in the preface to Book XI) also dates from the period of public service and is further evidence of a deepening of the statesman's involvement with religion. Nothing in the *De anima* itself forbids this interpretation.

On that note of uncertainty we come to the end of our

---

30. *Var.* 12.16 (before 1 September 537) and 12.22–24 (537/538, probably early winter at latest, since the harvest of 537 seems under discussion).

knowledge of the public career of Cassiodorus. Whether he relinquished office to a duly appointed successor or whether military events led to the breakdown of the Gothic civil government, we simply do not know. There is no record of any successor being appointed for Cassiodorus by Gothic authorities; the next Roman authorities in Italy that we know of were appointed from Constantinople.

For the remainder of the history of the life of Cassiodorus as a private person we rely on his own later writings. Their evidence is arguable in the extreme, and an evaluation of his later life, intimately bound up with the assessment of those texts themselves, is a task reserved for later chapters. What we know for certain is that Cassiodorus spent some time in Constantinople, probably doing most of the work on his Psalm commentary there, but settled into the monastic life at Squillace to pursue his second career.

2

Cassiodorus under Theoderic

CASSIODORUS' public career can most usefully be studied
in two parts, corresponding first of all to his years as panegyrist
and functionary under Theoderic and then (in the next chapter)
to his service as praetorian prefect in the war-torn years after
Theoderic.

There is a certain preciosity about everything Cassiodorus
wrote for publication during his public life. The letters of the
Variae, as we shall see, are mannered and baroque in style, almost overloaded with rhetorical frippery—so much so that the
ordinary government business they were meant to discuss can
almost be forgotten by the reader.

It is important to emphasize this preciosity before turning to
the formal literary productions of Cassiodorus in the reign of
Theoderic. There are three such works—the *Laudes,* the
Chronica, and the *Gothic History*—of which only the least interesting survives intact. Furthermore, the surviving fragments
of the *Laudes* are too short to judge very clearly.[1] The two
fragments that survive seem to be from panegyrics delivered on
the naming of Eutharic as heir apparent and on the marriage of
Witigis and Mathesuentha.

We are inclined today to disparage the panegyric as a literary
genre; historians who chafe at the allusive mention of otherwise
unrecorded events in such rhetorical set-pieces are not often
charitable to their authors. But the very existence of the form as
a recognized literary genre certainly goes a long way toward

1. There are about twelve pages of readable text fraught with lacunae,
edited by L. Traube as *Orationum Reliquiae,* in *MGH.AA.*XII, immediately following Mommsen's edition of the *Variae.*

excusing the individuals who made use of it; modern sensitivities are offended by the resolutely obsequious tone of such speeches and all too often refrain from appraising the literary performance of an individual by attacking the vices of the genre. When, as in the case of Cassiodorus, we know little more than that the speeches were written and that they conformed to the laws of the genre, we are likely to take them merely as evidence of the author's fawning subservience to the powers he praised.

Yet we know too little of the criteria by which such literary pieces were judged by their contemporaries. Clearly no one, neither author, nor subject, nor audience, expected anything other than praise of the panegyric's subject to issue forth. Since, moreover, the ordinary delivery of such an oration was not a gratuitous action of an enthusiastic citizen but a formally staged literary event at the royal court, the willingness to lend one's talents to the production of such a work was often little more than a declaration of active loyalty to the regime in power. It was to be expected that the praise contained in the speech would be excessive; the intellectual point of the exercise (and very likely an important criterion in judging it) was to see how excessive the praise could be made while remaining within boundaries of decorum and restraint, how much high praise could be made to seem the grudging testimony of simple honesty.

To the extent, moreover, that panegyric was not produced as part of a court's routine and was at times a spontaneous contribution of the author (perhaps submitted in written form), the same standards would be applied with the practical purpose of evaluating the talents and the loyalty of the individual making the submission; in that case the obvious purpose of such an attempt to call royal attention upon oneself was the advancement of one's political hopes. We are explicitly told that this was the technique by which Cassiodorus won advancement to the important post of quaestor while still in the vicinity of his twentieth year (*Ordo gen.*, lines 27–31). We are prone to assume that Cassiodorus and his rhetorical talents were unique in his land and time;[2] in fact, there were doubtless still numerous young men working their way into the fringes of the court possessed of more education than experience and looking for a way to make themselves conspicuous.

We would know more of the role of these orations in the career of Cassiodorus if more of them survived and if we could be absolutely sure that they were written by him. The two surviving fragments were obviously written in different circumstances almost two decades apart. The rise of Eutharic took place during the period of seeming obscurity between Cassiodorus' quaestorship and his appointment as *magister officiorum;* as we shall see, he was active on other, similar literary fronts at the same time. The marriage of Witigis and Mathesuentha, an effort to legitimize the rise of Witigis by a connection with the family of the Amals (Mathesuentha later married a nephew of Justinian, for the same sort of reason), took place during the difficult days of the war with Justinian's forces, when Cassiodorus was still at court as praetorian prefect. In this case particularly, the role of such fancy rhetoric was clearly to add to the formality of the occasion, to emphasize (probably for publication) the conclusions that the general public was meant to draw from the union extolled. How and when these documents were published (in other words, how they came to be collected in manuscript in such a way as to survive into our time) is not known. It is at least possible that the publication of such a collection, like the later publication of the *Variae,* was a deliberate propagandistic act, glorifying the Gothic regime in a time of crisis. This possibility is slightly reinforced by the way in which the *Laudes* in general are referred to in the preface to the *Variae:* "You [sc. Cassiodorus, addressed by anonymous friends] have often spoken panegyrical addresses [*laudes*] to kings and queens with the approval of all who heard; you set down Gothic history in twelve books, plucking a

---

2. The active career of Ennodius overlaps that of Cassiodorus only slightly and thus falls beyond our ken; but of course what he did is very much analogous to Cassiodorus' later panegyrics.

bouquet of happy memories. Since you were successful in *those* endeavors . . ." (*Var.*, Praef. 11, emphasis added). The collection and publication of the orations would have been easier to accomplish than the editing of the *Variae* and would logically have preceded the larger work, even if stemming from the same conception and purpose.

The literary panegyric was, we can conclude, an established literary form that Cassiodorus practiced for his own advancement as well as for the pleasure of the royal recipients of that honor. In the court of heaven, politicians may be held responsible for the literal sense of every burst of hyperbole they utter, but the custom in this world is to be lenient in settling such accounts.

No doubt it also pleased the Amal dynasty to be exalted by so traditionally Roman a form of rhetoric. The other two literary products of Cassiodorus' public career more explicitly ennobled the Goths in the light of Roman tradition.

The *Chronica,* first of all, publicly celebrated the great honor shown to Theoderic and his family by the emperor Justin in sharing his first consulship with the heir apparent to the Ostrogothic throne. Theoderic was in his sixties, without a son, when his daughter Amalasuintha married Eutharic in 515. Eutharic came from the royal dynasty of the Amals, descended through five generations from Hermanaric, the younger brother of Theoderic's ancestor Vultvulf (*Get.* 14.80). Shortly after the marriage, between 516 and 518, the son Athalaric was born, extending the Amal line into its seventeenth generation (according to the genealogy preserved by Cassiodorus). As events would have it, the fortunes of the dynasty were to be less happy than they seemed at this time, since Eutharic died before his father-in-law, and Athalaric only survived eight years of his regency, while his mother in her turn only lasted a few months before being murdered for her kingdom by Theodahad.

None of this could be foreseen in 519, however, and there was great joy in the Gothic kingdom on the consulship of

Eutharic and Justin. The ominous potential (for the Goths) of the reconciliation of eastern and western churches after the Acacian schism (which Justin put an end to upon acceding to the throne) had been overshadowed for the time being by the reestablishment and reaffirmation of concord between the Roman emperor and his loyal Gothic viceroy. *Romania* and *Gothia* had never seemed more happily united with such prospects of lasting harmony. In this joyful environment there appeared at least one of Cassiodorus' essays establishing the literary heritage of the union of Goths and Romans, namely the *Chronica*.

Nothing could be more suitable for the consulship of the Gothic heir than to present him with a formal listing of all the consuls of the Roman *res publica,* going back to the first Brutus. In fact, the *Chronica,* like earlier such documents compiled under Christian influence, adopted the synchronism established by Eusebius and began by naming Ninus the Assyrian as the first holder of great temporal power in order to unite all world history in one sequence of rulers. Thus twenty-five generations of Assyrian kings from Ninus, covering 852 years, gave way to the Latin kings from Latinus and Aeneas, who in turn yielded to the Roman kings from Romulus to Tarquinius Superbus. Then the consular *fasti* as such began.[3]

Most of what is contained in the *Chronica* is of little direct interest to us. The consular *fasti* are preserved in other sources, and the occasional notes of important events are sparse and derivative through almost the entire work. Cassiodorus as chronicler is dependent on other sources, through various intermediaries: the influence of Jerome, Prosper of Aquitaine,

3. It may be important that the preface to the *Chronica* indicates that Cassiodorus was writing in obedience to royal command. The preface is addressed, we deduce, to Eutharic himself: "Sapientia principali, qua semper magna revolvitis, in ordinem me consules digerere censuistis, ut qui annum ornaveritis glorioso nomine, redderetis fastis veritatis pristinae dignitatem." We need not take this claim too seriously, but it foreshadows a theme in all of the works of Cassiodorus' public life.

Aufidius Bassus, Eutropius, the Livian epitomators, and others can be detected.[4]

As the listing of the consuls approached Cassiodorus' own age, however, the propagandistic purpose of the work became more clearly apparent.[5] For as the Goths enter the stage of Roman history, the facts about their presence became gradually distorted. The first clear trace is in the note on the murder of Decius, the third-century emperor who launched a great persecution of Christians and whose stock was correspondingly low under Christian kings. Cassiodorus was careful to claim explicit credit for the Goths (a claim repeated in the *Getica*) as Decius' slayers (cf. *Get.* 18). Again, Cassiodorus makes particular mention (in 263) of the Goths for having ravaged Greece, Macedonia, Pontus, and Asia, while allowing that other provinces were shaken by an irruption of barbarians; by contrast, under A.D. 271, where Jerome credits Claudius with a victory over the Goths, Cassiodorus only mentions *barbari*.[6] Under 287, the rise of Manichaeism is mentioned, but nowhere is there mention of the origins of Arianism or any of the vicissitudes of that sect (to which the Goths still adhered). Under 380, Prosper's chronicle had spoken of Ambrose, who wrote "pro

4. Mommsen, *MGH.AA.*XI, 111–113. Cassiodorus' dependence on Livy gives an excellent example of the problems faced in untangling the relation of such an entirely derivative work to its sources. Certainly the information for much of the earlier consular listing follows Livy (in his original edition, Mommsen printed the consuls as given by Livy side by side with Cassiodorus' text to show the close parallel), but at what remove we did not know for a long time. There has since been unearthed a papyrus epitome of Livy from Oxyrhynchus which demonstrates that for the establishment of athletic contests at Rome in 186 B.C. Cassiodorus followed in his entry the wording of the Oxyrhynchus epitome, not that of Livy himself. See C. H. Moore, *AJP* 25(1904), 241–255, esp. 245, who also argued that Cassiodorus, Obsequens, and the Oxyrhynchus epitome go back to another parent chronicle in addition to Livy.

5. Mommsen, *MGH.AA.*XI, 113, hints that frequent mention of Roman games and other affairs of the city means that this work was compiled "in usum plebis urbanae." The material is suggestive, but of a different conclusion: a visit of the heir to the throne to Rome to celebrate his consulship, perhaps.

6. The invasion of Asia is also in *Get.* 20.

catholica fide"; Cassiodorus changes the phrase to "de christiana fide." Two years later, Prosper reported that Athanaric,
a Gothic king, was murdered at Constantinople, while Cassiodorus only admits that "Athanaric, king of the Goths, came to
Constantinople and passed away there."

In 402, Stilicho fought the Goths at the battle of Pollentia;
Prosper mentions only that the battle was fought with "slaughter on both sides," but Cassiodorus insists that "at Pollentia the
Goths defeated Stilicho in battle and put him and the Roman
army to flight." Finally, to the mention of the sack of Rome by
Alaric in 410, Cassiodorus adds a gratuitous phrase, that Alaric
behaved *clementer* in victory. Throughout this recording of the
earlier conflicts of Romans and Goths, Cassiodorus had a narrow row to hoe as an author attempting to celebrate the union
of these two peoples. He took the Gothic side in these disputed
cases in ways that would both flatter the Goths and establish a
record of achievement (implying virtual parity with the Romans) to which Goths could point proudly; whether Romans
were expected to be impressed by these past glories, as revised
and enhanced by Cassiodorus' selective pen, is not certain.
There is, to be sure, no clear evidence that Cassiodorus deliberately falsified his facts in the places where he diverged from the
earlier Roman chroniclers. We know too little of the specifically
Gothic sources that were available to him to know whether he
might not have had better information in some places. Furthermore, in the cases where his changes were a matter of soft-
ening the terminology (*barbari* for Goths at an embarrassing
moment, *christiana* for the sectarian *catholica* in another), he can
be accused of little more than sensitivity to the feelings of his
audience.

Similarly, constitutional questions surrounding Theoderic's
position in Italy were doubtless involved in Cassiodorus' reluctance to make much of the achievements of the western emperors in the fifth century. Under 423, for example, he makes
the remarkable claim that "Honorius died and Theodosius
alone commanded the Roman empire for twenty-seven years."
The gist of this assertion is that, although Cassiodorus later des-

ignates Valentinian III (who held the title of *Augustus* from 425 until 455) as "imp.," somehow the west became at this time a subordinate realm with an imperial primacy in the hands of the east. In this context, the perfectly accurate statement that Theodosius in 424 sent Valentinian and his mother "to take power over the western realm" still distinctly implies Theodosius' supremacy in the imperial college. The only other mention of Valentinian marks his return to Constantinople to marry Theodosius' daughter.

Cassiodorus takes advantage of the facts again when he reports for the year 451 that "the Romans under Aetius with Gothic auxiliaries fought [on the Catalaunian plains] against Attila, who retreated, overcome by Gothic might." That statement is literally true in every detail, but it distorts the truth on two points. First, it limits mention of the leadership of the western Romans to Aetius, thereby emphasizing the irrelevance of the western emperors at this time; it was into Aetius' shoes that Theoderic would eventually step. Furthermore, the Gothic auxiliaries who are credited with the decisive role were in fact Visigoths; no mention is made that the Ostrogoths, including Theoderic's father, were present on the same battlefield, fighting (albeit under some constraint) for Attila and the Huns.

Further imperial notices in the fifth century make light of the western emperors; for 461, Ricimer's role in creating a new emperor ("caused him to succeed to the kingdom," i.e., *in regnum* and not, to be noted, *in imperium*) is explicitly asserted. Henceforth for several years the deeds of Ricimer are recorded (for example, s.a. 464, 465) until Leo is credited with dispatching Anthemius from the east to accept the *imperium* in Italy. Ricimer's actions in destroying Anthemius and replacing him with Olybrius are condemned, but the *patricius* is still the center of attention (criticized implicitly for not showing the spirit of cooperation towards an eastern emperor upon which the Ostrogoths prided themselves). The end of the empire in the west is not emphasized, but it is clearly stated under 476 that Odovacer killed Orestes and Paulus and assumed the name of *rex,* "while using neither the purple nor other regalia."

After Odovacer's putsch there are only two short military notices interjected in the consular listing until the arrival of Theoderic in Italy in 489. From that point it is to be expected that the Ostrogoths will do no wrong in Cassiodorus' account. Specifically, rumors of treachery on Theoderic's part in the death of Odovacer are thrown right back at the presumed victim: "Theoderic entered Ravenna and killed Odovacer, who was plotting against him." After that the work celebrates the virtues of Theoderic, including his glorious visit to Rome in 500 (connected explicitly with his solicitous concern for rebuilding that city), his provision of new water supplies for Ravenna, and his seizure of lands in Gaul from the confusion caused by depredations of the Franks. For the year 514 there appears the note, quoted in the preceding chapter, in which Cassiodorus allows the implication to stand that it was through his own influence (and, for appointing him, that of Theoderic) that harmony was restored to the church in Italy.

The last entries in the *Chronica* focus logically on Eutharic, praising his marriage in 515, his acceptance of the consulship in 518, and finally his triumphant occupation of that office in 519. Mommsen's speculation about a Roman interest in the work is confirmed and illuminated by the contents of the last entry, which enumerates with what for this work is considerable detail the marvels seen at Rome during the ceremonies surrounding the consulship (still a Rome-centered honor itself) before ending with briefer mention of the joy felt when the royal party returned to Ravenna. Rome was still a magnet, a good place for triumph and pomp.

Finally, the formality of the roster of consuls is restored by a concluding note recapitulating the number of years in each of the periods of history; the work ends with a sentence that was clearly designed to make the addressee nod happily, impressed with himself and with the dignity of the glorious office he held: "And so the whole order of the ages down to your consulship is registered here in 5,721 years." If the Goths were upstarts on the stage of history, they had clearly arrived when they could see a noble Gothic name next to that of a Roman emperor at the end of a chronicle of over five thousand years of history.

The purpose and the technique of Cassiodorus' chronicle are unmistakable. He can still be reproached here for tinkering with the truth, but he was at pains to observe at least the letter of the historical record as he had it; but this sort of chronicle is a species of panegyric itself, as the last entries make clear. If it is panegyric, its profound purpose of praising the Gothic heir is then seen to conceal other more private motives. Cassiodorus at this time was not holding any office at the Gothic court, nor was he helping out the quaestors with any of their work (and he might have done that had he been regularly resident in Ravenna at the time). Instead he produced a document in honor of the consulship that comes out of the most solid Roman traditions, and he concludes with a notice that may be the record of what the author himself witnessed at the consular games at Rome. If this is so, there is room to speculate that Cassiodorus was still in Rome following his consulship five years earlier, perhaps making or renewing his acquaintance with Dionysius Exiguus, who was still teaching there. We cannot tell whether we are meant to take seriously the words in the preface alleging that the *Chronica* was prepared at Eutharic's own request; and we can only speculate whether such an effort to call attention to oneself, taken in connection with the surviving fragment of panegyric on Eutharic's rise, was the spontaneous gift of a man whose political position was secure or the calculated device of someone who had remained outside the mainstream a little longer than he had planned and who would be grateful for renewed royal favor.

To this uncertainty one further note can be appended about our knowledge of the *Chronica*. At some time after the first publication of the work, the manuscript tradition that we have received the addition of a full set of Cassiodorus' formal titles, reading: "Cassiodori Senatoris, v.c. et inl., ex quaestore sacri palatii, ex cons. ord., ex mag. off., p̄p̄o atque patricii."[7] Our

---

7. Sc. "Cassiodori Senatoris, viri clarissimi et inlustris, ex quaestore sacri palatii, ex consule ordinario, ex magistro officiorum, praefecti praetorio et patricii."

ignorance besets us again, penalizing us because we do not know at what date Cassiodorus became entitled to use the title *patricius;* thus we cannot tell whether the absence of a prefixed *ex-* for the designation for the prefecture might be an indicator that this recension of the work dates to that period (perhaps recirculated about the time Cassiodorus was compiling the collected set of *Laudes* and the *Variae,* for whatever propagandistic gain that might be had).

The most significant of Cassiodorus' extracurricular activities of a literary nature during his public life has been twisted by the whimsy of history into a complex enigma about which only the most tentative conclusions are really possible. Where originally there was a work in twelve books that was always referred to as the *Gothic History,* we know now only an acknowledged abridgment in sixty modest chapters, the *De origine actibusque Getarum* (or *Getica*) from the pen of one Jordanes. It is in itself a useful source for the history of the Gothic nation; indeed, largely due to the survival of the *Getica* we are better informed about the early history of the Goths than that of any of the other barbarian tribes. Nevertheless, our ignorance on points connected with the work is immense; of the author we know barely the name, but can only surmise where he wrote his works; nor do we know how much of what he wrote was his own, how much borrowed from Cassiodorus, or which of the explicit quotations from ancient sources were added by which of the authors. Thus is the scholar's craft of intelligent speculation set to its task very stringently.[8]

The first problem is to set the date of Cassiodorus' own full version of the work. The existence of the work is attested in the *Ordo generis,* in Athalaric's letter to the senate on Cassiodorus' appointment to the praetorian prefecture in 533, and in Cassiodorus' own preface at the beginning of the *Variae;*[9] it is not

---

8. The history of Jordanian studies is full of distinguished scholars, not always working at their best. The latest is best: N. Wagner, *Getica* (1967); the first chapter deals with our concerns particularly.

9. *Ordo generis,* lines 35–37: "scripsit praecipiente Theodoricho rege historiam Gothicam, originem eorum et loca mores XII libris annuntians." Athalaric's letter, *Var.* 9.25.4: "Iste Amalos cum generis sui claritate restituit,

mentioned, it should be emphasized, in any of Cassiodorus' writings after his retirement to Squillace, where the absence of any mention of the works of his public life is most glaring in a catalogue at the beginning of the *De orthographia*. The most germane points of the evidence are that at the several dates involved in these quotations Theoderic is explicitly mentioned as having in some way been the proximate cause for the work's composition, that the work extended to twelve books, and that it chronicled seventeen generations of the Amal dynasty. The earliest date suggested for its completion has been 519, the latest 551; those authors who favor a later date usually assume that Cassiodorus wrote one version of the work to which Athalaric could refer in 533, then later added to it the events of the Gothic kingdom as they transpired, bringing it to a conclusion shortly before Jordanes got hold of it.[10]

There are hitherto unrecognized arguments that add up to a strong probability that Cassiodorus last laid a creative hand on the *Gothic History* in (or very shortly after) 519; the arguments that it must not have been finished until later are fallacious. The commonest counterattack to a 519 dating is the remark of Athalaric about the seventeen generations, since by any reckoning Theoderic would have been only the fifteenth, Amalasuintha the sixteenth, and Athalaric himself the seventeenth.[11] This objection disappears if we return to consider the events of the year 519, when Eutharic was celebrating his consulship. In that happy hour, Athalaric was an infant of one to

---

evidenter ostendens in septimam decimam progeniem stirpem nos habere regalem." Cassiodorus' preface, *Var.*, Praef. 11: "duodecim libris Gothorum historiam defloratis prosperitatibus condidisti."

10. The argument has been most strongly pressed by A. Momigliano, *PBA*, 41(1955), 207–245.

11. The line of descent of generations is, as I read it: (1) Gapt, (2) Hulmul, (3) Augis, (4) Amal, (5) Hisarna, (6) Ostrogotha, (7) Hunuil, (8) Athal, (9) Achiulf, (10) Vultvulf (whose brother Hermanaric was the great-great-great-grandfather of Eutharic), (11) Valaravans, (12) Vinitharius, (13) Vandalarius, (14) Theudimer, (15) Theoderic, (16) Amalasuintha (marries Eutharic), and (17) Athalaric (*Getica* 14).

three years of age, but he already afforded the Gothic kingdom promise of unbroken succession of the Amal dynasty through two generations at least; all seventeen generations of Cassiodorus' reckoning were already known, and the consciousness of the Goths was focused on the happy resolution of the succession question. (If Athalaric had lived as long as his grandfather and had ruled in peace, he would have lasted until 590.) Athalaric's birth, moreover, would have meant the assurance of the succession to a direct descendant of Theoderic, placating any discontent there could have been with the selection of Eutharic as Theoderic's immediate successor.

The *Getica* as it survives contains important confirmation for dating the original work to 519. For Eutharic's name appears frequently in its pages, especially in the listing in Chapter 14 of all the generations of the Amal dynasty, and elsewhere during the period before the death of Theoderic, notably in Chapter 48, where there is a sentence obviously integral to the structure of the chapter about Eutharic, his marriage to Amalasuintha, and the birth of their offspring. Then there is interpolated a sentence that cannot come from any earlier than 550, concerning the marriage of Mathesuentha and Germanus of that year. Then, to recover from that digression, Jordanes says, "But to take matters in order, let us return to the offspring of Vandalarius, a threefold flowering" (*Get.* 48.252). But after this emphasis on Eutharic in the earlier chapters, he disappears completely at just the point where he becomes Theoderic's heir.

What happened instead is that Jordanes concluded Chapter 58 with his account of Theoderic's military politics in Gaul, noting that "there was no race left in the western realms which Theoderic had not befriended or brought into subjection during his lifetime" (*Get.* 58.303). The next chapter then begins abruptly: "But when he grew old and felt death drawing near he called the Gothic nobles together and decreed that Athalaric . . . would be king" (*Get.* 59.304). Eutharic only appears in a relative clause attached to Athalaric's name, where it is stated baldly that "he had been orphaned of his father Eutharic" (*ibid.*). At this point the last few pages recount, in two chapters, the history of the Gothic nation from the death of Theoderic to the marriage of Mathesuentha and Germanus in 550. What seems likely, therefore, is that the original *Gothic History* had made a transition from Theoderic's role as peacekeeper to the enumeration of the virtues of Eutharic and the happy events of his appointment in the succession and his production of yet a seventeenth generation of Amals to hold the throne. The concluding pages of the work would then have been a celebration of both the marriage a few years before, the production of an heir, the election of Eutharic to the succession, and the consulship, a happy occasion on which to celebrate all this good news. When Jordanes got his hands on the *Gothic History,* however, he would see at once that the emphasis on Eutharic at the end was embarrassing in view of his premature death, and so he left off copying and excerpting the original work just at the point now represented by the end of Chapter 58 (while omitting to delete earlier references to Eutharic, perhaps out of inattention). Then he added his own concluding chapters, revising the order of history to make the work celebrate, not the reunion of Amals, but the union of Gothic Amals and Roman Anicii in the marriage of Mathesuentha and Germanus and the fortunate progeny, the young Germanus, born in the spring of 551. It is a quiet but telling argument for putting the date of the *Gothic History* back to 519 that the public occasions for both the original full version and Jordanes' abridgment were essentially the same, including the three elements of a marriage in the Gothic royal family of a female descendant of Theoderic, the birth of a male heir, and the role of the father in protecting the new line of succession.

Dating the *Gothic History* to 519 fits all the information offered by the three explicit mentions of it in Cassiodorus' works cited above. It raises further the question of Cassiodorus' relations with the Gothic court during the decade between his terms as quaestor and as *magister officiorum*. Finally, it completes the pattern of literary activity surrounding the decisions on the royal succession: the public oration (of which a fragment survives) on the marriage, the *Chronica* (the record of Roman antiquity that is made to culminate in the Gothic prince), and the *Gothic History* (Gothic antiquity made Roman). The *Chronica* and the *Gothic History* are then particularly placed in parallel, recounting the whole of the histories of the two peoples whose union is reflected in the rise of Eutharic to the Gothic succession and the Roman consulship.[12]

The circumstances of the production of the abridgment we possess are little better known than those of the original work. From the explicit evidence of the text, we know that it was written by someone named Jordanes, who wrote a similar little treatise on Roman history; that he addressed the work to a friend named Castalius (but that he copied the prefatory epistle almost verbatim from Rufinus' preface to his translation of Origen's commentary on Romans); that his purpose was to abridge "Senator's twelve volumes," but that he had only three days to reread *(relegere)* Cassiodorus' work, which he had obtained from Cassiodorus' steward ("dispensatoris eius beneficio");[13] that he made additions of his own; and that he tells us a little (the import of which is mysterious) about his own ancestry and background. Furthermore, the text as it stands reports events down to the spring of 551 and is expressly laudatory of the marriage of Germanus and Mathesuentha and the birth of their son, "in whom the *gens Anicia* joins with the Amal heritage to promise hope for each race, God willing" (*Get.* 60.315).

On the basis of certain other documentation of extremely doubtful authority (chiefly the appearance of the name Jordanes in other connections at this time, though the name was not rare), there has been much speculation, and at times general

12. For the attractive but unfounded theory of Momigliano on the origins of the *Getica,* see Appendix IV.

13. *Get.*, praef. 3; H. Fuchs, reviewing Momigliano in *Museum Helveticum,* 14(1957), 250–251, hypothesized lacunae in Jordanes' statement and proposed emendations, with plausibility but without necessity.

agreement, that Jordanes was either a Goth or a bishop of
Crotona on the Ionian Sea not far from Squillace.[14] These
hypotheses can now be shown to be too grandiose for their
evidence;[15] however, the contrary argument of Mommsen, that
traces in the text indicate that it must have been compiled in or
by a native of the province of Moesia, can also be disre-
garded.[16] What remains is a strong likelihood that Jordanes was
living and writing in Constantinople at the time he was producing the *Romana* and the *Getica* (the latter was written as an interruption while he was working on the former) and that it was
there, in about 551, that he knew Cassiodorus.[17] As for Jordanes' origins, the mysterious passage in the *Getica* indicates
little more than that he may have been of barbarian family.[18]
The question of the three-days' use of the whole text of the
original work in twelve books has exercised the ingenuity of
scholars, impressed with Jordanes' ability as a researcher in the
days before photocopy; the likeliest solution is that he had read
the work before, probably even taken notes, and that it was only
when he came to publish his *précis* that he had recourse to the
original to check and correct the accuracy of his work.

The most pressing strictly literary question about Jordanes'
version of Cassiodorus' work is no more certainly answerable
than any of these related questions. We have Jordanes' word
that to the work of Cassiodorus he "added appropriate material
from some Greek and Latin historians, adding a beginning and
ending (and a number of things in the middle) of my own"

14. The Jordanes who was bishop of Crotona is known to have been in
Constantinople with Vigilius in 551 (Mansi 9.60), and the *Romana* of our Jordanes was dedicated to Vigilius. The attractions of the theory identifying
bishop and historian are as obvious as its weaknesses.

15. N. Wagner, *Getica* (1967), 5–16.

16. *Ibid.* Mommsen advanced his argument in the preface to his Jordanes,
but it was already rejected by C. Schirren, *Deutsche Litteraturzeitung,* 3(1882),
1420–1424.

17. N. Wagner, *Getica* (1967), 31–56.

18. *Get.* 50.265–266. Wagner, *op. cit.*, 5–16, collected similar evidence for
confusion of nationalities among people whom Jordanes claims to have known.

(*Get.*, praef. 3). There are in fact explicit quotations from other authors in the work, including one concerning the allegedly Gothic emperor Maximinus that comes from the *Historia Augusta* to Jordanes through the *Roman History* of Symmachus.[19] Scholars have tried to attribute sections of the work to each author, but such labor comes to dust very rapidly. Passages that refer explicitly to events after 519 may be tentatively ascribed to Jordanes, but apart from that we must content ourselves with bearing in mind that Jordanes must have made interpolations even if we cannot identify them. What we want most to do is to read the work as though it were the product of Cassiodorus himself; what we are in fact forced to do is to read it as Jordanes produced it.[20]

As the work stands, it draws (at least indirectly) upon a motley variety of sources.[21] Josephus, Tacitus, and Priscus have all been drawn upon to one extent or another. The most mysterious source, however, is a certain Ablabius, "descriptor

19. W. Ensslin, *Des Symmachus Historia Romana als Quelle für Jordanes* (1949). If Ensslin's hypothesis, taken up by M. A. Wes, *Das Ende des Kaisertums* (1967), is correct, of course it means Jordanes must have been the sole author of that part of the *Romana* covering events after Symmachus' death; thus it is not impossible that he might have done the same thing with the same period in the *Getica* after Cassiodorus' work left off. Notice that the passage in the *Getica*, 46.243, dealing with the end of the empire in 476 is a word-for-word repetition of the description of the same event in his *Romana*, 345.

20. One wonders, however, what the format of Cassiodorus' *Gothic History* might have been. Could it have been merely a collection of extensive quotations from earlier authors, not unlike the *Historia tripartita*? Compare the phrase "defloratis prosperitatibus," referring to the *Gothic History* (*Var.*, Praef. 11), to the similar use of "deflorata," *Hist. trip.*, Praef., 2, 3. At any rate, every allusion to the *Gothic History* speaks of Cassiodorus collecting his material from other authors (e.g., *Var.*, Praef. 11; *Var.* 9.25.5), and Jordanes may only be aping him. *Get.* 60.316, Jordanes' conclusion, might then be read as having been written by Cassiodorus himself (save for the very last sentence), which would put a wholly new light on the defense therein against charges of bias. Cf. n. 26 below.

21. Mommsen chronicles the sources precisely, *MGH.AA.* V, xxx–xli. This plethora of sources is consistent with a remark of Athalaric (i.e., Cassiodorus) that seems to indicate a reliance on literary rather than oral tradition; "lectione discens quod vix maiorum notitia cana retinebat" (*Var.* 9.25.4).

Gothorum gentis egregius" and "historicus" (*Get.* 4.28, 14.82).[22] There is no other evidence for such a writer's existence, and scholars are right to be suspicious of his testimony.[23] It is particularly important to note that his name is quoted as an authority at the end of Chapter 4 and again in Chapter 14, when Jordanes picks up the narrative again after listing the genealogy of the Amal dynasty. Now Chapters five through thirteen, neatly bracketed by these two mentions of Ablabius, are precisely the most fabulous portion of the entire work, in which the history of the Goths becomes completely intertwined with that of two other races with which Cassiodorus apparently identified the Goths, namely the Getae and the Scythians. It is probably foolish to doubt the existence of Ablabius altogether, but mention of his name in these suspicious circumstances lends strong credibility to the hypothesis that whatever his book was like, it was the source for most of this confused and confusing legend. In assuming this we may in part be guilty of attempting to absolve Jordanes, and through him Cassiodorus, of the blame for this unscholarly passage; but be that as it may, Cassiodorus seems to have accepted this story lock, stock, and barrel, repeating it with an apparently straight face.[24]

After the appearance in the narrative of the Amals, the *Getica* takes on a great deal more authority. From the point of view of Jordanes' position in Constantinople, one of the most interesting features is that in Chapter 25 the conversion of the Goths to

22. Cf. also *Var.* 10.22.2, where Theodahad called Justinian's attention to "Ablabi vestri historica monimenta." (This is an emendation by E. Meyer from the *abavi* meaninglessly transmitted by the MSS at this point.)

23. The name itself is not unknown; four others are listed in the first volume of *PLRE,* one a praetorian prefect (A.D. 329–337) who may have been the historian; from the reign of Odovacer, *CIL* 6.32169.

24. Taking the sixty chapters of the *Getica* and dividing them by twelve (the number of books in the *Gothic History*), it is not unreasonable to assume that each book of the original may be reflected in approximately five chapters of the abridgment. Is it then possible that the contents of Chapters 5–13 here brought under suspicion represent Books II and III (following the geographical-prehistorical book reflected by Chapters 1–4) of the original?

Arianism by missionaries sent out by the emperor Valens is rebuked (the word *perfidia* is used three times to describe Valens' part in the transaction); clearly the interests of the Gothic faction at the Byzantine court by 551 were such as required renunciation of Arianism (though one cannot conceive such a renunciation in a version of the same work published by Cassiodorus in 519) and the blaming of the Visigoths (who were still conveniently the enemy in far-off Spain) for that doctrinal aberration. It can also be noted that in Chapter 59 the truth is told about the murder of Amalasuintha by Theodahad; this story had been current in Constantinople since 534, and there was no point in covering up the indiscretion further. Instead it could be made to appear as a foul treachery against the Amals (even though Theodahad was an Amal himself).

It is necessary at the end of this survey of the *Getica* to make an attempt to evaluate what more we can learn of Cassiodorus' work from the contents of the abridgment. If our hypothesis for the date and occasion of the original work is correct, Cassiodorus' purpose was still as deceptively but honestly panegyrical as in the *Chronica* and the *Laudes*. Cassiodorus' own political involvement in the work would have ended with first publication in 519, however, and the more expressly political content of the *Getica* as it stands can be attributed to Jordanes; clearly the position of the Goths in 551 was serious, made more serious by the early death of Germanus just when his marriage with Mathesuentha had given some hope of a truly Romano-Gothic rule for reconquered Italy. By this time the Gothic royal party owing allegiance to the Amals had thrown in its lot with the Byzantine forces, even to the point of renouncing Arianism, against the claims of their actual successors as kings of the Gothic people in Italy, the relatively uncultured Witigis and his successors, Ildibad, Eraric, and Totila. Self-interest mixed with an attempt to win a peaceful settlement for the beleaguered Gothic people back in Italy in a desperate attempt to hold some place for specifically Gothic elements in the Mediterranean world. What Cassiodorus may have had to do with this movement at this time cannot be known; it is clear, however, that he cannot be held responsible for the contents of the *Getica* as such.[25]

One obvious Cassiodorian literary motif shines through the turgid prose of Jordanes, however, in the very last lines: "You who read this, rest assured that I have followed earlier authors as I chose a few flowers from a broad meadow of their writings, with which I might weave a chaplet [*coronam*] for the curious reader to the best of my abilities" (*Get.* 60.316). The metaphor of picking flowers from the meadows of other writers introduces one of the commonest Cassiodorian literary tropes.[26] In the preface to the *Romana,* finished shortly after the *Getica,* Jordanes uses a similar figure, but the same image also appears twice in the short preface to the *Historia tripartita* and, most importantly, in both passages in the *Variae* referring to the *Gothic History.*[27] The first, quoted above from the preface to the whole collection, had Cassiodorus' friends say that "duodecim libris Gothorum historiam defloratis prosperitatibus condidisti."[28] Then, in Athalaric's letter to the senate, after mention of the seventeen generations of the Amals, there is a

25. The three-days' loan of the original work still tantalizes. Was it, and the apparent secrecy of it, an effort to maintain Cassiodorus' appearance as a man of religion, holding himself above politics? Or was the short-term loan an effort by Cassiodorus' steward to get the work back into the house before the master noticed its absence? Was Cassiodorus thus innocent entirely of the production of the *Getica*? Or was he perhaps merely away from home at the time? Not all questions have answers.

26. L. von Ranke, *Weltgeschichte,* 4.2 (1883), 314–315, first pointed out the parallel between the passage at the end of Jordanes' *Getica* and Cassiodorus' preface.

27. T. Janson, *Latin Prose Prefaces* (1964), 82–83, characterized Cassiodorus' role in the history of flower metaphors in such prefaces. Such phrases were reasonably common; cf. Eugippius, *Epistula ad Probam* (ed. Knöll, *CSEL* 9.1, p. 2): "idcirco quaedam velut ex ingenti prato floribus asperso caelestibus ex librorum eius quae data est copia inops aegerque conlegi," describing his anthology of selections from Augustine.

28. Cf. W. Bessel, *Forschungen zur deutschen Geschichte,* 1(1862), 639–643, with *prosperitatibus* referring either to the felicity of Cassiodorus' rendering or, to me more probably, to the happiness of that history, as happy as the history indeed was if written in 519. After emphasizing the connection of the work for the best part of a chapter with the year 519, I should now point out that the

passage that is almost a verbatim allusion to the words of Jordanes' conclusion: "You made Roman history of the Gothic origins, gathering in one chaplet [*coronam*] the flowers of the seed which had been scattered on fields of books" (*Var.* 9.25.5).[29] This allusion hints that Jordanes, no master of Latinity,[30] depended on Cassiodorus for the greatest part of his own work, both in content and literary form; his own contributions are probably minimal, and the number of learned quotations he interjected probably should not be exaggerated.

In Jordanes' *Getica* we see Cassiodorus the panegyrist through a dark glass, obscured to our view but not obliterated. The lasting value of his contributions to the ennobling of the Gothic race may be denigrated easily; he himself did not seem to count them among his works of lasting importance.[31] They should not, however, be judged by such absolute criteria; they were works of an ephemeral and public, if not political, nature, important for their immediate impact and the advancement of the interests of the Gothic kingdom and its subjects. However darkly or lightly we choose to paint our picture of that king-

---

exact dates of composition may run for several years before or after precisely 519, according to how long the research took. I would only argue that it must have been finished and published before the death of Eutharic (date uncertain: before 526).

29. Athalaric concludes that letter: "Perpendite, quantum vos in nostra laude dilexerit, qui vestri principis nationem docuit ab antiquitate mirabilem, ut, sicut fuistis a maioribus vestris semper nobiles aestimati, ita vobis antiqua regum progenies inperaret" (*Var.* 9.25.7). The purpose of the *Gothic History,* to connect the Gothic nation with the Roman where possible, and to elevate it to equal rank where not, is apparent throughout these remarks.

30. On Jordanes' Latinity, see E. Wölfflin, *Archiv für lateinische Lexicographie und Grammatik,* 11(1900), 361–368; L. Bergmüller, *Einige Bemerkungen zur Latinität des Jordanes* (1903); F. Werner, *Die Latinität der Getica des Jordanis* (1908); and D. Bianchi, *Aevum,* 30(1956), 239–246.

31. Cassiodorus' own later disregard for his own works is attested by the evidence mentioned earlier that the MSS of the *Chronica* date back to a redaction while he was still in public life; that the *Gothic History* is not mentioned either in his list of his own works in the preface to the *De orthographia* or in the sections dedicated to historians in the first book of the *Institutiones;* and that the *Gothic History* could disappear at all, when virtually all of Cassiodorus' other works have fared better.

dom, it was by the standards of its age a sincere and partially successful effort to establish a just and peaceful society in Italy. Cassiodorus cannot be reproached *a priori* for having willingly involved himself in the politics (and even the propaganda) of that regime; if he is to be blamed, it is for his own particular actions during his public life, not for the decision to enter that life in the first place. For it is noteworthy that his unabashedly propagandistic work (excepting only the fragment of an oration on the marriage of Mathesuentha and Witigis) dates from the apparent halcyon days of the kingdom, before the suspicions of Theoderic's old age began to react upon the other elements of the mixture of forces in Italian politics of the time to precipitate a poisonous residue out of that delicate equilibrium. When Cassiodorus came to compile the *Variae,* he was at once less enthusiastic and more circumspect, as we shall see in the next chapter.

In the dark years at the end of Theoderic's reign, we cannot know with any certainty what forces motivated the king's actions. It is only speculation, but not implausible speculation, to suggest that Cassiodorus returned to office as *magister officiorum* on the strength of the favor he had won with his literary works.[32] If, however, the year 519 was the occasion of all the panegyrical works, this would imply the passage of four full years before Theoderic hastened to reward such loyalty. It is thus more likely that Cassiodorus acted in these matters of his own free will, whatever invitation he had received from the court (it is always good protocol on such occasions to intimate that one's writings were the king's own idea in the first place), with limited thought of personal gain. It would then appear that the years of obscurity at this point in Cassiodorus' career were more likely to have been filled with agreeable literary activity, probably at Rome, rather than with idle scheming at ways to return to the court at Ravenna. But the evidence is not conclusive.

32. There is no specific content to the mention (*Var.,* Praef. 11) that Cassiodorus' panegyrical works had a "secundus eventus."

3

The *Variae*

THE collapse of Ostrogothic Italy in the face of Byzantine reconquest casts a shadow over the most important literary product of Cassiodorus' public career. That career, dated according to the documents in the *Variae,* did not last beyond 537 or 538; his appointment as praetorian prefect had originally been made in 533 in the name of Athalaric under Amalasuintha's influence, but we have seen how that youth died less than a year afterwards, to be followed swiftly to the grave by his murdered mother, leaving Theodahad in control of the kingdom. Theodahad's reign lasted scarcely two years, for it was in 535 that Belisarius set out on the war of reconquest, and by 536 he had advanced as far as Naples and Rome; Gothic dissatisfaction with Theodahad's rule ended in his murder.

If we take the relatively cultured Theoderic and Amalasuintha as the norm of the Amal dynasty, Theodahad was a crude intruder whose efforts to acquire a patina of Roman culture were overshadowed by his murderous instinct for power. But to most of the Goths, Theodahad was an Amal like the rest, given over to the enfeebling pursuits of literature and philosophy and thus incapable of leading the nation in battle; the early successes of Belisarius confirmed this fear, leading to the rise of the more vigorously military Witigis. There was sense, apparently, in this choice of a new leader, for the Goths rallied behind him. He besieged the Byzantine army in Rome in 537, and as late as 539 recaptured Milan. It was not until 540 that Ravenna surrendered and Witigis was captured for delivery to Constantinople.

Even this blow did not put an end to the resistance offered

by the Goths in Italy. While Belisarius was absent in the east, the Goths found stability under the leadership of Totila, who ruled for eleven years (longer than any king since Theoderic), capturing Rome twice more from the Byzantine forces. Belisarius himself returned to Italy for several years, without much success; in 550, upon marriage with Mathesuentha, Justinian's nephew Germanus was placed in command of the Byzantine forces, but he died too quickly for the eastern empire to claim him as a representative of the legitimate Gothic line of succession as well as the legitimate imperial power in Italy. At length the eunuch Narses launched a successful campaign in 551, delivering the final defeat to the Goths under their last king, Teias, in 553. The reconquest was thus completed after an eighteen-years' struggle, and Justinian was free to reorganize the imperial administration of Italy; this he did in the so-called Pragmatic Sanction of 554.

Against this dark backdrop, Cassiodorus' career as a statesman came to an end. The years of the Gothic War began with Cassiodorus holding power as the leading civil official in Italy, continued by taking him on a voyage of geographical and intellectual discovery to Constantinople, and concluded by sending him back to his family's estates, no longer a great statesman but only a simple *conversus,* a man who had turned his life to God in the monastic community he had caused to grow up at Squillace. There is no great mine of information in any of his works to reveal to us the secrets of his soul at this period; instead, we are forced to trace with difficulty the external events of his life through these years, seeking acceptable grounds for speculation on what private thoughts may have accompanied them.

The *Variae* is a work in twelve books containing the collected literary products of Cassiodorus' years in office. It contains letters, proclamations, *formulae* for appointments, and edicts in which are recorded the military commands, political appointments, judicial decisions, and administrative orders of the Ostrogothic kingdom; most are written in the name of the

reigning kings, but some are in Cassiodorus' name.[1] Most of
these documents (about two-thirds of the total) are not datable
except by their position in the collection in relation to documents datable on internal grounds. Very frequently dates and
names have been excised from the documents as we have them
to make them more edifying and (to Cassiodorus' colleagues
and successors in administration) useful. As many of them as
can be dated, e.g., appointments to a particular office stated to
begin from a specific indiction, can be fixed to three periods:
507–511, 523–527, and 533–537. These, we deduce, are the
periods during which Cassiodorus himself was at Ravenna
holding office, in the first instance as quaestor, in the second as
magister officiorum, and in the third as praetorian prefect. We
assume that Cassiodorus' activity drafting letters for the king
would in each case roughly begin and end with his terms in
office, that Cassiodorus was only involved in the literary activity preserved in the *Variae* during those years when he was
holding appointive office. This in turn may imply that he did
not in fact normally reside at court except when in office; for as
we saw in the first chapter, his efforts as a ghostwriter for the
king during the last two periods of official activity were super-
numerary activities, undertaken as favors because of the high
esteem in which his literary style was held. Thus, had he been
at court while out of office, he would have been every bit as
capable of aiding the quaestorial staff as when holding an official appointment.

We saw in the *Ordo generis* that Cassiodorus entered public
life as *consiliarius* (a kind of aide-de-camp for legal affairs) to his
father during the latter's term as prefect. In fact, that post was
descended from that of the *assessores* in ancient Roman courts,
the jurists who sat next to the magistrate on the judicial bench
and gave him legal advice on the disposition of cases before

1. In Books I–X, there are 346 letters, 43 proclamations, 3 edicts, and 8
legal *formulae* (in Books VI–VII, 62 form-letters, 2 proclamations, and all 8 legal
formulae); in Books XI–XII (in Cassiodorus' own name), 52 letters, 11 proclamations, and 5 edicts.

him.[2] We know so little of the post in the sixth century that it is only a probable assumption that the holder of the office had to have had some legal training before such an appointment. We have seen, however, that Cassiodorus seems to have been unusually young at the time of his appointment, and it is natural to wonder whether most of his legal education might not have come to him on the job; that a father would be allowed to appoint his own son to assist in this way indicates that it was not a post under severe outside scrutiny.

As a result of the oration in praise of Theoderic that Cassiodorus presented at this time, he received his appointment as quaestor. It seems clear that the post was a reward not merely for the loyalty of a sycophant but also for the talent of a polished rhetorician. For the specific function of the quaestor in this age (as the *Notitia Dignitatum* informs us tersely) was literary: "Under the authority of the quaestor: drafting laws, answering petitions."[3] The *Notitia* adds that the quaestor did not have his own *officium* (bureaucratic staff), but could requisition help from other imperial bureaus as necessary. The formula of appointment emphasizes the quaestor's intimate relationship with the king, since it was he who put the desires of the monarch into words that were both rhetorically effective and legally valid (*Var.* 6.5). Much was indeed made of the importance of rhetoric as a weapon for insuring compliance with decrees by effecting the persuasion of the subjects that the decrees communicated were right and necessary; the quaestor's words should prevail "so that the sword of punishment should be made almost superfluous where the quaestor's eloquence has its way" (*Var.* 6.5.3). Certainly, great store would be set on presenting the commands of the king in as impeccably correct (both rhetorically and legally) and pleasing a fashion as possible. It was for this virtue, as well as the presumed knowledge of the law, that Cassiodorus, the youthful orator, must have been

2. Augustine's friend Alypius was an incorruptible *consiliarius* for a *comes largitionum Italicianarum* at a very early stage in his legal career: Aug., *Conf.* 6.10.16.

3. *Notitia Dignitatum,* Occ. 10.3–5 (ed. Seeck, p. 147).

selected.[4] Despite the intellectual demands of the post, the telltale absence of an *officium* marks the quaestorship as the least lofty of the posts carrying the rank of *illustris;* for it is an unchanging rule of bureaucratic government that one's dignity and worth are directly proportionate to the number of underlings on hand to do one's bidding.

It is a subject for much speculation and little certain knowledge, to what extent the role of the quaestor was more important under the Ostrogothic kings than under the late emperors. For it would seem that the quaestor's job was in large measure to put the best face on official pronouncements and to look after the sensibilities of the thin-skinned aristocracy. To these ends every appointment to a high office was accompanied by a letter to the senate announcing the appointment and expressing concern for the senators' desire that their company be augmented by the most worthy candidates.[5] Even if Theoderic was not illiterate, the presence in his retinue of a polished Latin rhetorician was a valuable asset; but we have no way of knowing how far Cassiodorus went in polishing and elaborating the monarch's thoughts. It is possible that Theoderic could understand little more than the gist of most of Cassiodorus' most polished productions; however that may be, it is clear that the eloquence at least, and perhaps a goodly part of the accompany-

4. Knowledge of law as a requirement is specified in *Var.* 6.5.4; for other characteristics of the quaestorship, see *Var.* 1.12.2 (it is a "dignitas litterarum"), 1.13.2 (the man must be a *iuridicus*), 5.4.1–2 (his qualities at some length), 8.14.4 (his function as a publicist—cf. the allusion to his status as ghostwriter in 6.5.2, where he is said to make a "gloriosa falsitas"). The ideal quaestor has a degree of moral independence, however, which Cassiodorus shores up with traditional authority at *Var.* 8.13.5: "Renovamus certe dictum illud celeberrimum Traiani: sume dictationem, si bonus fuero, pro re publica et me, si malus, pro re publica in me." But note that this version does not repeat earlier versions surviving from antiquity (Pliny, *Paneg.* 67.8; Victor, *Caes.* 13.9) *ad verbum,* nor do any of those versions refer specifically to the quaestor.

5. As we saw in Chapter I, at this time actual membership in the senate was almost exclusively conferred by appointment to a post of the rank of *illustris*. But see *Var.* 6.11 for an apparent method for conferring the rank—and actual membership in the senate?—without any accompanying duties.

ing philosophy about the nobler purposes of the king's rule, are directly attributable to Cassiodorus. We can recall, moreover, that on his appointment to the prefecture by Athalaric, the letter of appointment recalled Theoderic's fondness for laying aside the cares of state and indulging in philosophical conversation with his learned minister (*Var.* 9.24.8). Whether we choose to interpret this statement as exaggerated boasting by Cassiodorus, as evidence of the king's own relatively high level of intellectual ability, or as a carefully colored description of a relationship where a comparatively ignorant king listened in silence, if not awe, to the lectures of his bookish friend, the most important information seems to be that at least Cassiodorus thought of himself as a part-time minister of culture to the Gothic kings; that his literary efforts were sought after is the best and only confirmation that such a view has. One sees, however, that his employment as publicist for the court was good politics for maintaining good relations with the restive aristocracy. Theoderic must have found Cassiodorus a valuable tool for keeping him in contact with a faction in his kingdom that he might otherwise not have known.

Most of the letters written for the king in the *Variae* date to the period of the quaestorship. A total of 187 letters in Books I through V are commonly dated to the 507–511 period, and it is possible that the 72 *formulae* in Books VI and VII were composed at this time. From the first years as *magister officiorum* there are 42 letters written in the name of Theoderic. After Theoderic's death, Cassiodorus remained in office for little more than a year, producing the thirty-three letters of Book VIII and the first thirteen or fourteen letters of Book IX; many of those letters were announcements of the death of Theoderic and other documents related to the transfer of power. The remaining eleven letters in Book IX were written after Cassiodorus' appointment as prefect in 533 and before the death of Athalaric in 534. Book X contains all of the letters written in the names of the various monarchs during the last three years that Cassiodorus spent in office. Many of the first letters are pairs, e.g., one written by Amalasuintha to introduce

Theodahad, and one by Theodahad to acknowledge his own appointment. There are only four letters in Amalasuintha's name for the six months between her son's death and her own. Twenty-four letters appear in the name of Theodahad as well as two addressed to the empress Theodora by Theodahad's wife and queen, Gudeliva.[6] Finally, there are only five letters in Witigis' name: a formal announcement of his election to his Gothic subjects, three diplomatic pieces to Byzantine addressees, and one to all his bishops asking their support for a mission to Constantinople.

There was, therefore, a decline in the volume of Cassiodorus' ghostwriting during his term as prefect especially; but it was at this time that he was for the first time entitled to issue decrees in his own name, and these are collected (to a total of 68) in Books XI and XII of the *Variae*.

It is thus of comparatively little importance to the study of the *Variae* to consider Cassiodorus' activity as *magister officiorum,* since in fact no trace of his activities specifically undertaken as a function of that office comes down to us. It can be reconstructed from remarks about the office in Cassiodorian and other sources that the *magister* was something remotely like head of the civil service, involved in all the decisions of the realm insofar as they needed facilitating by the bureaucracy; and he frequently attempted to extend the scope of his action, but was not in fact a major force in the making and execution of policy.[7] In the *Notitia Dignitatum* the *magister* seems to be in charge of certain household troops (but whether this continued under the Goths is to be doubted), the *agentes in rebus* (a courier service largely replaced by Gothic *saiones,* probably under

6. Amalasuintha did not marry Theodahad, as some assume, but only associated him to her throne; the phrases she uses include "producere ad sceptra/ regnum," and "consors regni" for Theodahad himself; see *Var.* 10.3.2 and 10.4.1 for the latter phrase, which does not imply marriage in Latin. Theodahad was probably already married to Gudeliva, who appears officially as his queen after Amalasuintha's death.

7. Cassiodorus once calls the post of *magister officiorum* "quoddam sacerdotium" (*Var.* 1.12.4).

Gothic control), and the four principal bureaus of the court in charge of shuffling papers and pushing pencils: the *scrinia memoriae, dispositionum, epistolarum,* and *libellorum.* The distinction in function between these offices is difficult to recover at this date, though it surely resided in the form and content of the documents with which each was concerned. The *magister officiorum* also had charge of the system of post-horses maintained throughout the realm for official purposes (the *cursus publicus*) and the arsenals.[8] There is some trace in Cassiodorus' own *formula* for the office that the post had something of the functions of a modern ministry of foreign affairs (though his role in meeting foreign ambassadors may have been more a matter of protocol and hospitality than policy) and some authority over provincial governors (*Var.* 6.6). The office seems to have taken over, as time passed, more and more functions once exercised by the praetorian prefect, due in part to the ambition of the holders of the office, in part to a need to relegate routine bureaucratic functions to the *magister* while the bulk of the administrative, judicial, and financial authority remained with the praetorian prefect. We have seen how Athalaric related that Cassiodorus' service in this post was enlivened not only by his frequent assistance to the quaestors but also by his ready assumption of a military command when the shores of Italy seemed menaced and there was no one else at hand to do the job (*Var.* 9.25.9). This glimpse of the practical role of the office under the Goths seems to depict the *magister* as a kind of chief of staff for the whole government, in charge of making things work and taking burdensome administrative tasks away from king and prefect.[9] Of Cassiodorus' own performance in

8. Abuse of the *cursus* is deprecated in *Var.* 4.47 and 5.5. By the sixth century the *cursus clabularis* (ox-drawn wagons for heavy hauling) seems to have been abandoned, leaving only the *cursus velox* (horses and light carts); Jones, *LRE,* 830–834. The Ostrogoths may have maintained arsenals at some of the following sites mentioned in the *Notitia Dignitatum:* Concordia, Verona, Mantua, Cremona, Ticinum, and Lucca.

9. For the *formulae* may in part preserve traditional material about the offices and in part tend to exaggerate the glory of the office for the benefit of the individual to whom the letter is addressed.

this post, however, this fleeting glimpse is our only direct information.

For Cassiodorus' second extended period out of office, from the end of his term as *magister* in about 527 until his appointment as prefect in 533, we are more poorly informed than for the first. The evidence becomes generous again only when we examine Cassiodorus' performance as praetorian prefect. He was appointed in 533, apparently to take office from the first of September with the beginning of the official year; the letters concerning his appointment are contained in the *Variae,* drafted by their subject. Only at this point, a quarter of a century after Cassiodorus entered public life and almost a decade after Theoderic's death, can we begin to think of him as the leading figure of the Ostrogothic civil government. However useful he may have been as quaestor in publicizing and praising Theoderic's actions for a Roman audience, however skillful a manager of bureaucrats he contrived to be as *magister officiorum,* he was still undeniably outside the narrowest inner circle of power. Not only had he not held the prefecture (though the distinguished Liberius had reached that rank before the age of thirty, while Cassiodorus was nearly fifty in 533), he had not held any of the major portfolios in the financial departments. His actions had been limited in their significance to the government itself, rarely involving intervention in the affairs of the society at large. Even if his influence with Theoderic was as substantial as he himself would have us believe, it could only have been the influence of an adviser, and, to judge by the time he was allowed to spend away from court, an adviser less than vital to the interests of the monarch. And we are not without grounds for supposing that the comparatively hasty departure from office after the change of kings in 526 indicated some reshuffle in the royal cabinet after which Cassiodorus, willingly or not, found himself on the outside once again.

But Amalasuintha, the actual ruler of Italy in her son's regency, did bring back Cassiodorus to the highest rank in 533 and allowed him to publish flowery praise of himself in her son's name. His task can have been anything but easy during these besieged years, but the books of the *Variae* dealing with the period give the opposite impression. In Cassiodorus' own books, XI and XII, sounds of war are distant indeed;[10] the letters collected treat all manner of quite ordinary administrative topics. A large part of Book XI is devoted to letters of appointment for posts in Cassiodorus' own *officium;* in the same vein are edicts and letters of instruction to lower officials for the conduct of business under the new prefect—all of Book XI may date from the first few months of Cassiodorus' term. In Book XII there are ordinary matters of tax relief, an obscure property case, some construction orders, and a few more appointments. No fewer than four of the letters there have to do with the appointment of officials and the instructions given them for the procurement of delicacies for the royal table (*Var.* 12.4, 12.11, 12.12, 12.18). Mommsen dated these letters to the period of the prefecture in general, but it is likely that they can be attributed to the reign of Theodahad, who died in 536. For there is not much evidence of contact between Cassiodorus and the martial-minded Witigis (only the five perfunctory letters in his name in Book I), nor is there much reason to think that the new warrior king was much concerned with the consumption of royal delicacies in a peaceful palace—he had to spend too much time with the troops. Theodahad, on the other hand, always appears to have been a man who enjoyed the perquisites of the throne to the fullest.

Because he insists on including only matters of peaceful import and such a substantial body of material on the administrative details of his assumption of office, Cassiodorus gives us a good picture of the functionings of the *officium* of the praetorian prefect at this time. The picture is largely theoretical—that is, confined to a description of how things should run, rather than a record of actual performance. Since similar descriptions survive in the *Notitia Dignitatum* and in the *De magistratibus* of John

10. The famine in the last four letters of Book XII, once thought the result of the Gothic war, is now known to have been meteorological in origin: L. Ruggini, *Economia e società nell' "Italia Annonaria"* (1961), 321–341.

Lydus, we can perceive the structure and some of the functions of the office at this period.[11]

This snapshot of administrative structure shows how little really did change. There was some shuffling about of minor responsibilities from office to office, but in general the prefecture remained recognizably similar in the last days of the Gothic kingdom to what it had been more than a century before. The office was the only cabinet post to authorize the holder to issue directives in his own name; these included edicts on judicial affairs and price control (e.g., *Var.* 11.12). He also supervised the levying of the annual indiction, or general tax, payable in kind throughout the realm; this levy was so important that it was assigned directly to the prefect for collection rather than to a separate ministry (like the others that dealt chiefly with the royal monetary transactions—*sacrae largitiones*—and estates—*res privatae*). The indictional year began on the first of September, to coincide with the end of the harvest and the beginning of the collection of the tax on that year's crops. Since the entire realm depended on the efficient collection and redistribution of the harvests in the summer and fall before the onset of the winter closed off the seas (by mid-November at the latest) and the world settled down to a long season without economical means of transporation for bulky products, this function of the prefecture was central to the well-being of any government; not only must the troops on the frontier be supplied, but the corps of bureaucrats itself and the royal court had to be the objects of the prefect's efficient (perhaps his most efficient) attention.

The prefect also had important administrative and judicial functions. He appointed and paid provincial governors; and he was authorized to discipline them, as well as to offer direct re-

11. T. Hodgkin, *The Letters of Cassiodorus* (1886), 93–114, describes the *officium* of the prefect at length, appending a useful table comparing the pictures given by the *Notitia*, Cassiodorus, and John Lydus. Jones, *LRE*, 586–592, summarizes the material more lucidly; his information on the other details of the prefect's tasks is better than Hodgkin's.

scripts to their queries, some of which appear in the last books of the *Variae*. Finally, he was the highest judge of appeal in all legal matters; this was important under the Gothic kingdom, and still more so in the kingdom's last disorganized years, when royal justice was untutored in the ways of Roman law and not easily tracked down sometimes in the camps. To whatever extent the ordinary administration of the kingdom progressed in any ordinary way in the war years, the prefect, as the head of that administration, was a figure on whom much would, or at least could, depend.

As indicated, every praetorian prefect was in a position to issue documents in his own name; moreover, the occupant of the government's highest seat would have access to the records of preceding administrations.[12] A preoccupation with his own literary activity and the availability of copies of the documents that he had produced over the preceding three decades as quaestor and as informal quaestor's helper eventually led Cassiodorus to the notion of publishing a compilation of those documents as a monument to his public career. In the prefaces with which he adorned this compilation (one at the very beginning, and another before Books XI and XII to introduce his own prefectural documents) there are self-effacing apologias. While it is difficult to descry genuine literary motivations behind such a facade (where the urging of friends was introduced as the motive for publication), and indeed while such a facade may not be without some substantially accurate backing, the role of literary vanity in stimulating such a compilation seems undeniable. If from his earliest years Cassiodorus had been praised on all sides for the facility of his pen, it would be difficult for him to avoid thinking fondly of his accumulated literary production at the close of his career.

To impute such a motive to Cassiodorus, however, requires us to think that he did indeed foresee the proximate end of his public career while he was still at Ravenna with access to the

---

12. *Var.* 1.26.2 shows one generation of bureaucrats referring to their predecessors' files.

files; it is not in the ordinary course of events for a man in his early fifties to be thinking of imminent retirement. There seems, therefore, to be a definite, if completely unstated, air about the *Variae* of a man who realized that one phase of his life was coming to an end. Whether this was connected with a growing desire to turn to a more expressly religious style of life or with shrewd estimates of the inevitability of Gothic defeat and the absorption of Italy into a larger political structure in which Cassiodorus could not or would not find a place, the effect is the same. For all the likelihood, however, that such thoughts were occurring to Cassiodorus at this time, they, like the bloody war going on about him, leave no direct trace on the *Variae*.

For as much as the *Variae* is a document of the career of one statesman, it is also a semiofficial record of the kingdom itself. The original readers of the *Variae* were not so concerned with using it as a source to establish the dates and events of Cassiodorus' life, or even to learn about the affairs of the kingdom. Instead, readers in Italy (or even in the east, if such there were) perusing these pages around 540 would see spread out before them a varnished picture of the successes of the Gothic kingdom in Italy reaching back over three decades. The work covers a full generation of the politics of the kingdom and brings to life again in particular the acts and achievements of the dead and sorely missed founder of the Gothic experiment in government. When we read, for example, the first letter of the *Variae,* in which Theoderic speaks of reconciliation to the emperor Anastasius after a minor skirmish in 508, our attention is riveted on the event itself; to Cassiodorus the editor (as opposed to Cassiodorus the original author) and to his reading public, the letter was a painful reminder of the sad course that events had taken in the years since. In years when Rome was besieged by warring armies, captured and recaptured amid scenes of carnage and destruction, the lofty purposes of Theoderic in encouraging the rebuilding of the ruins of former wars would again evoke an echo of what might have been, what was in fact once beginning to be, before events overtook their shapers. The *formulae* in Books VI and VII, moreover, are a clear demonstration of the state of bureaucratic "normalcy" that once prevailed in the kingdom, whatever their use to future quaestors may have been.

But while the *Variae* is a testament to the virtues of the Gothic kingdom, it is a nonpolemical treatise, threading carefully through the events of the preceding decades, glossing over disturbances past and present, emphasizing only the happy and the successful. Thus the omission of any mention of the sad fate of Boethius and Symmachus may have been conditioned by more than Cassiodorus' own reluctance to reveal seamy details of his own advancement at his kinsmen's expense; the crime for which the two nobles were executed was alleged collusion with the eastern empire. Whether or not they had been guilty and whether Cassiodorus felt remorse at his own inability to alter their fates, that aspect of their lives was not an appropriate subject for inclusion in this dossier of success. In addition to literary vanity, then, this new motive appears for Cassiodorus' choice of literary forms for this work; the documents of past years, edited and selected carefully for innocuousness, had an impersonal ring to them that increased the ability of the work as a whole to mollify inflamed sentiments. If such a work was meant to be read in Constantinople and in Rome and in Campanian villas as well as in Ravenna, it would have been extremely difficult to make the case for the Gothic kingdom in the form of a treatise arguing the case as such; even a revised *Gothic History,* by virtue of its need to treat all of the historical events serially, would have been inappropriate for leading men's sentiments to reconciliation.[13] Instead, the *Variae* as it stands is a work with which no one in the Mediterranean world had reason to take deliberate exception. Theoderic, Athalaric, Witigis, and the Byzantine rulers appear in these pages without stain on their character, always acting honorably and fairly. The

13. The great difficulty that Cassiodorus would have faced in finding a way to record all the events of the period 519–551 without offending any of his potential audiences is, to me, another strong argument against Momigliano's claim that he kept the *Gothic History* up to date until 551.

only former starring character in the drama on whom any adverse light is thrown is Theodahad, but even this is most indirect; for in the palmy days of Theoderic's reign, letters were
addressed to Theodahad three times, and on two occasions the
letters were rebukes for the rapacious behavior of Theodahad's
men (*Var.* 4.39, 5.12).[14] In both cases, Theoderic makes explicit
the need for his own relatives to maintain higher standards of
behavior than others.[15] This hint of disapproval of Theodahad
(these two letters could as easily have been omitted) is undoubtedly a quiet rebuke for the man (already dead at the
time of compilation) who had been instrumental in the downfall of the kingdom by his murder of Amalasuintha and who
had been on the throne when Justinian opened hostilities. In
spite of this, acts of his administration are preserved, in large
part addresses to the emperor and empress at Constantinople
seeking peace and reconciliation. This careful inclusion of initiatives for peace (and the omission of letters, if any there were, of
a more belligerent nature) is all part of the attempt to establish
and maintain the record of the Ostrogothic kingdom as an enterprise dedicated to the well-being of its people and the empire of
which it still confessed itself a part.

We have spoken of the *Variae* as though it were such a dossier without being very clear about the intended audience. Here
again the evidence deserts us. Is it likely that this was a composition intended to win the attention of powerful figures in Constantinople? If so, whom? For ultimately only Justinian could
reverse the policy of reconquest; and it is difficult to see how

14. Procopius, *De bello gothico* 1.3.2, also knows of Theodahad's avaricious
ways.

15. *Var.* 4.39.1–2: "... avaritiam siquidem radicem esse omnium
malorum, ... Hamali sanguinis virum non decet vulgare desiderium, quia
genus suum conspicit esse purpuratum." *Var.* 5.12.1: "Si iustitiam colere uni-
versos et amare praecipimus, quanto magis eos qui nostra proximitate gloriatur,
quos omnia decet sub laude gerere, ut regiae possint fulgorem consanguinitatis
ostendere. haec est enim indubitata nobilitas, quae moribus probatur ornata:
quia pulchrum est commodum famae foeda neglexisse lucra pecuniae." Note
the isolation of *fama* as a commendable target for acquisitiveness, where money
is not.

much hope Cassiodorus could have entertained of having his treatise reach the emperor at all, much less of having it convince him to abandon a policy for rehabilitating the ancient glories of the empire that he must have seen, at that particular time, as an almost total success. If the work was not directed to the emperor, or to Constantinople, then to whom in Italy could it have been aimed? With what urgency? Those who had lived under the Ostrogoths must have by that time known fairly clearly what that rule was like; indeed, there must have been few Italians alive who could remember the days before Theoderic arrived almost half a century before, and fewer still who could remember the days when emperors ruled the west. Agents of an imperial ideology in Italy in the late 530's must have been men of great faith indeed, since the last years of the emperors in Italy had not been such as would inspire nostalgic yearning in those who had heard their history. In fact, whatever nostalgia for the empire there could have been in Italy at this time depended on what men had heard (and some possibly seen) in the contemporary empire in the east or what had been handed down by traditions from as far back as the grandfathers of the older men of that time.

One possible circumstance of composition needs to be observed, however. Procopius recounts a debate between Belisarius and Gothic ambassadors at Rome in 537 or 538. The arguments advanced by the Goths at this point resemble very closely the kind of position that Cassiodorus takes in the *Variae*.[16] The written work, coming out at just about the same time as the debate Procopius recounts, might then have been meant to appeal to the Roman aristocracy in land already occupied or threatened by Belisarius.

But such speculation aside, what then are we to make of the work itself? In part we must retreat to our notions of Cassiodorus' unquestionable literary vanity, and in part we must confess that he may have felt only very generally that the record was worth establishing precisely "for the record" while it

16. *De bello gothico* 2.6.14–22.

still could be done. In fact, both of these motives are the ones that appear, disguised in rhetorical coloring, in Cassiodorus' own prefaces.

The most extended apology for the work is the initial preface, where these motives must be pursued behind the billowing garments of Cassiodorian rhetoric.[17] Cassiodorus begins by attributing the idea for such a collection to learned men *(diserti)*, who thought he should collect the letters "so that posterity might recognize the burdens I undertook for the common good and the conscientious deeds of a man who could not be bought" (*Var.*, Praef. 1). To this, Cassiodorus replies that such publication might subvert the purpose of establishing his own reputation, if what he had written appeared foolish *(insubidum)* to later generations. After quoting Horace's dictum (*Ars poet.* 388) that what is to be published should be held back nine years to give the author ample time for reflection, Cassiodorus elaborates that his literary performance in public documents had been rushed and less than perfect; instead of nine years, Cassiodorus had had scarcely a few hours (*Var.*, Praef. 3–4).[18] He emphasizes for a long paragraph the cares that beset him in office, his solicitousness for the welfare of the people, and the consequent defects of his writing. In such words he purports to decline the suggestion to publish.

But the friendly urgings of learned men (never identified) are reintroduced at substantial length in what amounts to direct quotation. They begin by accepting and repeating with added praise the argument that Cassiodorus has been busy in his func-

17. Before even the preface, one scrap of text may be authentic and tantalizing without telling us much. In a single MS of the twelfth century there is transmitted the following elegiac couplet before the preface: "Iure Senator amans offert haec dona magistro/cui plus eloquio nulla metalla placent." (Fridh prints this on his reconstructed title page as we would a book's dedication.) The use of the single name Senator has the ring of authenticity; that the line is transmitted only in one copy may prove only that it was transcribed (even at considerable remove) from a single original exemplar, a presentation copy for a revered teacher.

18. "Dictio semper agrestis est, quae aut sensibus electis per moram non comitur aut verborum minime proprietatibus explicatur."

tion as prefect, and add a reference to his extracurricular activity as quaestor's helper; they praise his lack of corruption, which is compared to his father's integrity, and they add remarks alluding to his intimacy with Theoderic and the long hours spent in conversation with the monarch. They turn the initial argument in on Cassiodorus, insisting that men already know how busy he was, and that if he could produce anything worth reading under such circumstances, his reputation will be doubly enhanced. They add that his work can serve as a teacher for both the well-prepared and the unprepared holders of offices in the *res publica;*[19] moreover, if he does not act, he will allow the acts of his kings to be obliterated in forgetfulness. "Do not, we pray, let those whom you have addressed on their promotions to the rank of *illustris* be overcome forever in silence and obscurity" (*Var.*, Praef. 9). For all this, they ask, "do you still hesitate to publish what you know can be of such great use to others? You are hiding, if we might say so, the mirror in which every future age could examine the quality of your mind" (*Var.*, Praef. 10). The appeal to vanity is capped by a remark that, while sons are often very different from their fathers, "one never finds a man's speech unreflective of his character" (*Var.*, Praef. 10).[20] They conclude that after his earlier successes of a literary nature (the *Laudes* and the *Gothic History* are enumerated), there is no reason why he should resist the persuasion to publish his records.

In the face of such argument, Cassiodorus owns himself a beaten man. "Be merciful, my readers," he pleads, "and if there is any temerity and presumption here, blame these friends

19. T. Hodgkin, *The Letters of Cassiodorus* (1886), 136, erred in his note by assuming that a negative has dropped out of this line; he misses the parallel and contrast between *rudes* on the one hand and those *praeparatos* to serve the republic. The text is: "deinde quod rudes viros et ad rem publicam conscia facundia praeparatos labor tuus sine aliqua offensione poterit edocere . . ." (*Var.,* Praef. 8).

20. "Oratio dispar moribus vix potest inveniri." An aged commonplace; cf. Seneca, *Ep.* 114.1: "hoc quod audire vulgo soles, quod apud Graecos in proverbium cessit: talis hominibus fuit oratio qualis vita."

rather than me, for I am in complete agreement with my de-
tractors on these points" (*Var.*, Praef. 12). A description of the
work's contents then follows.

For Cassiodorus has collected "whatever I have been able to
find written *(dictatum)* by me on public business while I held
office as quaestor, *magister*, or prefect,"[21] and arrayed the material in twelve books. To protect others from the "unpolished
and hasty addresses" that he is conscious of having produced
himself all too often in honoring new appointees, he justifies
the inclusion of the sixth and seventh books containing the *formulae*, "for my own use, late as it is in my own career, and for
my successors who find themselves pressed for time" (*Var.*,
Praef. 14).[22]

The contents are reflected in the title, and he devotes the
remainder of the preface to explaining his title, *Variae*,[23] which
he chose "because we could not use a single style to address
such a variety of audiences" (*Var.*, Praef. 15). He identifies
three classes of individual readers to whom the individual letters could be addressed, including those "multa lectione
satiati," those "mediocri gustatione suspensi," and those last "a
litterarum sapore ieiuni"; each must be addressed in a different
way "persuasionis causa," so that "it sometimes becomes a
kind of artistry, the avoiding of what learned men would

21. Cassiodorus is not likely to have used his terms loosely in bureaucratic
connections; *dictatum* recalls precisely the function of the quaestor's office as
quoted above ("leges dictandae," see note 3, above), thus canceling any impression this sentence might give that there was an essential connection between the
offices held and the documents drafted in the king's name; as mentioned before,
the contents of Books I through V and VIII through X are indistinguishable
from one another in the sense that the same subjects are treated throughout
irrespective of the offices Cassiodorus held at different times.

22. This line probably confirms that Cassiodorus was still on the job as
prefect when compiling the *Variae*, and thus in touch with the royal archives
(and secretarial assistance). But was he phasing out his activity and thus more at
leisure than (as he reminds us throughout these prefaces) was his custom while
serving as prefect?

23. "Librorum vero titulum . . . variarum nomine praenotavi;" cf. *Ordo
generis*, line 14.

praise" *(ibid.)*. The preface concludes with a largely artificial and irrelevant attempt to connect these three kinds of audience with the three traditional levels of ancient style (high, middle, low); this particular schematization is not reflected in the letters themselves.

The other preface included in the *Variae,* at the beginning of Book XI before the books of Cassiodorus' own publications from his prefecture, seems to postdate the earliest preface by some time, though it is not necessary to assume that earlier portions of the work had been published separately. The evidence for a lapse of time is the mention only here, and not at the beginning where it might rightly belong, of the addition of the treatise *De anima* to the twelve books of the *Variae;* that treatise is mentioned here in terms that echo the opening lines of the little treatise itself.

The remainder of the second preface consists chiefly of an excuse for not having more in the way of judicial decisions to include. Cassiodorus had, he explains himself, the assistance of one Felix, a young lawyer whose talent he praises highly, who removed much of the burden of such work from Cassiodorus himself. In particular, his help is credited with having enabled Cassiodorus to give fuller and less fatigued attention to the higher affairs of state *(regales curae).* Finally, Cassiodorus drapes this praise of Felix with the further admission of his own deficiencies and the arrogance of any author so bold as to publish such material. Here again the excuses ring truer than at first glance if read carefully.[24]

However successful the prefaces were in their literary intent, they leave open some questions that we would have been glad to have answered. The most pressing is that of the comprehensiveness of the contents. In the passage quoted above, Cassiodorus claims to have included whatever he had been able to find ("quod . . . potui reperire") of those things dictated while he

---

24. Cassiodorus is scrupulous about the inclusion in the *Variae* only of pieces he has himself written; it would have been easy to include some of Felix's work without admitting that someone else had written them.

held office as quaestor, *magister,* and prefect. Are we to take this literally? Is this collection a complete anthology of all such surviving documents? If we assume, as we probably must, that Cassiodorus was still in Ravenna and probably still in office at the time of compilation, and then assume that he had access to the files of the court for gathering these documents, do we then accord to this work credit for being a full chronicle of the public acts of the Ostrogothic kingdom for those years? On balance, we cannot.

First, according to our interpretation of the circumstances in which Cassiodorus came to be involved in quaestorial activities during his last two terms of office, he was almost certainly not involved in *all* of the literary activity of the quaestor's office; moreover, for the eleventh and twelfth books, he explicitly states that legal decisions were largely drafted by his aide (his *consiliarius?*). Second, there is an obvious conflict between the express purpose of presenting documents that make either the author or the subject (or preferably both) look good and the claim to have included everything Cassiodorus could find of his compositions. Moreover, a very clear impression comes from reading this work that nothing, nothing whatever, of a controversial nature has been allowed to remain. The most heatedly debated events of the kingdom's history appear indirectly if at all; thus the letter inviting the elder Cassiodorus back to court is itself the major link of evidence in the hypothesis that the prefect Faustus fell from favor as a result of his actions in office at about the time certain of these letters were written; but nowhere is Faustus explicitly criticized.[25] Of course the deaths of Boethius and Symmachus are nowhere hinted at, though they appear as addressees of flattering letters; and one would scarcely know, from the exaggerated formality and courtesy of the diplomatic letters, that there were wars being fought in these years. The nearest one gets to warfare are letters reestab-

25. The sequence of letters (*Var.* 3.20, in which Faustus is mentioned as prefect, and *Var.* 3.21, in which he is addressed only as "V.I."—which rank would remain if the office were removed) has inspired suspicion, which then fastens on the sudden appearance of the older Cassiodorus in *Var.* 3.28.

lishing peace and letters involving the equipping and mustering of troops (included because they reflected well upon the civil officials involved). Left to ourselves, and convinced that these letters represented a balanced picture of the Ostrogothic kingdom from 507 to 537, we would immediately conclude that so peaceful and so happy a realm never existed on the face of the earth; if our attention were then called to the sounds of war echoing from Italy at the very moment of publication, we would be most disagreeably surprised.

From all that we have said so far in this chapter, therefore, it becomes evident that what we have here is an edited transcript of the public record, not the unexpurgated whole. We have already suggested the main lines of the propagandistic purpose that this work was expected to serve, as is apparent from both the contents themselves and Cassiodorus' own prefaces. It is worth repeating that the only one of the major characters on the scene of Italian politics in the sixth century to appear at all to a disadvantage, and that only indirectly, is the dead and—to both sides—discredited Theodahad.[26] Theoderic, Amalasuintha, and Witigis all used murder as an instrument of policy; but only Theodahad's action was universally, if not reviled, at least disclaimed by 537 or 538. If motives apart from literary vanity are to be accepted for the *Variae,* as I think they must, Cassiodorus' own explicit claim that his purpose was to enshrine the memories of the notables chronicled therein becomes a declaration of that propagandistic intent, a clear enough statement that the work was seen to seek reconciliation, at the price of a little self-inflicted blindness to the seamier side of affairs.

---

26. The case of Argolicus, urban prefect from 510, is only an apparent exception. Appointed in *Var.* 3.11, recipient of five more letters in Books III and IV, he is rather sharply rebuked in 4.29 for a fairly ordinary-sounding bit of profiteering in office; he is seen again in 4.42 in unrelated business. Argolicus' reputation was clearly slight enough to be sacrified to show Theoderic as a corruption-fighting king. By contrast, *Var.* 8.20, appointing Avienus praetorian prefect, cast aspersions on a nameless predecessor in that office (who almost surely must be Abundantius—cf. 5.16, 9.4).

More of this propagandistic purpose appears in the way in which the collection was arranged. To begin with, the only chronological force demonstrably existing in that arrangement was the division between Cassiodorus' terms of office (though this was violated for a purpose with the last two letters of Book V) and the distinction of monarchs under which they were originally written. Thus, as stated before, the first four books contain documents from Cassiodorus' quaestorship under Theoderic (507–511); Book V, except the last two letters postponed from 511, contains the letters from his term as *magister officiorum* while Theoderic was still alive;[27] Books VI and VII, the geographical center of the work, separating Theoderician books from those of his successors, contain the *formulae dignitatum;* Book VIII and the first half (letters 1–13 or 14) of Book IX record events of the remainder of Cassiodorus' term as *magister* (526–527); the remainder of Book IX, terminating in the two letters of his own appointment, contains documents of his term as prefect under Athalaric (533–534); Book X contains the diverse letters, taken in rough chronological order, under the several monarchs of the remainder of that term (534–537/8); and Books XI and XII contain his own letters as prefect (533–537/8).

If the arrangement of letters in the individual books is not strictly chronological, however, there is still a discernible literary pattern.[28] (Cassiodorus himself describes the actual composition of the books as involving conscious *ordinatio* on his part [*Var.*, Praef. 13].) The principle at work is that the positions of honor in each book are at the very beginning and at the end.

Books I, II, VIII, and X all begin with letters addressed to the emperor at Constantinople. In Book I, the letter treats for peace after the skirmishes of 505–508; in the second book, the

27. One suspects that many letters in Book V, however, may still date from the period 507–511; but this cannot be proven.

28. Note that 2.27 and 4.43, as well as 3.23 and 4.13, are pairs of letters that have gotten separated by inadvertence. Another slip of the compiler is the presence of both 1.39 and 4.6, which are verbally identical descriptions of two similar cases (Cassiodorus was using *formulae* of his own all along, no doubt).

first letter merely announces the consul for the year (and is followed by the other two letters in the dossier on that particular appointment, to the appointee and to the senate); while Books VIII and X each begin by announcing the succession to the throne of a new ruler, Athalaric in the one case, Theodahad in the other. On the other hand, Books III, IV, V, and IX open with letters to barbarian kings. In Book III, there are four such royal communications, all attempting to keep the peace in Gaul; Book IV begins with two unrelated letters to different kings (of the Thuringians and the Heruli); and Books V and IX begin with isolated letters of that nature.[29] To confirm the importance of the opening spot in each book, there are no letters to Constantinopolitan emperors that do not hold that spot, except in Book X, where no fewer than ten of the book's thirty-five letters are directed to Justinian and five more to Theodora; but this exception proves the rule, since Book X is the only one written under more than one monarch, and the broad chronological outline takes precedence.

Obviously Books XI and XII could not open with addresses to emperors or monarchs; again the chronological motive seems to take over, since Book XI begins with Cassiodorus' collection of letters announcing his own appointment (though he may obviously be using the place of importance to call attention to his own virtues a little more), and Book XII begins with a relatively general set of instructions to various officials.

If emperors only customarily appear in the first spot in a book, barbarian kings can appear elsewhere, but only in one specific location: at the end of a book. Thus Gundobad and Clovis, who are both addressed in letters at the beginning of Book III, also appear as addressees of the letters at the ends of

29. *Var.* 9.1 is the only letter to a German king after Theoderic's death; Besselaar, *Cassiodorus Senator en zijn Variae* (1945), 124, points out how this letter, full of threats and recriminations, exemplifies the decline of the policy that Theoderic had pursued towards his neighbors, which had led Cassiodorus, as abridged by Jordanes, to claim that, "nec fuit in parte occidua gens, quae Theoderico, dum adviveret, aut amicitia aut subiectione non deserviret" (*Get.* 58.303).

Books I and II, respectively. Furthermore, Transimundus, king of the Vandals, is sent two letters that appear in the *Variae* at the end of Book V. This apparently deliberate positioning of the non-imperial royal letters calls our attention to the last letters in other books, to see by what right they hold that position. The results are at first diverse. Book III ends with a letter to a *comes privatarum* named Apronianus, directing him to welcome an *aquilegus* (water-diviner) coming from Africa; the letter contains a long digression on that special art of divination. Book IV, on the other hand, concludes with a letter to Symmachus, praising his work in reconstructing damaged edifices and particularly commissioning the rebuilding of a theater; then the letter digresses on the nature of the theatrical art, with frequent reference to the science of etymology. Books VI and VII, following the hierarchical order of the offices they describe, conclude with minor offices. The last letter in Book VIII is a directive to one Severus, *vir spectabilis,* to put down riots in connection with rural, apparently pagan, celebrations in the province of Lucania (not far from Squillace), and contains a digression on a miraculous fountain there; the two preceding letters, also to Severus, also digress readily in praise of various amenities of Cassiodorus' home territory. Book IX is completed by the two letters to Cassiodorus on his elevation to the prefecture. Book X, always pedestrian, ends with the distressingly plain letters ascribed to Witigis. In Books XI and XII, Cassiodorus chooses to end his personal books with impersonal documents; in the first case with a general amnesty, very possibly issued at Easter 534 during Cassiodorus' first year in office, while in the second case the last four letters dealt with, and the very last letter is an edict establishing remedies for, famine in northern Italy.

Despite their diversity (their "variousness"), it is possible, I hold, to see clear threads connecting these letters.[30] To begin

---

30. Besselaar, *op. cit.*, 163, identifies the two positions of honor, but claims that elevation of style is more important than addressee. As I show, content takes precedence over style and is on a par with addressee in determining position.

with, the first several books end on letters carrying as a unifying theme ideas about various arts and sciences. In Books I and II, the letters to German kings are covering letters for gifts of clocks in the one case and a musician in the other (in both cases furnished by Boethius), while Books III and IV deal with the science of divining and the art of theatrics, respectively. Book V's concluding letters show Theoderic, in his last appearance in the *Variae,* at his best in reaching a peaceful settlement of an international disagreement; this is the very virtue that is the last thing for which Theoderic was praised in the *Getica* (*Get.* 58). Books VIII and IX both end with letters on subjects dear to Cassiodorus himself, namely his own home province and his own career's advancement. This self-indulgence is paralleled by the ends of Books XI and XII, both of which show Cassiodorus the prefect to his best advantage, dispensing legal mercy in the indulgence at the end of Book XI, and working diligently to remedy the evils of famine in Italy in Book XII.

Both halves of the *Variae,* therefore, feature letters at the end of each book designed to put the very best possible face on the Ostrogothic kingdom for its sophistication of culture as well as its benevolence in government. The first five books reflect most favorably on Theoderic himself, while the last five books seem to be centered more and more on the person of Cassiodorus himself, a tacit recognition that the kingdom was not so well governed at that epoch as to merit making the later kings heroes in quite the way that Theoderic was. It is even possible to see an ironic twist (or *apologia pro vita sua*) in this transition, perhaps even a hint that with Theoderic gone, Cassiodorus himself was the last guardian of the old values left in the government. If the first letters in each book demonstrate the public grandeur of the kingdom in its negotiations with great monarchs, the last letters give an elegant picture of the whole life of the kingdom and its society. Moreover, by including in these concluding letters the flattering missives to Boethius and Symmachus, Cassiodorus is at least making an attempt to reconcile their mourners to the Gothic kingdom; the praises of his favorite province are couched in a repression of pagan rites that no doubt would please a Byzantine audience still not sure just how fully Christian these people in Italy had remained under Arian rule. And pointing out the amiability of his own administration and his concern for the well-being of the greatest part of the people allows Cassiodorus to show how a besieged regime merits the acceptance and support of his audience, whether Roman or Gothic, Italian or Byzantine.

The frame placed around each book in this way further conditions reactions to the contents of the whole, giving honorable dealings with foreign powers and correct ideas of civilization at home as the poles between which the affairs of the kingdom are set.[31] The remainder of the contents, for all their variousness, are remarkably true to the overall guidelines thus tacitly set out. This consistency leads us to believe that all the letters in this collection were chosen according to definite limiting criteria.

More letters dealing with appointments to *illustres dignitates* appear in the *Variae* than with any other subject. Some of those honors were virtually empty (cf. the case at *Var.* 2.15–16), but most are real offices by which the civil affairs of the kingdom were administered. Since for all the highest honors there exist letters in the books of *formulae* as well as personal efforts in the rest of the work, we are justified in assuming that not every appointment was treated with the same personal touch. Very many of the families honored with personal letters appointing their members to high office are indeed the greatest families of the Ostrogothic realm; these letters commonly provide an occasion for recalling the virtues of ancestors and relatives who have already served the kingdom well.

After the appointments, the next commonest type of letter in the *Variae* is the decree on a given administrative matter of a

---

31. The beginning and ending letters are tied together most closely in the first three books, where Books I and II end with letters to Gundobad and Clovis (probably written almost simultaneously) offering attractive bribes furnished by Boethius as bait to win favorable consideration of peace initiatives; Book III begins with the dossier of letters that followed these gifts by some time, in which the motives of diplomacy are more explicit and, as events proved, more hopeless, however noble.

more or less routine nature, whether issued spontaneously or in response to a petition. The most common subjects of these documents are private and ecclesiastical lawsuits, with frequent cases involving the conflicting claims to property of feuding heirs or even churches. In one instance, for example, a minor's guardian had apparently accused the youth's brother-in-law of engineering an unfair division of inherited property; the two letters preserved require the parties to come to court and have justice done; a third party is directed to supervise the execution of that justice (*Var.* 1.7–8).[32] Without fail, such cases are adorned in Cassiodorus' letters with the king's solemn promises that he will recognize his duty to protect the weak and secure justice.

Apart from judicial determinations, there is a large collection of royal orders on the interconnected subjects of commerce, transport, taxes, and the grain supply. Here the end in view is the welfare of the people and the establishment of a fair method for providing the fisc with its revenues. Thus, one case agrees to allow the annual payment of the *tertiae* (tax in lieu of land for Gothic settlers) to be lumped together by its payers with taxes already being paid, since their land had been independently declared immune from actual confiscation and the annual payment will continue indefinitely (*Var.* 1.14). In another instance, the bishops and *honorati* of a district left anonymous are charged to cooperate with royal agents in putting an end to speculation in grain that is causing the *possessores* of the region to suffer (*Var.* 9.5). Frequently the topic is of particular interest to the court: once Theoderic is heard complaining about an interruption in the supply of *sacra vestis,* the royal purple cloth (*Var.* 1.2); other letters speak of procuring delicacies for the king's table from those parts of Italy that have special treats to offer.

Such documents provide the most mundane reading in the *Variae.* Scattered throughout the first five books, the last half of

32. These two letters may date to before and after the appearance at court and may be meant to show the workings of the king's justice in some detail. Our view is distorted because we can see only the indictment and/or the execution, never the legal process itself.

Book VIII, and throughout Book IX, they provide the background of ordinary benevolence on which the Gothic rule was based. Taken together with letters ordering an end to various abuses of the public post, they fill up the gaps between the more remarkable discussions. For in addition to these ordinary affairs, three other subjects stand out, two of special interest to a specifically Roman audience.

The topic of most general interest is the succession to the throne. Half of Book VIII is filled with documents of Athalaric's succession, including notifications to virtually every constituency (beginning with the emperor Justin) of the death of Theoderic and the orderly transfer of power. Since Athalaric says when appointing Cassiodorus that there were in fact some military scares at this time, we may assume that these letters served at that time a function analogous to that which the *Variae* was expected to perform a decade later—the self-justification of the Gothic rule.

The two Roman topics have to do specifically with the circus (and circus factions) and the interest that Theoderic had in the rebuilding of structures damaged in Italy's wars. In the last half of the *Variae,* the only document concerning rebuilding is Cassiodorus' own letter ordering repair of the Flaminian Way (*Var.* 12.18). Under Theoderic, however, there had been more leisure and opportunity to attempt (as civilized monarchs should) to repair what Italy had lost, and especially the city of Rome. Twenty-five letters deal with subjects ranging from the ordinary (clearing vegetation from a watercourse [*Var.* 5.38]) to the decorative (mosaics for Ravenna [*Var.* 1.6]) to the strictly cultural (the letter to Symmachus praising his earlier rebuilding efforts and enjoining the reconstruction of the theater of Pompey [*Var.* 4.51]). In one case, Theoderic explicitly allows the use of scattered stonework fallen from ruined buildings in these rebuilding activities, and several other letters involve arrangements for the transportation of materials; clearly the enterprise was one that was both necessary after decades of warfare and neglect and at the same time willingly undertaken. There can be little doubt that such a policy was good politics, since its result would be to associate in the public mind the Gothic regime with the new and refurbished structures it caused to be built throughout Italy. Theoderic's private motives—how much of this was simple expedience, how much royal vanity, and how much a sincere concern for the ancient glories of noble Italy—are hidden from us. Furthermore, the frequent appearance of these letters in the books dating from Theoderic's reign (they exceed 10 percent of the letters in those five books) may be exaggerated by Cassiodorus' own practice of selection; certainly any letters that he could find in which Theoderic appeared as the dedicated rebuilder of Roman Italy would have a strong claim to inclusion in a collection published shortly after the Gothic siege of Rome sustained by Belisarius. Whatever Theoderic's policy really was, the *Variae* makes it clear that Cassiodorus wanted his king remembered for his unflagging concern for the renovation of Italy's damaged splendor. In this and other respects, Theoderic's reign is made to seem a golden age, and one not long past at that; by implication, it was a golden age recoverable by prudent men.

The other rulers in whose names Cassiodorus wrote do not appear fully enough, or enough to their own advantage, for us to derive a consistent picture of the image that Cassiodorus meant to create for them. It must have been difficult, in the first place, to do this for Athalaric, whom everyone knew to have been in fact a child, and for Theodahad and Witigis afterwards, the documents of whose reigns were too much constrained by circumstance to allow much scope for the display of virtue (though Cassiodorus' selection at least removes almost all the blots from their records, a negative but effective device). Theoderic, on the other hand, does succeed in becoming attached in our minds to an image of the kind of king he was (or was represented to be). Whatever he may have been in real life, the king we meet in the *Variae* was a gentle man, always happy to praise his subjects for their faithful service to his kingdom and, *a fortiori* (and the way in which the logical connection is made to seem obvious is usually the acme of Cassiodorus' art as propagandist), to virtue and justice. When he has reason to reproach his subjects, it is with sorrow rather than anger: the voice is that of a gently chiding father, calmly reviewing the principles of good government, finding them sadly lacking, and quietly but forcefully urging the rectification of the unhappy situation.[33] We are entitled to believe that Theoderic may have been more vigorous in expressing himself when seen in life; but we see him always in the *Variae* as Cassiodorus would paint him for us, or rather for the angry, strident warring parties of the time in which he published his anthology.

In every way, then, the *Variae,* read as a work of contemporary history, presented a picture of life in Italy as it once was—and as it still could be—and which contrasted sharply with the quickly deteriorating reality. There was once a time when a learned king sent erudite directives to his subjects, ruled moderately and justly, and was solicitous of the health and happiness of his kingdom through happy decades. There is not much way of knowing whether this portrait comes close to the truth; but its purpose was not, in fact, objective truth, but the counteraction, by a kind of genteel polemic, of the angry prejudices that were displayed on all sides in the Gothic war. The *Variae* is thus a kind of final effort in the genre of panegyric by Cassiodorus, but panegyric of a considerably more sophisticated form than any of his earlier efforts. Judged as history the book exhibits many faults; but it is a kind of panegyric of the past that has striking and lasting value. That it succeeded in some measure is best remarked by observing how thoroughly our own present ideas about Theoderic and his kingdom have been conditioned by this one work; even if our suspicions are aroused, it is still against this text alone that they can be tested.

A literary analysis of the book (which must be balanced between considering the works as individual documents and as elements in the whole collection) throws further light on the nature of the work and its particular successes and failures. Some such analysis has, in the past, been based on attempts to

33. *Var.* 1.35, the sucking-fish letter (discussed below) is a good example of the gentle chiding at which Theoderic excelled when Cassiodorus wrote the words.

identify the literary genre in which the *Variae* can be formally located.[34] It is valuable to begin such a study of the *Variae* by observing the mixed position it takes between various traditional uses of the epistolary genres. For example, the *Variae* partakes both of the ancient tradition of the literary epistle as practiced by Pliny or Symmachus (the letters of appointment to high office resemble the documents by which the earlier authors had practiced the *religio* of polite society), but at the same time it has the formality of chancery rhetoric of more ordinary royal and imperial documents of the sort that survive in bulk from all ages. In fact, the strictly literary use of the epistolary genres dies out for most of the middle ages, reviving only with the twelfth century; in Cassiodorus, however, two different kinds of letter-writing have been welded together to form a new kind of document. For, in fact, late antique chancery style, such as we know its existence, was not as consciously literary as the letters in the *Variae*. The kind of letter contained in the *Variae* seems almost to have been invented by Cassiodorus to combine business and pleasure. Each individual letter was from the beginning a little piece of propaganda, as well as an instrument of government. Receiving one of Cassiodorus' letters from the royal messenger denoted the favor one found in the eyes of the king, gave opportunity to delight in a pleasing literary style, and for both reasons inspired reflection on the wisdom and cultivation of the magnanimous monarch.

Thus the propagandistic thrust of the *Variae* as a published collection was not something altogether new imposed by artful selection and editing at the time of publication; from the first, these letters had been fulfilling many of the purposes that they were then meant to fill again for a new audience when Cassiodorus published the collection. Furthermore, this idiosyncratically propagandistic use of the royal chancery was a skill at which Cassiodorus was particularly adept, beyond the range of

34. The over-sensitive distinction between *Brief* and *Epistel*, which Besselaar, *Cassiodorus Senator en zijn Variae* (1945), 127, applies to Cassiodorus (stemming from theories of A. Diesmann), has been confuted by Å. J. Fridh, *Terminologie et formules dans les "Variae"* (1956), 3–4.

the ordinary quaestor. We should note, moreover, that we only see Theoderic granting benefits (e.g., agreeing to hear a legal case or granting tax relief), never denying them. Requests that the bureaucracy (or even the king) rejected were probably not honored with a royal letter of reply. The image of generosity was thus encouraged with no conscious effort at deception and selection of material, for the *Variae* in fact began with dozens of day-to-day decisions years before.

With the *Variae* there are many different styles, adapted chiefly to the subject of the letter and the occasion of composition. As stated earlier, it is difficult to see a direct relationship between a recipient's level of education or social status and the level of style of the letter addressed to him; nevertheless, there is doubtless substantial tailoring of the more important letters to the individual recipients in a way that is inaccessible to us, since the private details of the relationships between these people (particularly the high potentates of the court) and their king are lost to history. The most obvious cases of this tailoring are the letters to Boethius and Symmachus, where the whole point of the letters is to flatter the aristocrats by asking their advice and assistance on cultural matters; the king wants to show an interest in such affairs, while deferring to the vanity of those who felt themselves the particular guardians of culture. Of a different nature are the letters at the end of Book VIII to Severus, governor of what is now Calabria, in which Cassiodorus goes on at length about the beauty of his home province; similarly, in the extended description of Squillace upon which we drew in Chapter 1 above, Cassiodorus' addressee has obviously come to expect that the good prefect will grow a little long-winded and lyrical when he has the chance to write about his home town.[35] As political documents, these letters in particular may have had some effect in maintaining good rela-

35. Letters that pause to praise Cassiodorus' home province (Lucania et Bruttii) include 3.8, 8.31–33, 9.3–4, 11.39.3 (the first "for example" that comes to his mind), 12.5, and 12.12–15; this probably shows a combination of native bias and a half-random search of the files. See also 2.29–30, clearly pulled from the "Milan" file together, though otherwise unrelated.

tions with the folks back home, but that was undoubtedly minimal compared with the simple literary delight that Cassiodorus would take in the act of composing them. By contrast, when the time came to publish the *Variae,* these descriptions of a happy and fertile country could doubtless also be read as evidence of the prosperity of Italy under the Goths.

The literary resources that went into composing these rhetorical tours de force were considerable. The most famous example, a favorite with all Cassiodorus scholars, is the query directed to the prefect Faustus about a delay in the arrival of the grain supply (*Var.* 1.35). The ships in which the grain is to be transmitted are the focus of the trope, which becomes outright allegory. The king wonders aloud what could cause the delay when such favorable weather attends the season for sailing; could it be, he supposes, the sucking-fish that has fixed its teeth in his ships, or the conch from the Indian Ocean? Perhaps the sailors are themselves made languid by the touch of the stingray. "Truly," the king concludes, "men who cannot move must have suffered some such attack." But then, he adds, the sucking-fish is really procrastinating venality, the bite of the conch really insatiable cupidity, and the stingray is fraudulent pretence. "They manufacture delays with corrupt ingenuity, pretending to encounter adverse conditions." The prefect is then strictly directed to look into this situation quickly and make the needed amends, "lest famine might seem to be born of negligence rather than drought."

This letter also contains one of Cassiodorus' trademarks, discussion of natural phenomena. The effect of the various marine creatures on the ship's course is discussed carefully in view of the behavior of the animals, and the figure stands in close relation to the thing allegorized. This attachment to natural history is one of the commonest themes of Cassiodorus' digressions.[36] He has at least ten such lengthy digressions on subjects ranging from storms and elephants to the production of purple cloth

36. H. F. A. Nickstadt, *De digressionibus quibus in Variis usus est Cassiodorus* (1921) on the digressions; see also Å. J. Fridh, *Terminologie et formules dans les "Variae"* (1956), 18–19.

and the production of amber.[37] A large number of these digressions have been shown to derive from the *Hexameron* of Ambrose, including the case discussed in the paragraph, where Cassiodorus was drawing on a similar treatment in Ambrose of the various fish.[38]

It should not be thought that Cassiodorus is not capable of integrating digressive material harmoniously into his work. Two elegant examples demonstrate this. One of the simplest, shortest letters in the collection is a proclamation "to all Goths and Romans and those who command harbors and castles," dating from Cassiodorus' quaestorship (*Var.* 2.19). In an unknown locality, certain slaves have murdered their own master and dishonored the funerary rites. Theoderic is grieved, comparing human behavior to that of birds: "Alas, the pity men abandon is found even among birds. The vulture, who lives on the corpses of other creatures, for all his great size is friendly with lesser birds and protects them from the attacking hawk, beating him away with his wings and gnashing his beak: and yet men cannot spare their own kind" (*Var.* 2.19.2–3). This is more than a zoological metaphor chosen arbitrarily to illustrate the cruelty of men to men; Cassiodorus did not leave the metaphor at that, but instead integrated it neatly with the final statement of Theoderic's judgment: "So let him be food for the vultures, who can cruelly seek the slaughter of his shepherd. Let him find such a sepulcher, who has left his master unburied" (*Var.* 2.19.3). No one, not even Cassiodorus, would call this letter a masterwork of literature; but such a piece, unambitious yet neatly suited to its circumstances, with the verbal details of its metaphorical structure completely worked out and adroitly executed, is perhaps comparable to good lyric poetry for its scope and workmanship, if not for its theme.

It is not, therefore, surprising that Cassiodorus could be as effective and competent in one of his longer efforts with a more consciously literary purpose. The letter to Boethius at the end

37. *Var.* 5.2.15 cites Tacitus' *Germania* on the origins of amber.

38. Ambrose, *Hexameron,* 5.10.31; Nickstadt, *op. cit.,* 22–23, showed the connection to Ambrose and listed parallel passages.

of Book II, requesting that a musician be found as a gift for Clovis the Frank, is one of the longest letters in the *Variae*. The business of the letter is transacted in a few lines at the beginning and end; the bulk of the text is a little treatise *de musica,* with historical and technical material in abundance. The digression begins with the third sentence of the letter and continues for over 120 printed lines (*Var.* 2.40.2–16). At the end, Cassiodorus calls this little treatise a *voluptuosa digressio,* then gives Boethius his instructions: "Please name the *citharoedus* we have requested from you; he will be another Orpheus, taming the hard hearts of these foreigners [*gentiles*] with sweet music" (*Var.* 2.40.17). But this precisely calls into question the digressiveness of the whole letter. For the theme of the discussion of music has been its capacity to impart peace to the soul, to represent the peace of celestial harmony; and it is precisely peace that is the goal of the gift itself. In fact, no more competent and learned case could have been made for the suitability of just such a gift at just such a time.

In the same letter there is a parallel case of a well-integrated bit of apparently digressive material, in the story of Odysseus and the Sirens. The familiar tale is repeated, mainly to show the power of music, culminating in Odysseus' successful escape from the Sirens. As Cassiodorus finishes this passage, he has also completed one section of his discourse on the effects that music has on men; he wishes to turn to the music of the Psalter as his next subject. His transition is effected by means of the mythical tale just concluded, turning from the last sentence of the tale to the next topic thus: "He had himself bound to the mast so that he could hear the Sirens' songs with his own ears but still escape the dangers of the sweet voices, prevented as he was from plunging to the foaming waves. In the same way, let us pass from the example of the crafty Ithacan to speak of the Psalter sent from heaven" (*Var.* 2.40.10–11). The transition is not strictly logical, but the neatness of the figure and its integration into the structure of the letter makes it possible, almost inevitable, that we overlook that. Our attention is propelled along happily without being too explicitly bothered about where it is being headed next.

A more doubtful example of the functional utility of rhetorical figures, and a more revealing specimen of Cassiodorus' practice, is a short letter to Faustus, the praetorian prefect, enjoining tax relief for inhabitants of the Cottian Alps suffering from the depredations of marching Gothic armies; to his command Theoderic adds the brief metaphorical statement that "The river continuously scours its channel and sterilizes it, leaving the surrounding country more fertile for its passing" (*Var.* 4.36.2). The figure is a neat one again, offering to modern readers, for example, a new way of considering what the effects of such an army's passing must have been like; it is less certain that Faustus really needed to be told such things. What has happened here, instead, is that the format has become fixed, requiring that every letter to come from Cassiodorus' pen have some literary pretensions.

The apparatus of classical learning is another bit of fretwork added to the more colorless business at hand. It is surprising, however, that there is so little formal classical allusion in the *Variae*. Apart from the silent use of such presumed sources as Ambrose or Pliny for the substance of digressions, there is very little dropping of classical tags, with or without acknowledgment. From the whole work, for example, there are only five explicit mentions of Vergil, three with quotations; and the quotations are not quite verbatim, thus probably from memory.[39] The explicit and implicit allusions in the *Variae* are almost exclusively from Latin literature, with only three allusions to Homeric events to demonstrate any familiarity with Greek legends.

Cassiodorus' other major literary habit is a taste for etymology common in late antiquity and almost extinct today. That this particular trait was Cassiodorus' own is best seen when he

39. See Vergil slightly misquoted from memory in *Var.* 5.21.3 and 5.42.11, for example.

makes extensive use of the science again in his *Expositio Psalmorum*, written far from the dictates of chancery style. One scholar has catalogued etymologies in the *Variae* ranging from the months of the year to musical terms to the names of provinces; as usual in late antique authors, they contain a mixture of fact and fiction.[40]

When all this literary baggage had been collected and Cassiodorus set out to produce one of his little masterpieces, the final effect achieved was neither unpleasing nor ineffective. From the preamble (frequently taking the form of a first premise of a syllogism developed by the letter) through the exposition of the subject (with time out for illuminating digression) to the final determination of the king's will, the line was actually very clear and direct.[41] Brevity is the reigning characteristic of the individual documents. The longest letters are those in which Cassiodorus had a personal interest; the longest in the whole collection is only 154 lines long in the most recent edition.[42] After that, the longest letters are to Boethius to provide a musician for Clovis and to the senate on the merits and ancestry of Cassiodorus' own father (*Var.* 2.40 and 1.4). Few of the other letters run to more than a hundred lines; the average length is approximately thirty-five lines. There is a certain tedium that affects modern readers of the *Variae* for two reasons, one unrelated to the original composition of the letters, the other unrelated to Cassiodorus at all. First, the original letters came to their audience only in small doses; while Cassiodorus argues in his preface that the variousness of the collection makes it read more quickly, even the first readers of the whole work must have felt some discomfort with such a vast collection of short, disconnected letters. But second, the origi-

---

40. Besselaar, *Cassiodorus Senator en zijn Variae* (1945), 145–147, identified forty-three uses of etymology (not all noted in Traube's index to Mommsen's edition).

41. On the preamble to the typical letter, see my remarks above and Å. J. Fridh, *Terminologie et formules dans les "Variae"* (1956), 30–59.

42. *Var.* 11.1, in which Cassiodorus announced his own appointment as prefect to the senate.

nal letters had an attraction that does us little good—that is, their strong topical interest. For us, to whom the events described are long ago and far away, and to whom the individuals are names only a few of which we recognize with any enthusiasm, the main attraction of the work for its contemporary readers is lost. If we can presume for this work, moreover, an audience still in love with rhetoric, the presence of its ornaments in these letters in such liberal and diverse portions was an added attraction of no little merit.

The formal shape of the letters has been altered in the course of compiling the whole collection in two ways that lessen their interest for us but that in fact increased their aesthetic attraction in Cassiodorus' eyes. First, there has been a wholesale deletion of names and dates to increase the timelessness of the letters published. Most names of legates to whom diplomatic letters were entrusted are gone, but in one case the names of two barns involved in a lawsuit have been reduced to "illud et illud" anonymity as well (*Var.* 3.29.2). But by no means are all dates missing, or all names; Cassiodorus the compiler functioned erratically on this one point.

Second, we have also lost the attached *breves* by which were transmitted particular details of the case for many of the more complicated issues treated.[43] In one case the letter preserved in the *Variae* is almost without significant content, merely exhorting the recipient to obey the commands specified in the attached *breves;* in another letter the attachment would have given the list of names of persons affected by the royal action (*Var.* 4.21 and 5.31.1).

Hard linguistic evidence both confirms our estimation of the kind of work this was and gives independent testimony to the

43. For this practice in the strictly personal letter-writing of late antiquity, see J. F. Matthews, "The Letters of Symmachus," in J. W. Binns, ed., *Latin Literature of the Fourth Century* (1974), 48–99, esp. 63–81. He shows how our valuation of trivia and substance is exactly the reverse of the late antique taste; we think the elegant letters preserved intentionally are trivial, hankering after concrete information that the disdainful ancients consigned to their attached memos.

level of culture still attained by educated classes of the sixth century. The language of the *Variae* has been studied from several aspects;[44] the sum total of the research demonstrates that the work's ties to Latin literary traditions are as strong in language as in rhetoric and style. Only two Germanic words are used in the whole work, both nouns for specific technical needs (*saio* for the kind of court functionary who replaced the *agens in rebus,* and *carpa* for a fish). There are a great many more words that occur for the first time to our knowledge in Cassiodorus, often formed by adding standard endings to old words to form new nouns (ending in *-or, -tio, -tas, -ius*) and otherwise orthodox in their Latin derivation. Moreover, very many recently coined nouns in *-tio,* adjectives in *-lis,* and adverbs in *-ter* are used. The most characteristic feature is the use of increasingly abstract words to replace existing words; the new words (whether coined by Cassiodorus or drawn by him from the usage of his day) are weaker in force but (superficially) more specific in meaning than classical equivalents. In addition to all of this, there is the importation of numerous Greek words (though none in such a way as to indicate that Cassiodorus himself knew Greek at this time).[45]

In syntax, Cassiodorus similarly represents the trends of the consciously literary language of his age. He runs into occasional trouble on matters of form (his use of the royal "we" is some-

44. On the language of the *Variae,* see Å. J. Fridh, *Terminologie et formules dans les "Variae"* (1956); also his *Études critiques et syntaxiques sur les Variae de Cassiodore* (1950), and his *Contributions à la critique et à l'interprétation des Variae de Cassiodore* (1968), all prolegomena to his Corpus Christianorum edition (1973). There are several dissertations from the Catholic University of America on Cassiodorus; for the *Variae,* see B. H. Skahill, *The Syntax of the Variae of Cassiodorus* (1934); M. J. Suelzer, *The Clausulae in Cassiodorus* (1944, but based on Garet's 1679 text, so compare H. Hagendahl, *La prose métrique d'Arnobe* [1937], 79–83, 257–260); and (best of all) O. J. Zimmermann, *The Late Latin Vocabulary of the Variae of Cassiodorus* (1944).

45. See O. J. Zimmermann, *op. cit.,* for the material in this paragraph. He points out that there was very little afterlife in Latin prose for most of the apparent neologisms in Cassiodorus (only 16 of 129 were ever used again by other authors).

times inconsistent even within a given letter), but he is clearly in command of the language to the extent that anyone was in his age. The vocative case is disappearing, to be replaced by the formal third person (e.g., *magnitudo vestra*), and the general use of demonstrative pronouns is far more abundant than in Caesar and Cicero. But nothing Cassiodorus does is without precedent in Silver or Late Latin, in the church fathers, or in other acceptable representatives of later style. His is a rhetoric of the schools to a fault, resulting in a highly artificial kind of work.[46] There is a tendency, difficult to isolate, to depart from the periodic style in favor of a monotonous alignment of clauses, against the boredom of which the excessive use of consciously flashy figures and language attempts to militate.[47]

Whether chancery style was a cause or an effect of some of these developments in the language is an unanswerable question. Certainly there was generally a shrill respect enunciated by all emperors for literary values that they did not always understand fully. Thus government language becomes characterized in general by euphemism and vagueness.[48] As an author, Cassiodorus does not transcend the literary faults of his environment; rather, he may be said to have attempted to find ways to circumvent them, to make virtues of the vices that had crept into the language he had been taught. The mannered style of late antique rhetoric was a home for him, a way of reacting against the boredom that sets in when an austere style becomes too familiar and thus contemptible.[49]

The most obvious thing about the language of the *Variae*, however, is perhaps the most important for an understanding of the work as a whole; namely that the language is clearly that

46. Skahill, *op. cit.*, can be squeezed to produce this paragraph.

47. Å. J. Fridh, *Études critiques et syntaxiques* . . . (1950), 82.

48. R. MacMullen, *Traditio,* 18(1962), 364–378. See Besselaar, *Cassiodorus Senator en zijn Variae* (1945), 179, for a table of the frequency of formal verbs, contributing an air of authority and an appropriate number of syllables for a clausula, but little more, in the *Variae* and the *Institutiones.*

49. E. R. Curtius, *European Literature and the Latin Middle Ages* (1953), 273–301, for the mannerist theory of late antique and early medieval Latin.

of Cassiodorus himself, uninfluenced by Gothic elements. This is an important consideration for answering the most important question about the *Variae,* namely the degree to which these letters reflect the actual policies of the Gothic kings in whose names the bulk of the individual letters were written, and how much they simply show Cassiodorus playing with his rhetorical toys. Some scholars are too ready to assume that the letters can be taken as is to reflect the thoughts of the monarch in whose name they were drafted; others too skeptically assume that Theoderic was an illiterate who could scarcely understand the purport of the letters drafted for him, much less appreciate the literary art. It seems, in light of all that we know about Cassiodorus and Theoderic, that a middle position does least violence to the evidence.

There is unquestionably triteness in even the most intellectually central concepts that appear in the *Variae,* and with it further evidence of the evisceration of the natural force of language. It has been traditional to see this process at work in the concept of *civilitas,* which even the most superficial treatments of the *Variae* have distinguished as a central idea of Theoderician government. Indeed, if Theoderic were entirely responsible for the words uttered in his name, the presence of such a concept would be praiseworthy in the policies of a barbarian. But it is Cassiodorus to whom we must assign responsibility for the intellectual framework of the *Variae,* and we can be less lenient with triviality on his part. *Civilitas* is in fact part of a larger scheme of slogans that springs from the whole pattern of denatured language with which Cassiodorus loaded the *Variae.*

For it must be remarked that, for all the literary care that has gone into the *Variae,* the effect is not memorable; there is nothing so well put anywhere in these letters that it would bear remembering. There is everywhere in Cassiodorus a nostalgia for the epigrammatic brilliance of Silver Latin rhetoric, but this emotion is couched in a growing wordiness. Every epigram is taken out, examined from all angles, and belabored to death. In the preface to Book XI of the *Variae,* for example, Cassiodorus quotes a pithy anecdote to Cicero's rhetorical practice: "For that fount of eloquence is said to have declined an invitation to speak by saying that he had not read anything the day before" (*Var.* 11, Praef. 8). In the context of Cassiodorus' preface the remark has point and purpose, for he is pleading for mercy from his audience for the failings of his own ill-considered, hastily-published writings. But Cassiodorus is not content with Cicero's remark; he must elaborate it through six more sentences. "What can happen to others, if such a marvel of eloquence has to demand the assistance of *auctores*? Talent grows ever rusty unless refreshed by reading." (This sentence in particular is limited to saying just what Cicero has already been quoted as saying, but saying it less memorably.) "The barn is quickly emptied unless replenished by continuous additions. The treasury is readily emptied unless refilled with money." (Illustrating the line of Cicero, Cassiodorus adds two gratuitous analogies.) "So human invention, when it is not stocked with other people's sayings, is quickly exhausted on its own." (He summarizes the main point again, perhaps misunderstanding it slightly—Cicero would have sought ideas, not words, from his reading. "Anything sweet-smelling in our prose is the flower of our studies, which nonetheless withers if cut off from its source, assiduous reading" (*Var.* 11, Praef. 8–9). (Finally a connection back to the thread of the preface's argument is made.)

In part the nature of the documents preserved in the *Variae* is responsible for this rhetorical weakness at the knees. Very many indeed are the royal letters in the *Variae* whose punch is pulled at the last moment with a final qualifier, in particular in legal cases where the facts admit of some doubt and Theoderic wants to circumscribe the effects of his rescript (e.g., *Var.* 2.29.2); in a more modern bureaucratic jargon, if anything goes wrong the monarch must preserve his "deniability" and shift the blame that may result from the case onto the shoulders of a bureaucratic underling.

As a matter of simple language, enervated terminology is everywhere apparent, particularly in certain terms that recur frequently; these words are almost totally devoid of denotative content, but they act as signals of royal approval or disapproval. It is precisely the famous slogan *civilitas* and its parallel terms that provide the best example of this linguistic spinelessness. *Civilitas* itself always refers in Cassiodorus to the actions of a citizen (as etymologically it should, as Cassiodorus would see). Behaving like a good citizen was something that Theoderic wanted to preach to his Goths, whom he was teaching to pay taxes; his remark, "*Civilitas* preserved is an honor for the Goths," was addressed to a Gothic military governor in Sicily (*Var.* 9.14.18).[50]

But Theoderic spoke more often of his own virtues than of his subjects', and in edicts and letters laying down the law, more often of wrongdoing to be avoided than virtue to be practiced. As a king and as a representative of Roman imperial traditions, Theoderic would not prescribe *civilitas* as a model for his own behavior; when he wishes to describe his own magnanimity, the term chosen more often than any other is *humanitas*— whether as a general quality or as a term for specific acts (even used occasionally in the plural in that restricted sense). This slogan is Ciceronian, of course, though it never really caught on in Latin, perhaps precisely because it was too vague and watery for most political purposes. But Cassiodorus must have thought it appropriate for giving a folksy touch to a lofty monarch, assuring the audience he addressed that the king was at heart decent and kind. At any rate, by a rough count *humanitas* and its immediate derivatives appear about as often in the *Variae* as *civilitas* and its derivatives.[51]

A word that appears about four times as often as either of these terms for the kind of behavior one hopes to cultivate is the blanket term for behavior one wants to discourage: *praesumptio.*[52] Etymologically, the term means a taking for oneself of something; in the *Variae* it usually means to do so in an unlawful or wrongful way. In particular it is a term favored in edicts to describe proscribed behavior; it appears eight times

50. "Gothorum laus est civilitas custodita."
51. By thirty-four times to thirty-one.
52. With its derivatives, *praesumptio* appears about 125 times in the *Variae*.

(*civilitas* appears twice) in the *Edictum Athalarici* in Book IX, and it appears three times, balanced with three appearances of *humanitas,* in the edict that ends the *Variae* (*Var.* 9.18, 12.28).[53] On the rare occasions in the *Variae* where the word does not refer to wrongdoing, it still has the sense of undertaking something vaguely undesirable; a general getting a new assignment is reminded that youth is benefited by such a task: "Iuvenum siquidem virtus praesumptione laboris animatur . . ." (*Var.* 5.25.1). In another case, the presumption is that of the king, presuming the loyalty and integrity of a fiscal officer (*Var.* 8.23.8).

In the generally negative sense of the *Variae, praesumptio* is often tied to *cupiditas* as effect in action of a cause in spirit.[54] *Praesumptio* can include crimes up to and including murder, but in later life Cassiodorus will use the same word to describe the blunders of scribes (*Inst.* 1.15.6–16). Thus the word has not been strengthened by Cassiodorus in the *Variae* to serve as a strong rebuke against criminal behavior; rather the rebuke has been weakened so far as to be summarized in the equivocal term.[55]

And so the pattern of cliché is complete: *humanitas* is the kind of behavior the king promises on his part; *civilitas* is the behavior he preaches as desirable from his citizens; and *praesumptio* is what he deprecates. These are not the catchwords of a vital political conception or a strong central administration; they are moralistic slogans, slogans that fail to inspire, bits of euphemism that assume definite meanings from being used so

---

53. See *incivilitas* equated with *praesumptio, Var.* 7.39.2.

54. This is explicitly the case at *Var.* 7.9.3, often implicitly elsewhere.

55. One other term appears as a feeble prod to motivate good behavior: *fama* (cf. note 15, above). A desire for *fama* will preserve one from too much desire for lucre (*Var.* 1.4.8), for it benefits a patrician to seek that "quod et famam vestram possit augere" (*Var.* 2.11.3). This idea is never elevated to the rank of slogan, but it seems to contain a shrewder insight than many other trite expressions of the work. In approving a love of *fama,* however, Cassiodorus was closer to classical antiquity than to the church fathers. Augustine, *De civ. Dei* 5.12–15, was even shrewder than Cassiodorus in observing the way a love of glory replaced (sublimated?) lesser cupidities in the Roman scheme of values.

often but that in turn at least partially deflate what is being said in the name of verbal nicety.

It is thus in Cassiodorus' clichés that we find the traces of his policies. That the soul of his political purposes was thus entrusted to weak and hackneyed language, fortified with euphemism and shored up with triviality, was not a sign of any great strength of purpose or confidence in execution of design. To what extent this weakness mirrored an insecurity of Theoderic we do not know; it may have been imported gratuitously by Cassiodorus, since we have no certain knowledge of the roles that king and courtier played in drafting these documents and the ideas that lay behind them. But Theoderic was apparently pleased by the fainting language in the documents he was given to sign, and it is certain that in the end the weakness of the kingdom did in fact come to reflect the weakness of the language in which it was extolled. Whether it was Theoderic who got the kind of propaganda he deserved, or whether it was the propoganda that was as ineffectual as the government, we do not know.

In either case, the documents were the same precious little things, rhetorically and literarily self-conscious, meant to please, to edify and (usually) not to offend, and similar in their individual purposes to the purpose to which they would be put when collected into the *Variae*. For their function was nothing less than the justification, in the course of everyday business, of the Ostrogothic rule in Italy, on the grounds of political and imperial legitimacy, and the demonstration of the success of the kingdom when left to its own devices to establish and maintain an orderly society under a humane monarch, in spite of the barbarian origin of its leaders and many of its people. In a sense, therefore, the *Variae* began as panegyric but ended as a serious brief for the constitutional legitimacy of the whole kingdom, carrying the arguments and the supporting evidence in favor of the continued existence of the kingdom within the Roman empire. For the tragedy of the Ostrogothic kingdom is that precisely that subject of so much modern scholarly speculation, the constitutional position of Theoderic, was never clearly established; the Ostrogoths always occupied an ambiguous, delicately balanced position, in danger of overthrow at any time from several directions. In the end, the most fearful power decided to put an end to the ambiguity. As this was happening, Cassiodorus brought a lifetime of statesman's work to bear in this last work, presenting the case for the Ostrogothic kingdom as strongly and diplomatically as he could. But the forces then in motion were too great, too much beyond the control of individuals, to be called back by the voice of reason and the winged words of rhetoric.

As long as we witness Cassiodorus in his public *persona* as spokesman to the Latin literary world of the Ostrogothic kingdom, we are only allowed to see him as a diligent optimistic bureaucrat. His concerns are consistently those worldly problems of the conscientious public servant, diversified only by occasional, touching attempts to maintain as much external pomp of the Roman traditions under the new regime as possible. Thus the last letter we have in the collection written in the name of Theodahad, just before that king's murder and replacement by Witigis, just as Italy began again to know the ravages of war after Belisarius' invasion, is a marvelous, erudite, and even amusing discussion of the condition of certain bronze elephants on the *Via Sacra* at Rome that had fallen into disrepair (*Var.* 10.30).[56] When the king wants to have them repaired, he illuminates his letter with all the hoary legends about the elephant that were handed down from one ancient writer to another (Cassiodorus has what Pliny had, but is independent of him as well). For example, we are told that "a wounded elephant remembers the offense and is said to revenge himself on the perpetrator long afterwards" (*Var.* 10.30.6). Cassiodorus' elephants adore their creator and serve only good princes, opposing evil ones. In the midst of war, the king took time to speak of these things, and he concluded, "Do not let

---

56. From 535/536; this was probably placed at the end of Theodahad's documents for the reasons enunciated above for placing similar letters at the ends of whole books.

these images perish, since it is Rome's glory to collect in herself by the artisan's skills whatever bountiful nature has given birth to in all the world" (*Var.* 10.30.8).

This hopeless effort to preserve a memento of empire at the heart of Rome epitomizes much of what Cassiodorus had been trying to do for thirty years. There is quixotic nobility about this that weighs disproportionately heavy in any assessment of the virtues and vices of the man. If Cassiodorus was not, for most of his career, the most outstanding figure in the rank-conscious society of Romans at the Gothic court, he was still a consistent presence, loyal and ingenious after his own lights, and clearly still faithful until virtually the very end.

4

Conversion

IF the *Variae* was a defense of Gothic rule in Italy, it is the last such document to survive. Dependent as we are on Cassiodorus for our knowledge of the internal affairs of that kingdom, our view of the reconquest is obstructed by a major shift in the character of the evidence that Cassiodorus provides at this period. Sometime in 538, as he concluded the publication of the *Variae* and departed from public life, Cassiodorus published a short treatise *De anima,* choosing a new genre and a new focus for his literary interests.

The political and military situation in Italy after 537 did not admit any great sphere of activity for intellectual bureaucrats.[1] Witigis besieged Rome, then lifted the siege in 538; in 539 the Goths recaptured Milan, but Belisarius, in spite of his feud with Narses, captured Ariminum. Finally, Belisarius captured Ravenna in 540 and with it the chief part of the Gothic nobility, including Witigis himself.[2] These important captives Belisarius took with him to Constantinople, inspiring Justinian to bedeck himself with the title Gothicus. But the war was only beginning back in Italy, for after a brief interregnum of divided leadership, the young Totila took the Gothic throne and began an impressive series of victories. All through the 540's he more than occupied the Byzantine forces in Italy, capturing Rome twice, eventually going down to defeat in 552 before Narses,

1. Belisarius already had a praetorian prefect of his own, one Fidelis, at Rome in early 537 (Proc., *De bello gothico* 1.20.19–20), whose authority probably increased along with Byzantine control of Italy.

2. Belisarius was first invited by the Goths to accept their kingship; he pretended to agree to win access to the city, then reneged and proclaimed his allegiance to Justinian.

by then sole Byzantine commander in Italy. In 553 the last Gothic ruler, Teias, was defeated and slain, and the Ostrogothic kingdom passed from the stage of history.

Because the *Variae* ends with letters from 537, we perceive, perhaps rightly, a change in the tone of government after that date. When Cassiodorus refuses to be our guide any longer, we see only a trackless waste of war and destruction. The pretence of *civilitas* was too expensive a luxury to maintain in the midst of battle.

We know little of Cassiodorus in this period with certainty. If we assume that the *Variae* was published while Cassiodorus was still in office or at least still in contact with the files of government, then it follows that its contents give a good *terminus post quem* for either retirement or publication, whichever came first. The opening of the *De anima,* which speaks of the compilation of the *Variae* as a task completed shortly before, also seems to imply that the author's retirement was due to literary pursuits. Certainly there are none of the whining complaints about the pressures of office that characterize the prefaces in the *Variae.* The likeliest sequence, therefore, seems to be that Cassiodorus ceased to function as prefect in late 537 or early 538 (whether because he was dismissed by the Goths, because there had ceased to be tasks for a civil servant to perform in the Ostrogothic government at war, or because of a simple desire to seek retirement unconnected with the particular crises of the time—and the last of these is the least likely) and more or less immediately set himself to compiling the *Variae* for publication.[3] This was a task that might not unreasonably be expected to have taken some months, perhaps a year or so, if it involved searching through the files to collect material, then editing and arranging it, and finally composing the prefaces and taking some steps to see that the work reached whatever audience Cassiodorus had in mind.

3. It has been suggested that Cassiodorus resigned in protest against Witigis' murder of senators given in hostage by the besieged Romans in 537. There is (1) no evidence for this, and (2) little likelihood that the *Variae* would have grown out of so acrimonious a parting of the ways.

Thus, by some time late in 538 or early in 539, Cassiodorus was at last truly at liberty, though apparently still living at Ravenna and not immediately desirous of moving from there; for Ravenna was still an island of comparative safety, and it may not have been clear how lenient the Byzantine forces would be with someone who had served the Gothic government in such high positions. The *De anima* seems to have been written in this milieu, almost surely before the capture of Ravenna in the spring of 540. The first sentence of the preface of the *Expositio Psalmorum* refers to an increasing interest in scriptural studies while Cassiodorus was still in Ravenna: "After I had rid myself of the duties of office at Ravenna, weary of all the world's foul-tasting woes, then when I tasted of the heavenly Psalter, a honey for souls, I plunged myself into their study greedily, to banish the aftertaste of bitter deeds with sweet verses" (*Ex. Ps.* Praef. lines 1–5).[4]

Thus the composition of the *De anima* occurred between late 538 and early 540. In reality we come here to a serious lacuna in the evidence for Cassiodorus' activities. We do not next have definite knowledge of his whereabouts until 550, when he was in Constantinople in the circle of persons known to Pope Vigilius during that pontiff's long stay in the eastern capital. We will discuss the nature and extent of Cassiodorus' stay in Constantinople in the next chapter in connection with the Psalm commentary, which was largely composed there. For the moment we must concern ourselves simply with the narrower question of how Cassiodorus got from Ravenna before its capture to Constantinople sometime in the 540's. In the complete absence of direct evidence, hypotheses must be confected.

The commonest reconstruction of Cassiodorus' career at this

4. This preface to the Psalm commentary, it should be noted, was clearly written some years after the events described. Thus the conventionally antithetical opposition between the bitterness of secular cares and the sweet delights of the Psalter probably represents accurately only the sentiments that had developed over the years following the period described. There is no contemporary evidence that at the time of the transition from public to private life Cassiodorus was motivated by any notable spiritual distress.

point has argued that he returned to his family estates at Squillace upon his retirement from office; there, the theory pro-
gresses, he founded at least some forerunner of the later monastic community and was busy on most of the Psalm commentary. Then he went to Constantinople with other refugees from
the military activity of Totila in about 547/9, at about the same
time as Vigilius made the same trek.[5] There are two military
difficulties with this thesis. First, it assumes that the chief civil
official of the Ostrogothic kingdom was not only released by
the Byzantine forces but that he was allowed to pass un-
molested down the entire length of Italy to his family estates on
the extreme shore of the southernmost province. Furthermore,
it assumes that at a later date Cassiodorus, the lifelong sup-
porter of the Gothic regime, fled in fear from the approach of a
Gothic army. It is certainly conceivable that Cassiodorus
changed his coat completely on the approach of the Byzantine
armies; but there is not one slightest shred of evidence, direct or
indirect, for any such event. Our whole interpretation of the
Variae as a pro-Gothic dossier compiled on the eve (or morn) of
Cassiodorus' retirement runs counter to such a view.

The alternate view does seem simpler.[6] If we allow Cassiodorus to remain in the comparative safety of Ravenna until
its capture in 540, the probability then increases that he would
have left Italy at that time with Belisarius and Witigis. He
might or might not have gone voluntarily. If he was still interested in politics he may have thought that Constantinople
was the place where the fate of Gothic Italy might most profitably be settled; but if he was entirely devoted to religion, a
desire for the relative security of Constantinople might well
have been enhanced by a desire to acquaint himself with the
ecclesiastical institutions of the eastern church. He may simply
have had no choice. Some combination of both political and

5. See A. van de Vyver, *Speculum,* 6(1931), 244–292.

6. The long sojourn at Constantinople thesis began with J. Sundwall,
Abhandlungen zur Geschichte des ausgehenden Römertums (1919), 154–156, and was
accepted by M. J. Cappuyns, *DHGE,* 11(1949), 1349–1408.

religious motives, volition and constraint, may well have obtained.

If our dating of Cassiodorus' birth in the mid-480's (made possible by the discovery of the *Ordo generis*) is correct, then Cassiodorus was in his early fifties upon the fall of Ravenna; not only is this an age still adventurous enough to go off to Constantinople for considerations at least partly still political, but it enables us to place the date of his final return to Squillace at around 554 and his age at that time at about sixty-five to seventy, a reasonable age for genuine retirement in any century.

Thus we provisionally accept the hypothesis of a prolonged stay at Constantinople, lasting from 540 to 554. In the next chapter we will see that there is indirect evidence to support this belief further. Nevertheless, the question does not, it must be emphasized, admit of certain proof in either direction. Our choice of probabilities must in part be conditioned by a sense for the tenor of the life we have seen Cassiodorus creating for himself and a preference for the simpler hypothesis.

It is customary (and reasonable) to see in the *De anima,* the first religious treatise that Cassiodorus wrote, a document of his "conversion" from the life of a public statesman to that of a private man of religion. It is important, however, not to be misled by modern notions of what "conversion" involves; furthermore, we should take into account again what little we do know of Cassiodorus' religious life before his retirement. Some of the evidence for religious leanings in Cassiodorus the statesman was blotted out for us, partly by reticence in the first place, and perhaps partly by later self-censorship at the time of compiling the *Variae,* because of the difficult relations between Arian Goths and Catholic Italians. While Theoderic is praised as a model of tolerance by his contemporaries and by modern readers of the *Variae,* he was still a hated Arian to, for example, the so-called Anonymus Valesianus chronicler. What image of religious peace there was in Italy is at least partly a creation of the tacit agreement of all concerned to say nothing about the subject in public.

To be sure, Dom Cappuyns saw signs of increasing religious devotion in Cassiodorus' years as praetorian prefect.[7] The only firm pieces of evidence to which he could point, however, the letters at the beginning of Book XI addressed to Pope John II and the bishops of Italy, are not strong testimony (*Var.* 11.2–3). We do not know how customary such professions of faith and loyalty by new prefects were, nor how hollow they were in practice. Furthermore, similarly respectful rhetoric had been written by Cassiodorus and addressed to bishops and clergy of the orthodox church in the name of Arian rulers long before that time. There is no reason why the conventional cannot be sincere, but the presence of the conventional cannot be taken as proof positive of special sincerity.

On the other hand, one piece of evidence from a later date for Cassiodorus' growing interest in religion somewhere around this time is more substantive. The whole effort of Cassiodorus to found a school of Christian learning at Rome in concert with Pope Agapetus (elected 535, died 536) will be discussed at greater length in Chapter 6; but this kind of activity (which may have begun before 533 and before Agapetus was pope or Cassiodorus prefect) is clear evidence of an interest in Christian intellectual activity, whether newfound or long-established. The only other evidence for Cassiodorus' religious development at this time indicates that the concern was some time in developing. The enthusiastic praise in the *Institutiones* for the talents and the work of Dionysius Exiguus indicates that Cassiodorus was personally acquainted with the Scythian monk. As we have seen, opportunities existed for the two men to know each other, either as teacher and student or simply as brother scholars, both before Cassiodorus' public life and during the years from 511 to 523, some part of which, at least, Cassiodorus seems to have spent at Rome. Thus the education of Cassiodorus, and even his intellectual pastimes in adult years

7. Cappuyns, *op. cit.*, 1355. Cassiodorus was one of eleven *illustres* urged by Pope John II to oppose Nestorianism (*PL* 66.20–24); but he was addressed there in his public capacity.

spent out of office in semiretirement, may well have been directed toward the Christian life of learning for decades before his term as prefect. The sudden desire to found a school may be evidence, not of new concern for religious affairs, but rather of a newly developed consciousness of his ability to carry off such a project, which depends more on financial resources, likeminded cosponsors, and a certain amount of the confidence of mature years than on simple religious fervor. Thus while the notion of Cassiodorus' growing religious concerns during these years remains unproven, it can plausibly be replaced by a picture of a more lasting and developed interest.

It is therefore useful to speak of the process whose outward product was the *De anima* as one of conversion if we take care to understand that term. Current usage in English commonly limits "conversion" to the adoption of a particular religious creed by an individual or group formerly outside the community of faith thus entered; other uses are analogical. There is a strain of evangelical Christianity that speaks of conversion even in cases of individuals who have been brought up within organized Christianity; this is actually a revival of some of the original content of the concept.

For "conversion" in early medieval Christianity is not a simple event, a declaration of allegiance comparable to the acquisition of naturalized citizenship by a legal process. Instead, the term, rooted in the etymological notion of a turning towards God, had extensive use for many sorts of religious experience. To take the most familiar case, the young Augustine had been brought up by a Christian mother and enrolled as a catechumen; his chief religious activity as a young man was with the peripherally Christian Manichaeans, but by the time of his acceptance of the chair of rhetoric at Milan he was willing to attend orthodox Christian services while remaining officially a catechumen. Thus in the modern sense of the term, the event that took place in the garden at Milan in 386, and that has become the archetype for "conversion" discussions ever since, could be treated merely as the decision of a man who had been in Christian milieux all his life to accept baptism; even this is not so remarkable as it would be today, since late baptism was common.

But clearly Augustine treats his experience in Milan as a conversion, by which he has reference more specifically to the spiritual content of his life than generally to legal formalities. This distinction is central to early medieval notions of conversion.[8] The best evidence for the importance of this notion is found in the textual history of the *Regula* of Benedict, buried beneath a mountain of misplaced philological effort.[9] In several places in that text, Benedict speaks of "conversion" as something central to the life of the monk. In Chapter 58, with the enumeration of the vows that the new monk is to make, the subject is emphasized; the novice is made to promise obedience, *stabilitas,* and *conversatio morum suorum.*[10] The philological difficulty is with the word *conversatio.* That it is only a philological difficulty is best attested by the palaeographical information that in the places in the rule were *conversatio* should be taken in the sense of "conversion," the medieval monks and copyists who lived under the *Regula* simply changed their text to read *conversio,* following the spirit and sense of their founder's command, rather than the letter.[11]

8. For a good study of early medieval *conversio,* see P. Galtier, *Revue d'histoire ecclésiastique,* 33.1(1937), 1–26, 277–305.

9. The exact meaning of the three vows of the Benedictine *Regula* (Chapter 58) is much debated. The two schools of opinion (*conversatio* in Chapter 58 does/does not mean "conversion") can be found most carefully presented in the notes to the edition of the *Regula* by J. McCann (1952), who discusses the question extensively and sensibly, concluding that *conversatio* does roughly equal *conversio* in the crucial passages; for the opposing view, see H. Hoppenbrouwers, *Graecitas et Latinitas Christianorum Primaeva,* Supplementa, Fasciculus 1 (1964), 47–95, who gives a fairly complete bibliography (no less than fifteen studies) of the quarrel.

10. *Reg. Ben.* 58: "suscipiendus autem in oratorio coram omnibus promittat de stabilitate sua et conversatione morum suorum, et obedientiam. . . ."

11. The issue of terminology has grown simpler with the years. Hoppenbrouwers has reduced his point of view to arguing that "morum suorum" is not a mere redundancy (leading to limp translations like J. Chapman's "monasticity of behavior" for the whole phrase), but an epexegetic genitive; it is un-

The explanation for Benedict's use of *conversatio* has been obscured in the later history of the term and the ideas it represents; for Benedict's *conversatio* had connotations of durative action lacking in *conversio.* Thus its initial use directly implied an obligation on the part of the monk whom Benedict was describing to continue throughout his life the process begun with the taking of the monastic vows. The term, then, not only focuses attention on the spiritual life of the monk, rather than his external acts, but demands a continuing process of turning to God anew each day, rather than a simple, once-and-for-all event at one stage of his life. This emphasis is directly attuned to the whole purpose and nature of monastic life, something that seeks new perfections each day. In a similar vein, in the seventh chapter of the *Regula,* Benedict listed twelve "steps of humility" for the monk to climb, envisioning a continuing effort at perfection that will only have its ultimate success in the next life, but that must be labored at diligently in this.

Thus in late antiquity one could still speak of the conversion of a heathen, and even of a heretic (e.g., a Gothic Arian), when all that was meant by it was the acceptance of catholic Christianity by an individual. But by the extension fostered in the manner just described, the term could also be used of actions taken by men who were already, to all appearances, loyal Christians. Thus we begin to hear of men who are called *conversi* (Cassiodorus in later life, for one); these are men who, after a life dedicated to public or military service, have turned to a more explicitly religious way of life. The term can refer both to those who do so in the midst of home and family (in a kind of heightened experience of the more exclusively literary

---

clear whether in this case that term is anything more than a euphemism for redundancy, however. The main thrust of the case McCann expounds seems to prevail by showing (1) the existence of other passages in the rule where *conversatio* clearly does have the sense of "conversion," (2) the medieval acceptance of *conversio* as the reading for *conversatio* in the crucial passages of the *Regula,* and (3) the silliness of all attempted translations denying the equivalence. If *conversatio* does not mean something more than simply *mores,* we make of Benedict and ourselves only hairsplitters.

retirement of earlier aristocrats grown weary of public life) and to those who make formal profession of membership in an organized monastic community.

The final stage of religious ascent to which the notion of conversion could be applied was that of devoted cenobitic monks who chose to retire to the eremitic life; both Benedict and Cassiodorus recommend the hermit's life, when prudently and wisely undertaken, as the highest life open to man.[12] Hermitage thus culminates a ladder of external experiences of the religious life that gave practical realization to the different levels of conversion that men could undergo in their interior spiritual life.

The theology of conversion could be seen under two different aspects as well. First, the point of view could be God's rather than the individual's, in the context of the relationship of grace. The prophet's words, "Convert us to you, O Lord, and we will be converted" (Lam. 5.21), could be a summary of this understanding.[13] But in that narrow context, the terminology of conversion was influenced by Luke: "If thy brother sin against thee, reprove him: and if he do penance forgive him. And if he sin against thee seven times in a day, and seven times in a day be converted unto thee, saying, I repent; forgive him" (Luke 17.3–4). Obviously, here the term is referring to little more than ordinary penance; but it is important to notice the iterative quality of this kind of penance and to recall how it reflects the repeated and continuous nature of Christian conversion at the highest level.

Conversion could also be understood, not from the point of view of temporal things, from which one is expected to turn towards God, but from that of eternity. The goal, the ideal state

12. *Reg. Ben.* 1: "heremitarum . . . qui non conversationis fervore novicio sed monasterii probatione diuturna . . . contra vitia carnis vel cogitationum . . . pugnare sufficiunt." Cf. *Inst.* 1.29.

13. Augustine, *Soliloquia* 1.1.6, for example, uses *converto* actively of God's effect on men. The same idea is fully developed by Thomas Aquinas, *Summa Theologiae,* Ia, 1, 62, art. 2, ad 3.

of man's life, is thus *stabilitas,* the state eventually reached by conversion when it shakes the soul loose from attachment to (and repeated turnings away from God as a result of attachment to) unstable temporal things. It is no coincidence that the vow that appears in grammatical parallel with that of *conversatio morum suorum* in the *Regula* of Benedict is that of *stabilitas;* this kind of monastic stability was only, to be sure, a faint echo of the kind of stability ultimately sought, but its appearance is strongly figurative of that other stability. Cassiodorus himself summarized this doctrine very neatly in the *De anima:* "Clearly the soul in this world can gain and lose goodness, converted by an unstable and shifting will, nor does it always abide in one firm purpose of the will, but even against its own disposition is changed in its orientation [*se conversione mutare*]" (*De an.* 4.214–218). Conversion is thus the action of the soul, understood temporally, intended to counteract the adverse influence of temporal things, while *stabilitas* is the state to be achieved by that motion, beyond temporality, in the next life.

The life of a *conversus* (of one "correcting his evil ways, doing good, pursuing the reward of good works," as Isidore of Seville would define him [Isidore, *Sententiae* 2.7.7]) is thus a life deliberately (and somewhat ostentatiously, to be sure) ordered along Christian principles. In this broad sense, it is not incorrect to speak of Cassiodorus as a *conversus* from the time that he began writing the *De anima* and studying the Psalter, though he only used the term of himself at a later date. Given the limitations of our evidence, there still seems to be a direct and connected progression from Cassiodorus the public servant active in reconciliation between warring parties to Cassiodorus the author of the short philosophical treatise to Cassiodorus the commentator on the Psalms and the founder of monasteries. We are, to be sure, not in possession of any direct biographical testimony for this period, nor can we tell what vicissitudes may have disturbed this apparently smooth and direct passage.

What we do know of the *De anima,* however, should caution us to avoid making too much of the discontinuity between the last works of the politician and the first of the *conversus*. First of all, the *De anima,* despite its clearly religious content, is not one of the works listed in the preface to the *De orthographia* as the fruits of Cassiodorus' life of conversion; that list, written perhaps about 580, begins with the "Psalm commentary, to which, with God's help, I devoted my first efforts at the time of my conversion" (*De orth.* 144.1–2). Thus, however justified we are in speaking of Cassiodorus' conversion as beginning, or appearing to begin, with the *De anima,* very late in his life Cassiodorus was not putting the date back quite so early.

The second consideration limiting our estimate of the religiosity of Cassiodorus' intentions at this time is the explicit connection between the *De anima* and the *Variae.* We have already noticed that the *De anima* is mentioned in the preface to Books XI and XII of the *Variae* as the work that immediately followed the compilation of the *Variae* (*Var.* 11, Praef. 7).[14] The reason for making mention of the *De anima* at that point was to justify its inclusion in the same volume with the *Variae,* as almost a thirteenth book; the treatise does in fact survive in one family of manuscripts, following immediately on the last page of the *Variae.* The same thing is stated explicitly in the Psalm commentary, which refers to something "in the book about the soul, which is the thirteenth book in the *Variae*" (*Ex. Ps.* 145.30).[15]

An appreciation of the state of Cassiodorus' mind on religious matters at the time of the composition of the *De anima* must thus take into account this connection with the *Variae.*

14. *Var.* 11, Praef. 7: "Sed postquam duodecim libris opusculum nostrum desiderato fine concluseram, de animae substantia vel de virtutibus eius amici me disserere coegerunt, ut per quam multa diximus, de ipsa quoque dicere videremur."

15. The connection between the *De anima* and the *Variae* is further strengthened by the rubrics used at the beginning and end of the shorter treatise. The *incipit* of the *De anima* attributes the work to "Magnus Aurelius Cassiodorus Senator." This is the same form of the name as the one given in the rubrics of the *Variae;* it is used consistently in the manuscripts of the *De anima,* at the beginning and end of the work.

First, the *De anima* must have been completed before the preface to the last two books of the *Variae* was written; thus the two works seem to have been in production simultaneously. Second, the state of Cassiodorus' mind before and after his retirement is not therefore drastically changed. There is a certain very gentle irony (not emphasized at all) in placing this philosophical disquisition, with its chapters on how to detect good men from bad by their appearances, at the end of a long work in which a great many good and bad men are seen in the midst of temporal affairs. But there is no reason to think that Cassiodorus was undergoing any more than a very gradual change of mind during this period. If Cassiodorus was always a devoted man in religious matters, a horrible war that he had long sought to avoid would make those religious concerns more visible to his neighbors and his literary posterity; they would not necessarily in themselves bring about radical change. Moreover, the evidence as it stands for the period 537–540 does not logically require us to assume anything more than this unveiling of concerns hitherto hidden by chance and literary circumstance.

The Cassiodorus of 537–540 is therefore a man who, in the loosest early medieval sense of the word, is in the first stages of a conversion. Whether, however, he was aware of this very strongly himself is not known to us. At this time more than at any other in his life, the literary *persona* through which Cassiodorus speaks to us obstructs almost completely our view of what we would like to believe is the real man. There is certainly none of the self-revelation of an Augustine before us, nor will there ever be. Very quietly, behind all the literary smoke screens, Cassiodorus continues to develop out of one phase of his life and into another by a quiet and continuous process, no more theatrical or melodramatic than the couse of a gentle river to the sea. If there is something for us to grasp here of the character of the man, we must do so gently to avoid crushing our catch with the vigor of our own analysis. The simplest thing to say is that the conversion we are witnessing is only a conversion in the medieval, gradual sense. By modern standards, the development is too subtle, too deliberate, too unspectacular.

Thus as we turn to the text of the *De anima* to see what its author would have us learn from it, the great surprise is the absence of surprises, the simplicity and straightforwardness of the treatment of a comparatively unexciting subject. Our task must be to determine the particular interest that this topic aroused in Cassiodorus' mind and how the composition of this book seemed to him to be a beneficial contribution to his own intellectual development and to his audience's understanding of the truths of faith.

But as soon as we look for testimony about the origin and purpose of the work, we run into a familiar feature: a rhetorical preface in which the demands of friends are represented as the real source of the work. "While I was rejoicing in the happy conclusion of the work I had undertaken, and the quiet harbor took me in battered from the ocean of those twelve books, whence I had arrived freed from, if not always praised for, my labor, a thoughtful group of friends drove me out again onto the sea of thought, demanding that I discuss some of the things which I had read in theological and secular books about the soul and its powers, since the soul is a key which unlocks secrets of greater things; they said it is silly of us to be ignorant of that through which we know so many other things, since it is always useful to know how it is that we know" (*De an.* 1.1–10). This weighty, not altogether attractive sentence tells us much and little. The temporal connection between finishing the *Variae* and beginning the *De anima* has already been noted; the "group of friends" is suspiciously reminiscent of the earlier preface to the *Variae;* and the expressed philosophical purpose has already been alluded to in the preface to Book XI of the *Variae.*

If we must hesitate to judge how much truth there is in the preface to the *Variae* on the matter of the anonymous friends, we are so much the more on shaky ground here. To hear Cassiodorus tell it, he had never yet in his life had an original idea for a literary work; his panegyrical-historical works were all inspired by his kings, and now the *Variae* and the *De anima* are produced grudgingly at the behest of friends who remain hidden from us. The bulk of the first little chapter of the *De anima* is placed in the putative words of the friends, who expound a little their notion of the subject and enunciate twelve questions for Cassiodorus to answer. It is this last point that offers the surest grounds for doubting the genuineness of this supposed dialogue; for the twelve questions so elaborated follow from one another so neatly and comprehensively that they must have been worked out, at the very least, by the true author in conjunction with, perhaps, philosophically inclined friends. If we admit that the entire device of the curious friends may be fictitious, we then conclude that in fact what we have before us is only a rather hackneyed introduction to the larger work. In either case it is a clumsy beginning.

The pretext for the work is a bit of sophistry implied in the passage quoted above. The purpose of the friends' questions is to know more about that thing, the *anima,* through which the human mind obtains knowledge. To justify this theme, a distinction is drawn between the pursuits of *mundani doctores* (from whom we seek to know the courses of the planets, the height of the heavens, the measure of the earth, and the four elements) and more enlightened students of theology. The curiosity of the *doctores* is hypocritical: "for when we are taught by the sages, 'know thyself,' how far can it be tolerated that we should be thus ignorant of ourselves?" (*De an.* 1.16–18). There is much to this argument that is mere quibble, but something more is present, imperfectly expressed in the stilted prose. For the contrast presented in the first sentence between the things to be discovered about the *anima* in the *libri sacri* and those found in *libri saeculares* presents to us for the first time what is probably the most fruitful (if not original) idea that Cassiodorus ever had, the one that moved to the center of his life's work within a few years.

Already in his years in public life, he had sought, together with Agapetus, the establishment of a school for sacred, as opposed to secular, studies. The first words of the *Institutiones,* written at least fifteen to twenty years after the *De anima,* reflect the attitudes of the last years of Cassiodorus' public career and the very words of the preface of the *De anima.*[16] The contrast vaguely stated by the friends in the preface to the *De anima* between the wide-ranging concerns of the worldly men of learning and the more subtle discourses that they were demanding of Cassiodorus surely shows the same discomfort that Cassiodorus expressed more clearly after settling at Squillace. For the meantime he was trapped in wartime Ravenna, probably conscious that his first effort at founding a school had failed. At this time the intellectual activity of Cassiodorus was guided by the same principles but supported by little of the confidence with which both the Roman school and the later enterprise at the Vivarium were undertaken.

The *De anima,* then, undertook the study of a philosophical issue from a point of view not strictly philosophical, making reference to scriptural texts. Unlike Augustine's early works on the soul, which argued from the conclusions available to un-aided human reason, Cassiodorus argues from authority. Un-like Claudianus Mamertus' *De statu animae,* which borrows heavily in its second book from worldly philosophers, Cassiodorus argues from specifically Christian authority (Augustine is the only author he cites by name).[17]

16. *Inst.,* praef. 1: "Cum studia saecularium litterarum magno desiderio fervere cognoscerem, ita ut multa pars hominum per ipsa se mundi prudentiam crederet adipisci, gravissimo sum, fateor, dolore permotus ut scripturis divinis magistri publici deessent, cum *mundani auctores* celeberrima procul dubio traditione pollerent" (emphasis added).

17. There has been a general assumption prevalent that Cassiodorus' *De anima* depends heavily on the fifth-century *De statu animae* of Claudianus. But Halporn has argued (*CCSL* 96.508–509), and by independent investigation I concur, that there are no detectable verbal reminiscences of Claudianus' treatise in Cassiodorus. A. Souter, *Texts and Studies,* 9.1 (1922), 322, stated without reference that Claudianus is referred to in Cassiodorus' revision of Pelagius' commentary on the Epistles; I have been unable to verify this claim. J. H. Waszink, in the first published version of his edition of Tertullian's *De anima* (1933), 16–17, thought that Cassiodorus had been greatly influenced by Tertullian's work; in the second edition (1947), 49, Waszink retracted that claim completely.

Any overt religiosity of purpose, however, is not very clearly represented in the outline of the work proposed; the subjects are clearly of a philosophical order, though capable of theological answers. It is of course typically Cassiodorian that there should be exactly twelve questions proposed and answered in order. In the original Cassiodorian edition of the work, these twelve questions were the chief structural features. In the manuscript tradition there is a further division of the work into seventeen or eighteen *capitula;* the seventeenth-century edition of Garet preserves a twelvefold division of chapters (from a less populous family of manuscripts) that tries to reflect Cassiodorus' intentions more faithfully. However, it is probable that the twelvefold division was left implicit in the most primitive form of the work, the form in which it first left Cassiodorus' hands, and that all chapter divisions are later interpolations, even if by the author himself.[18]

The division into eighteen chapters comprises two introductory chapters presenting the queries of friends and the reply of Cassiodorus (a similar dialogue in the preface to the *Variae* was not divided into chapters), twelve chapters corresponding to the twelve questions answered, two further chapter-divisions interpolated into the answer of the twelfth question, a *recapitulatio,* and a concluding *oratio.* For the purposes of content, the chapter titles interpolated over the answer to each question are superfluous. See, for example, the end of the fourth chapter (the end of the second response): "Now let us go on to treat the soul's *substantialis qualitas* in well-chosen words—you recall that this was your third question" (*De an.* 4.227–229). With that, the intervening title, "De qualitate animae," is superfluous and

---

Now M. Hofinger, *Cassiodors und Tertullians De Anima* (1970), has investigated the relationship at considerable length; he also concludes that no dependence existed.

18. H.-I. Marrou, *Mélanges J. de Ghellinck,* 1(1951), 235–249, has argued that the chapter headings in Augustine's *De civitate Dei* are similarly interpolated on the basis of a list of topics prepared by the author. Cassiodorus in the *Hist. trip.,* praef. 5, makes explicit mention of his interpolation of headings in that text as a special case.

less informative than the preceding sentence. Rather than being
an isolated event, this case is in fact typical of the work. At the
end of every single one of the first eleven responses there is a
similar sentence (most have the word *nunc* directing the reader's
attention) providing an easy and natural transition to the next
chapter.[19] The most interesting case is that of the beginning of
the very first answer, where Cassiodorus almost seems to
forget that the questions were set for him by someone else and
begins to speak of what he must treat before he enters on the *res
expetita;* but in fact this prolegomenon is only the first of those
very things suggested by his friends.

After the discussion of the future state of souls in the answer
to the twelfth question, another transition is prepared in the
text: "Now we must put aside this bundle of questions and
summarize our complex and wordy argument under a few
headings, so that we can add up our conclusions briefly and
store them away in the barns of memory" (*De an.* 16.60–63).
This sentence confirms that the discussion of the questions has
included everything up to this point; it also makes the insertion
there of the next chapter heading, "Recapitulatio," superfluous
and uninformative again. That chapter is taken up partly with a
listing of the twelve conclusions reached in the work, but it
quickly becomes a concluding discourse that praises the virtues
of the *anima* and then a prayer addressed in the second person
to the Lord.[20] After this had gone on for a page or so, the
author of the eighteenfold division noticed that recapitulation
had become prayer, so he interrupted our reading once again
with the unhelpful title, "Oratio." In this case, the last of these
intrusions, otherwise moderately helpful in signaling the contents of the work for impatient modern readers, is simply misplaced.

19. It is true, as Professor Halporn has pointed out to me, that similar preparations are often found for new chapter headings in the *Inst.*, e.g., at the end of
I.9. I only find it probable that the chapter titles were not present in the *De
anima* as it was originally composed.

20. The use of the second person singular pronouns to address God begins
at *De an.* 17.40, about halfway through the "Recapitulatio."

At the beginning of Cassiodorus' part of the work he is faced with his friends' final request: "Tell us these things in order, God willing, so we may follow you easily and so you may earn the title *doctor*" (*De an.* 1.51–53). This would not be Cassiodorus if he did not first protest against such implicit praise. He pleads the difficulty of the subject, arising specifically out of the sophistry by which it was introduced; just as the eye sees stars, but not itself, so the *anima* knows all things save itself. This, of course, does not actually stop Cassiodorus, but it lets him complain that "these matters do not resemble the royal commands with which we have lately busied ourselves, but befit serious and abstract dialogues which speak not to corporeal ears but to the purified hearing of the inner man" (*De an.* 2.1–4). Moreover, he claims, he is fatigued by the effort of producing the *Variae*: "What sort of thing can I write, wearied as I am from the work I have just been hurrying to finish?" (*De an.* 2.12–13). But his friends, as we suspected all along, are relentless, and he wins only the reprieve of a few days *(aliquot dies)*. The work is tolerable, indeed almost pleasant: "But now I find it unburdensome to be urged to speak of matters which, if I handle them truthfully and with God's help, will invigorate my audience and illuminate my own understanding as I make the argument" (*De an.* 2.23–26).

Whereupon he truly begins, first by distinguishing the inconveniently similar terms for different things that often confuse men. Thus the first question thoughtfully provided for him is an etymological one, which he enjoys as is his wont. *Anima*, he claims, derives from *anema*, signifying dissimilarity to blood, which is the source of the life of beasts; *animus* is conversely derived "apo tu animu," namely the wind, since its cogitation is similarly swift.[21] With soul and mind thus distinguished, he adds almost gratuitous differentiations from other terms. *Mens* is defined, but the distinction from *animus* is not made explicit. *Spiritus* is defined, and opposed to *anima*, in three ways. Thus, he concludes, "the soul is defined as a spiritual

21. Augustine and Claudianus Mamertus did not rigorously distinguish the two similar words.

substance which in no way perishes" along with the body (*De an.* 3.34–36).

With his terminology settled, Cassiodorus turns to defining the *anima* philosophically. He begins by presenting various opinions, first from *magistri saecularium litterarum*, who "say the soul is a simple substance, a natural shape, separate from the matter of its body, a divisible whole, having the power of life" (*De an.* 4.1–4). This contribution from the oracles of secular wisdom, the straw men of Cassiodorus' argument, is not wrong but incomplete. "The soul of man, as the opinion of truthful scholars has it [*ut veracium doctorum consentit auctoritas*], is a unique spiritual substance created by God, enlivening its body, rational and immortal, but capable of converting itself to both good and evil" (*De an.* 4.4–7). The first definition echoes Chalcidius' Plato and Aristotle, while the opinion of the *veraces doctores* depends on Augustine's *De quantitate animae*, at least indirectly. It is this more comprehensive, and at the same time more religious, definition that Cassiodorus proceeds to analyze in detail. The chapter that does this, and on which the rest of the work is to be based, is longer then any of the other responses and approximately three to four times as long as all but the ninth and the twelfth. For this definition "is set out before us like a hen's egg, containing within the life of the unborn bird and the pleasing array of feathers. Now we will unpack that definition because men learn more readily what appears clearly divided in parts" (*De an.* 4.7–11).[22] Each term of the definition of the *veraces doctores* is then elaborated at some length.

The first topic is the createdness of the soul, on which for the first time in the work scriptural authority is cited (from Ecclesiastes and Isaiah) in two passages that state straightforwardly that God is the source of *spiritus* and *omnis flatus* (*De an.* 4.18–20). Another paragraph explains the association of the soul with the body and its quality as spirit, again quoting the authority of scripture. And so Cassiodorus proceeds through

22. Cf. Macrobius, *Saturnalia* 7.16.

the definition; his longest section is reserved for the discussion of the immortality of the soul. In this case his procedure imitates that of the work as a whole: first he presents the syllogisms of the *auctores saecularium litterarum,* but then he states, "We have no trouble confirming the immortality of the soul on the authority of inspired texts," and he alludes to Genesis 1.26 to argue that immortality is a necessary consequence of creation in the image and likeness of God (*De an.* 4.127–132). To this argument are then added for support only refutations of objections that might be brought against such an interpretation of the Genesis passage; for example, it might be objected that image and likeness entail the power to create, so Cassiodorus refutes this in hopes of leaving his original argument erect. With such explanation he passes on to the last elements of the definition, arguing the soul's convertibility towards good and evil on the basis of common experience. Finally this point is used to conclude the section by showing how this convertibility is what formally distinguishes for us between the soul of man and that of God.

The third response, concerning the *qualitas* of the soul's substance, only refers at the beginning to secular *auctores,* but the first theory presented is clearly pre-Christian, to which again Cassiodorus responds with scripture and echoes of Augustine. The remainder of the questions from this point on are of a philosophical nature, always colored with this desire to show how the Christian answer differs from (mainly by improving upon rather than refuting) the view of the secular authorities. Thus the fourth section concludes that the soul does not have corporeal form, the fifth that the moral virtues are the riches of the soul struggling against corporal impurity. Justice in this view combats the *prava vel iniqua* in which man is susceptible, while prudence defends against *confusa* and *incerta;* similar claims are made for fortitude and temperance. Thus the cardinal virtues are made a fourfold shield against the onslaughts of vice. Cassiodorus concentrates on the cardinal, rather than the theological, virtues, infusing the old classical ideas with Christian meaning rather than transcending them completely. Thus these moral virtues are contrasted only to the natural virtues of the soul, which we would call its characteristic powers.

The most theological chapter treats the origin of the soul and attempts to understand the scientific facts represented by the scriptural account of creation.[23] Since the chapter itself begins with reference to scripture, there is no mention of secular views, and indeed the question is taken in such a way as to preclude its ever having been asked by secular authors. More traditional is the longest dispute, spread over two chapters, on the *sedes animae* and the arrangement of the body to perform the soul's bidding. These chapters are the least scriptural of the work, but the most obviously dependent on the commentaries of earlier Christian writers.[24]

This discussion completes the scientific section of the work and affords a return to moral issues. Two curious chapters come next, without much foundation in known sources, on the ways of identifying good and bad men: "De cognoscendis malis hominibus," and "De cognoscendis bonis hominibus" (*De an.* 12, 13). The first chapter describes the fall of man through sin, then asserts that there are certain obvious indicators by which evil men betray themselves. They are sad-eyed, easily distracted, and worried over what other people might think of them; moreover, they have literally an evil odor about their persons. Good men, the next chapter reveals, are forgiving, humble, self-effacing images of what unfallen man might

23. This was a point on which Augustine expressed strong uncertainty; see *De libero arbitrio voluntatis* 3.21.59 (and elsewhere), where he reviewed four theories: that all souls descend from Adam's soul, that they are created specially for each person, that they are pre-existing entities sent by God, and that they are pre-existing entities that come of their own free will. Augustine concludes, "aut enim nondum ista quaestio a divinorum librorum catholicis tractoribus pro merito suae obscuritatis et perplexitatis evoluta atque illustrata est; aut si iam factum est, nondum in manus nostras huiuscemodi litterae pervenerunt." Cassiodorus notes this uncertainty at *De an.* 9.21–24; it is the first occasion in the treatise where he cites any authority by name.

24. At *De an.* 11.115, the chanting of the Psalter is cited as the characteristically noble act of the human body and soul, performed in spite of the ills that afflict man.

have been (and they have a good odor besides). These laudable traits are not remarkable "in sexu validiore," but Cassiodorus professes himself unable to explain the virtues of virgins and widows (De an. 13.90–94).

It is easy to chuckle patronizingly at this kind of naive belief that good and evil men can be distinguished by external characteristics, but there is considerable psychological truth to the observations recorded in these chapters. They will not avail the reader much if he stands on a street corner scrutinizing the faces of passersby, but they will enable him better to look into his own soul and his own life. What are identified here are trivial external characteristics that spring from deeper moral qualities and can be symptoms of much more significant things. There is a higher spiritual discipline in repressing and correcting trivial bad habits, both as an inherently valuable practice and as a way of getting at the more serious interior failings. Thus a concern for other people's opinion of oneself is not in itself a great sin, but it is frequently a sign that temptations to vainglory have not been altogether successfully resisted. Similarly, the virtues enumerated in the chapter on good men are the little signs by which genuine, thoroughgoing moral excellence can be recognized in other people. Cassiodorus is not suggesting with these chapters that men can or should judge one another by these criteria, but he shows how easily one's own failings and other people's virtues can be recognized by attention to detail.

The last long chapter in three parts, on the state of the soul after death, is second in length only to the definition chapter. *Saeculares auctores* have been forgotten, and Cassiodorus promises to speak on the basis of a *diversa lectio*. He first describes death scientifically (by sixth-century standards), then the approach to judgment: "There we are burdened no longer with toil, we are no longer refreshed by food, nor are we daily beset by hunger; but abiding without end in the soul's true nature we shall do no good or evil deeds, but until the day of judgment only grieve for our past misdeeds or rejoice in our probity" (*De an.* 14.6–11).

The bulk of this section describes the state of life in the

futurum saeculum. The identifiable verbal parallels here go back to the last books of Augustine's *De civitate Dei,* where the subject was similar. Oddly, Cassiodorus does not depend at all on the descriptions of heaven and hell provided in scripture, perhaps out of a preference for attempting to rephrase familiar ideas. For the damned, hell is affliction without hope; for the just, heaven is a place where "the stable mind does not hesitate, is not vacillating, does not move, and is fixed in such a stable peace that it neither thinks nor seeks any good save contemplation" (*De an.* 15.44–47). This heaven, echoing the Augustinian formula, is a place where the soul is not able to sin (*De an.* 15.52–53). From here on, the work becomes palpably less and less a philosophy treatise and more and more a rhetorical evocation of, first, the conditions of the future life and, second, by an imperceptible transition, God Himself. To believers painfully conscious of how little they really could know of God, these verbal formulas were masterpieces of what the human intellect could achieve in cooperation with divine revelation; for they achieved the impossible: they captured something of the divine in mere words, enabling men to reach some part of the unspeakable mystery of God.

It is an interruption in an exulting contemplation for Cassiodorus to call his readers back to a mundane summary of the contents of the work here concluding, but he does so as briefly and concisely as possible. His only comment is on his use of the number twelve, which is the number of the zodiac signs, of the months of the year, of the principal winds of the earth, and of the hours of each half of the day's cycle.

After that short paragraph the remainder of the work is one final admonition growing gradually into a heartfelt prayer. "Now it remains, learned and astute readers, to transcend the material world and speedily offer ourselves to the divine mercy which illuminates all who behold it" (*De an.* 17.26–29). It is in that subjection to God that victory for the understanding will be found; "in Christ's service no heart which gives itself wholly up to Him is ever found untouchable, nor can it fail to see what it seeks, nor can it lose what it is given in reward for loyalty"

(*De an.* 17.33–36). The second person of apostrophe to the divinity enters easily and naturally, still in the course of a praise of divine mercy in revealing such things to men. This in turn leads to worshipful consideration of the redemptive function of God in Christ.

The "Oratio" (as so designated in the MSS) begins with a plea to Christ for assistance.[25] For the serpent is everywhere troubling all men: "he casts the evil eye, alas, on such great peoples, because there are two of them, and still persecutes the time-bound men whom he makes mortal by his impious efforts" (*De an.* 18.10–12).[26] This one sentence has received more comment than any other in the *De anima* because scholars have been unanimous in seeing in it a reference to contemporary events; just how the content of that reference is to be interpreted, scholars have been far from unanimous. The two main possibilities are that the two peoples so pitied are the Ostrogoth-Roman kingdom of Italy and the Byzantines (argued by van de Vyver, and followed by Besselaar, Cappuyns, and Ludwig), or that they are the Catholic Romans and Arian Goths in Italy itself (Mommsen, followed by Schanz).[27] If there is a contemporary reference in this passage, the two poles of opinion seem to me to blur an important reality, namely the connection between the Catholic Romans in Italy and the Catholic Romans coming from the east. Thus both opinions can be true, but neither complete, if the reference is to the whole pattern of oppositions between peoples brought to a head by the Gothic war, but going back to all the attempts to justify and establish the position of the Gothic kingdom in Italy over the preceding de-

25. *De an.* 18.4–5: "Dona quod offeram, custodi quod exigas ut velis coronare quod praestas," with echoes of Augustine.

26. "Invidit, pro dolor, tam magnis populis, cum duo essent, et adhuc temporales persequitur quos impio ambitu fecit esse mortales."

27. The history of this controversy is summarized by Halporn, *CCSL* 96.506, n. 14; Halporn himself avoids taking a position. See a faint echo of the phrase at Jordanes, *Get.* 48.246: "dum utrique gentes [sc. Ostrogothi et Visigothi] . . . in uno essent." I cannot help but wonder, however, whether the passage in the *De anima* is not a glancing allusion to Augustine's two cities.

cades. In this view the two parties are simply those who do and do not accept the rule of the Goths in Italy as legitimate; the whole crisis of identity which that kingdom suffered throughout its history is here encapsulated. Thus the theory is an attractive one; but it is dangerously undersupported by the flimsy text on which it is built. Some scholars have even professed to be able to date the composition of the work to within a few months on the basis of this passage almost alone; that is surely folly. The allusion is, in the end, obscure. The thought of the passage in which it is couched is a simple and nonpolitical one: that the devil is still active in the world to the detriment of men.

Having sought general assistance in this prayer against the devil, the emphasis turns personal and the pronouns become first person singular: "Lord . . . save me from myself and preserve me in you. . . . Then shall I belong to myself, when I truly belong to you" (*De an.* 18.19–22). Only in God will we understand ourselves and our troubles and successes. "All things rush to ruin when they revolt from loyalty to your might" (*De an.* 18.28–29). To love God is to be saved, to fear Him is to rejoice, to find Him is to grow, to have lost Him is to perish. Then another apparently contemporary reference: "It is in the end nobler to be your servant than to gain all the kingdoms of the earth" (*De an.* 18.31–32). This passage has also leapt out of the page and into the hands of scholars interested solely in the text as an (albeit unsatisfactory) historical source, telling them that Cassiodorus was profoundly disenchanted with public life and emotionally and spiritually in the process of a drastic conversion from a worldly to a spiritual life. Perhaps there is a special sight that reveals such hidden mysteries to some scrutinizers of ambiguous, conventional texts of this sort, which many a public servant of the age could have written only to return directly to the most distasteful political or military chores; if there be such a sight, I do not possess it and the text says nothing extraordinary to me. There is nothing in what we know concretely of Cassiodorus' public life to make us think that he ever lost sight completely of the superiority of heavenly to earthly kingdoms. The value as historical evidence of any such statement, moreover, is sharply reduced by its presence in a profoundly confessional rhetorical text such as this.[28] There is no reason to suspect that merely because it echoes the conventional, it is false; but neither are there grounds for seeing in it dramatic personal revelation. The whole tone of the work, with its extremely reserved self-representation, militates against such a conclusion.

The tone of self-abnegation reaches its height in the last paragraph of the prayer, where God's action in human life is extolled and sought after (*De an.* 18.52–54). Finally, a last short statement directly by the author to the reader completes the motif of humility, excusing the inadequacy of the treatment on grounds of the author's weakness, attributing the virtues of the work to his written sources.[29] "They can speak of these things blamelessly who have shown by the quality of their life that they have been purified in divine service" (*De an.* 18.58–60).

If we may for a moment ignore the author's petitions for forgiveness of his faults, what has this little book achieved? First, it has summarized the orthodox doctrine of the church in the sixth century on the human soul, arguing not from reason, nor again from secular authority, but from the authority of scripture and the fathers of the church. Second, more importantly, it has made the forbiddingly dry philosophical topic lead, as if naturally, into moral and theological considerations of the highest order, leading from the soul to its ultimate fate to the God that directs that fate. Third, it has embodied some stage or other in the spiritual development of its author. Concerned about the popularity of the *saeculares doctores* and the way they came to dominate philosophical discussion even in the Christian empire (as in Boethius' theological tractates, for

28. "Confessional" in the dual sense of praise of God, blame of self, as in Augustine's great work.

29. *De an.* 18.57: "alma lumina veracium litterarum," echoing the contrast with secular *doctores*.

example), Cassiodorus' work in the form we see it represents an epoch in the progression that will lead eventually to the monastic and intellectual enterprise at Squillace.

But we can comprehend the *De anima* no better than primitive man understood a rainbow. However attractive and unique the work seems to us to be, we are as unprepared to untangle with accuracy the circumstances of its composition as the primitive was to explain the refraction of light through suspended raindrops. We should be careful lest our desire to know more and more about Cassiodorus himself should lead us to skip over the simpler pleasure of observing his creation. Thus the period of this work remains for us a mystery, illuminated only by fleeting rays. We have arrived at a working hypothesis for Cassiodorus' movements at this time, determining that he may well have left Ravenna, perhaps under constraint, with the party in which Belisarius took Witigis to Constantinople, and that he settled in the eastern metropolis for over a decade. In the next chapter we will pursue the fragments of evidence that tell us about his stay in Constantinople, and we will look closely at the literary monument that he produced in that curious exile.

5

The *Expositio Psalmorum*

THE study of Cassiodorus' public life has focused our attention on the centers of power in Ostrogothic Italy. With his retirement and departure from Ravenna the scene begins to
change; the horizon of his experience first expands as we study
his years in Constantinople, then contracts rapidly around the
monastic foundations at Squillace. This chapter examines the
years in the eastern capital.

If Cassiodorus had never been out of Italy before his retirement, he had lived his whole life in a land that had impercepti-
bly become a backwater. No longer did all roads run to Rome;
even Theoderic, the ruler of Italy for a third of a century, only
made the journey across the Apennines down to Rome once in
all that time.

Constantinople was an altogether different case, for the land
and sea routes of the Mediterranean had brought the New
Rome to center stage. Rome had always been a republican city
bearing imperial pageantry a bit uneasily; Constantinople was a
city of, by, and for the emperors. Physically the imperial palace
was the center of the city, with private connections to the
forums of public life—the great circus and the great church.
Particularly in Justinian's day, if not again thereafter, the view
from Constantinople extended to the farthest horizons in all
directions, to the frontiers with Persia, to Egypt, Africa, Spain,
and Italy, as well as up through the Black Sea to the western
edges of the great steppes. If in Italy men were preoccupied
with finding new ways to settle the politics of their corner of
the Mediterranean world while a few aristocrats dreamed of
past glory, in Constantinople visions of the past were alive and
real with a still glorious future. Moderns are harsh with Jus-

tinian for having failed to cut back on imperial pretensions at a time when such prudence could well have made permanent the Roman claims around the *orbis terrarum;* but it was not a lack of vision that kept Justinian from bringing the barbarian kingdoms into a peaceful and mutually profitable association with the empire, but rather too many visions, and too grandiose ones. Justinian may very well be forgiven for believing that with just a little extra military vigor the empire that had maintained so much of itself with such indifferent leadership for so long could once and for all settle things according to the old plan.

But what a contrast Constantinople must have meant for Cassiodorus! Not long since honored himself with the highest rank his country could offer him, in Constantinople he became a cipher, no doubt astonished and a little abashed in the face of the pomp and splendor of Byzantine ceremony and city life. It is perhaps the greatest pity of all for students of Cassiodorus that we do not know more about this period in his life, the contacts that he made in Constantinople, the intellectual currents in which he wet his feet, the ones in which he swam, and the particular influences that shaped his actions when it came time to leave.

But first we must consider the length of his stay in the capital. In the last chapter we saw evidence from an Italian perspective to indicate that he arrived in Constantinople in about 540 and stayed until 554. Now further evidence is available from an eastern perspective.

There are first of all two pieces of direct evidence from the last years of Cassiodorus' stay; their coincidence in date (and that of a third piece of evidence now known to have been erroneously dated so late) was the strongest explicit evidence for assuming that Cassiodorus' stay in the capital was brief and late. First, Jordanes, who probably composed his own works in Constantinople, obtained a copy of Cassiodorus' *Gothic History* from Cassiodorus' own steward, obviously at Constantinople, in 550 or 551, when composing his *Getica* (*Get.*, praef. 2). Second, Cassiodorus is named in a letter of Pope Vigilius, dating

also from 550, which excommunicates two of the pope's followers, Rusticus and Sebastianus, for their obstinate opposition
to the ban on the Three Chapters, in which condemnation Vigilius had acquiesced in 548.[1]

The third apparent contact in Constantinople of which evidence survives was with Justinian's quaestor, Junillus (or
Junilius Africanus, as some style him). It was until recently believed that Junillus' little pamphlet, the *Instituta regularia divinae
legis,* was written in 550–551. Cassiodorus later recommended
this book as one of the most important basic handbooks for the
interpretation of scripture (*Inst.* 1.10.1). But more importantly,
the pamphlet represented the Nisibean style of interpretation,
which Junillus had learned at Constantinople from Paul the
Persian, who had lectured at Nisibis; and the enterprise of
Nisibis is mentioned on the first page of Cassiodorus' *Institutiones* as one of the examples of organized Christian scholarship and teaching that inspired Cassiodorus' own venture. It
thus seems likely that Cassiodorus had personal contact with
the author of this work; if it was written in 550–551, moreover,
that would further confirm the late date for Cassiodorus' presence. However, there is now conclusive evidence to believe that
Junillus died in 548 or 549 and that his treatise was composed in
542.[2] Nisibean ideas would probably have been unhealthy to
publish after 543 or 544 in the middle of the Three Chapters
controversy.

But Cassiodorus' own position in that controversy, the prin-

1. *PL* 69.49A–B: "Sed quia semel et secundo adhortatione nostra per fratres
nostros episcopos, id est, Ioannem Marsicanum, et Iulianum Cingulanum, vel
Sapatum filium nostrum atque diaconum, nec non et per gloriosum virum
patricium Cethegum, et religiosum virum item filium nostrum Senatorem,
aliosque filios nostros commoniti noluistis audire, et neque ad ecclesiam, neque
ad nos reverti, sicut omnia facitis, volvistis detestanda superbia." Zacchaeus,
bishop of Squillace, is also known to have been in Constantinople with Vigilius,
subscribing to the pope's *Constitutum de tribus capitulis* (May 14, 553: Mansi
9.106A) and mentioned in a letter of Vigilius at about the same time (Mansi
9.359B); probably this is mere coincidence.

2. E. Stein, *BARB,* Ser. 5, 23(1937), 365–390, esp. 378–384; Stein also
marshaled the evidence on Junillus' name in the same article.

cipal theological amusement of the capital through the 540's and early 550's, was always an ambiguous one.[3] When writing his *Institutiones* back in Squillace and away from the court's power, he had no hesitation in recommending Junillus' little book and in mentioning the Nisibis school favorably; but we have already seen that at Vigilius' urging, sometime in 549 or 550, he was active in attempting to reconcile two rebellious westerners to accepting the ban on the authors in question. In his own *Expositio Psalmorum,* written through this same period and revised somewhat at Squillace, he made use of the *Defensio trium capitulorum* of Facundus of Hermiane, published in February 548 before Vigilius' decision to approve the emperor's condemnation. Most scholars have assumed that the citation of Facundus must date the conclusion of the work to the period between Facundus' publication and Vigilius' condemnation, especially since the whole commentary is dedicated to a *pater apostolicus* who can only be Vigilius.[4] Given Cassiodorus' ambiguous attitude, however, no such razor-sharp dating is possible; the potential significance of this citation of Facundus will concern us when we come to discuss the Christology expressed in the Psalm commentary.

We must also remark the association of Cassiodorus' name in Vigilius' letter with that of Cethegus. Cethegus was the recipient of the original version of the document that was condensed to make the *Ordo generis Cassiodororum;* he had been a leading figure in the Roman senate since his consulship in 504; and he made his own way to Constantinople sometime in the 540's. The contrast that Vigilius makes between the two men, citing Cethegus as a *gloriosus vir* and *patricius,* while Cassiodorus is called a *religiosus vir* and *filius noster,* is the clearest definition we have of Cassiodorus' position in Constantinople. For he could with ease have been called *gloriosus,* and he was certainly entitled to the rank of *patricius;* but these honorific name-tags are something that Cassiodorus begins to shed after his retire-

3. On the Three Chapters controversy, see Fliche et Martin, 4.457–477.

4. Facundus is cited at *Ex. Ps.* 138.548–552; the dedication to Vigilius at *Ex. Ps.,* praef. 121–124.

ment. That he is called a *religiosus vir* seems to indicate that the
"conversion" that seemed to begin about the time of the composition of the *De anima* had continued to such an extent that
the religiosity of his life became at this time a defining characteristic, sufficient to distinguish him from his friend Cethegus.
Furthermore, the mention at the very beginning of the *Expositio
Psalmorum* that his interest in the Psalter began to be serious
while he was still at Ravenna would confirm the presumption
that it was at Constantinople that he composed his great commentary (just as it would be in the same city a few decades later
that Gregory would undertake his *Moralia in Job*). On the other
hand, the term *religiosus vir* is not narrowly limiting in its denotation; there is no mention of Cassiodorus being either monk or
priest, nor of his living in any organized religious community
under a rule. In fact, the indications are just the opposite.

First, we recall that Jordanes mentioned that Cassiodorus had
a steward from whom he had obtained a copy of one of the
works that Cassiodorus published during his career as a statesman. Cassiodorus was thus still in charge of some sort of
household in order to employ a steward; moreover, he still had
and cherished a copy of his *Gothic History*. Since the work itself
has now perished, since it is never mentioned during Cassiodorus' Squillace period, and since other original works
known to have been produced during the Squillace period have
of course survived, it seems reasonable to assume that Cassiodorus himself grew careless of it at some point, presumably
in connection with a loss of interest in public affairs. That he
still kept a copy in Constantinople implies that he was not yet
completely and formally immersed in a life of religion.

The date for Cassiodorus' departure from Constantinople is
every bit as uncertain as the other dates of his stay, but it can be
approximated. We last know for certain of Cassiodorus in Constantinople in 551, the time of Jordanes' publication; at this time
Italy was in flames with the last throes of the Gothic war.
Narses was sent to mop up the situation, and he destroyed Totila in 552 and Teias in 553. In August 554, Justinian issued the
Pragmatic Sanction reorganizing the government of Italy under

Byzantine control.[5] The Pragmatic Sanction seems to have been a signal for the general return to Italy of refugees, partly because it ratified the pacification of that country. Moreover, the struggle over the Three Chapters had come to an effective conclusion when, in late 553 or early 554, Vigilius bowed to the Council of Constantinople in condemning the three authors disputed once and for all without cavil. The controversy was not in fact concluded with this official decree, but the formalities were for the moment settled. With military and theological peace throughout Italy and the empire for the first time in two decades, then, it is logical to assume that Cassiodorus found his way home with the others.

If this reconstruction is correct, then Cassiodorus' longest book was written while he sojourned in Constantinople. The *Expositio Psalmorum* is the only formal commentary on the entire Psalter surviving from the patristic era. Because, however, it tells us more about the Psalms than about Gothic or monastic history, it has been the least fully studied of all Cassiodorus' works.[6]

There is in fact still room for much further study of patristic and medieval exegesis. The great work of Henri de Lubac has revolutionized our understanding of the theory of interpreta-

5. The Pragmatic Sanction: *Corpus Iuris Civilis* (ed. R. Schöll and W. Kroll), Novellae app. VII (Aug. 13, 554).

6. The best study of Cassiodorus' *Expositio* is R. Schlieben, *Cassiodors Psalmenexegese* (Dissertation, Tübingen, 1970); an abridged version is also available: R. Schlieben, *Christliche Theologie und Philologie in der Spätantike* (1974), but all my references are to the fuller version. See also, less impressively, G. A. Löffler, *Der Psalmenkommentar des M. Aur. Cassiodor Senator* (Dissertation, Freiburg-im-Breisgau, 1920). A somewhat more technical, but very useful approach was taken by U. Hahner, *Cassiodors Psalmenkommentar: Sprachliche Untersuchungen* (1973); the first section, "Sprachliche Mittel der Exegese" (pp. 17–172), analyzes Cassiodorus' exegetical terminology, while the second, "Sprachlich-stilistische Untersuchungen" (pp. 173–325), analyzes his strictly linguistic habits. This very competent volume reached me after this chapter had been substantially completed; I will refer the reader to some of Hahner's discussions, since I have chosen not to use the material myself lest this chapter be swollen further.

tion, but we still need demanding critical study of the practice
of hermeneutic.[7] We still do not possess a cumulative understanding of the rhetoric of this exegesis sufficient to enable us
to evaluate and compare different commentaries on the basis of
the presuppositions that controlled them. There is still something of the puzzled novice in all of our treatments of medieval
exegetical writings, due simply to the lack of adequately broad
common scholarly experience in giving to works of exegesis
the kind of sympathetic attention that Lubac's work has made
possible. Thus when we approach Cassiodorus' *Expositio Psalmorum,* we are attempting to do things that the human race has
forgotten how to do; we must attempt to teach ourselves to
read all over again, to look to this bulky book to tell us things
that we are unaccustomed to hearing in ways that we are not
used to following. As is the case so often in the analysis of
forgotten modes of intellectual activity, we must suspend every
instinctive adverse judgment in order to pursue the unique
form of human thought that lies behind the (to us) discordant
surface features.

This study will approach the Psalm commentary from three
different directions. First, we will be concerned with the
sources on which Cassiodorus drew, especially Augustine's sermons on the Psalms, but also the many other works cited
fragmentarily that give us clues to the circumstances of composition. Second, we will study the exegetical technique with
which Cassiodorus worked, following the gymnastics of his
mind in coming to grips with an individual text and producing
the commentary on it. Third, we will look at the content of the
exegesis, that is, at the subject matter discussed in connection
with the Psalm texts.

The circumstances and purpose of the composition of the
Expositio are the first topics of the work's preface. The opening
sentence states that Cassiodorus avidly sought the honey of the
Psalter after the *amarissimae actiones* of his public life, while still

7. H. de Lubac, *Exégèse Médiévale* (1959–1964).

in Ravenna. This new study of the Psalter was hindered, however, by the obscurity of the text, which he found veiled in parables (*Ex. Ps.*, praef. 6–7).

The solution to this difficulty Cassiodorus found in the sermons of Augustine, the *Enarrationes in Psalmos:* "Then I took refuge in the delightful work of our most eloquent father Augustine, in which I found such a densely packed flood of sage remarks that I could scarcely remember what I saw expounded there so abundantly" (*Ex. Ps.*, praef. 10–13). The *Enarrationes* of Augustine was a collection of his sermons delivered on various occasions, selected and ordered so that they covered the entire Psalter. There is some irregularity of coverage, some duplication of explanations; moreover, when the compilation was made, Augustine discovered that he did not have a sermon on the extraordinarily long Psalm 118, so a separate treatise was composed for the purpose.[8] The most important feature of Augustine's work is just its homiletic quality; rather than a systematic commentary on each verse, Augustine's work was an interpretation of the text for an audience listening to the oral presentation. Moreover, Augustine's collection was simply enormous beyond all convenience.

Mindful of all these things and of his own inadequacies, Cassiodorus was inspired to take up the pen himself, to "draw this ocean sprung from the Psalms themselves, with God's help, into shallow streams," the better to serve the student (*Ex. Ps.*, praef. 15–19). It is unlikely that Cassiodorus could have written this work at Squillace in possession of his library there, for he did not have a full set of Augustine's *Enarrationes.*[9] Since, however, the explicit quotations in Cassiodorus' commentary from Augustine's original are taken from remarks on Psalms in every decade of the Psalter, it is clear that the commentary must have

8. The Vulgate is used exclusively in this chapter for numbers of Psalms and names of biblical books.

9. *Inst.* 1.4 (written in the 560's): "in omnibus tamen beatus Augustinus studiose nimis latiusque tractavit; ex quibus iam duas decadas Domino praestante collegi."

been compiled at some place where Cassiodorus had regular access to the full Augustine, and therefore not at Squillace.

Cassiodorus was, however, more humble than precise in asserting that his work only summarized Augustine's; while he admitted adding certain things of his own, he deliberately left the impression that his work's virtues were all borrowed from Augustine. In fact, the relationship between the two works is not as close as Cassiodorus pretended, nor as distant as modern scholars believe. The scarcity of citations and allusions indicated by the index to the only modern edition of Cassiodorus' commentary (discerning only seventy-six such allusions in the entire work) is in fact radically misleading. Proof for such an assertion can be given economically by presenting a sample case; let us take Psalm 81.

There is no explicit mention or quotation of Augustine in Cassiodorus' treatment of this Psalm; no allusion was detected in the modern edition. Nevertheless, the entire exposition of this Psalm seems clearly based on Augustine's original treatment. Augustine's approach to the Psalm, on a straight verse-by-verse basis, beginning with the *titulus,* is obscured by Cassiodorus' more formal pattern. To begin with, Augustine asserts that the name Asaph in the *titulus* was placed there as a figure of the *Synagoga (Enarr. in Psal.* 81.1). Cassiodorus believed firmly, but Augustine did not always accept, that every Psalm was actually written by David, and that other names in the *tituli* are only there for our edification. In this case, Augustine and Cassiodorus agree; for Cassiodorus states that "these names are placed in the *tituli* for us to interpret; in this case Asaph represents *Synagoga" (Ex. Ps.* 81.2–4). In treating the first line of the Psalm, Augustine explains the term *Synagoga:* it represents for him *congregatio,* while *Ecclesia* stands for *convocatio*—the former is proper of beasts, the latter of men. Cassiodorus: "*Synagoga* is basically translated *congregatio,* an assembly but not specifically one of human beings; *Ecclesia* is a genuine *convocatio" (Ex. Ps.* 81.11–13).

At an early stage of Cassiodorus' exposition of the first

verse, he quotes scripture: "One stands in your midst whom you know not" (John 1.26). Augustine's own explanation of the first verse runs on at some length, but toward the end, he too quotes the same line of John. Nor is this the only such case; apropos of verse 4, both authors quote the line, "They are mute hounds, they cannot bark" (Isaiah 56.10). In treating verse 5, both recall the passage, "For if they had known Him, they would never have crucified the Lord of glory" (I Cor. 2.8), and both cite a passage of Matthew for that same verse. Such coincidences of citation are too close to be accidental; they constitute the strongest proof that Cassiodorus had the text of Augustine's *Enarrationes* under his hand when composing his own. This is important, since Cassiodorus, his own man, could easily have differed from Augustine on individual points of interpretation, while at the same time making use of the earlier author. Thus where a particular proof text seemed apposite, he could quote it as Augustine had; for him to have found such a pattern of parallel proof texts for one short Psalm independently of Augustine is beyond belief. It would not be worth denying that Cassiodorus brought his own fundamentally sound intellectual and religious training to bear on the commentary he wrote; but at the same time, it could be demonstrated more clearly than has been done before that he did indeed rely on Augustine's work as a guide for the entire length of his endeavor. [10]

But Cassiodorus also had other resources than Augustine to bring to bear on the subject. The first and most obvious was the remainder of the text of scripture itself; for all the parallelism between Augustine's and Cassiodorus' use of individual passages, Cassiodorus used many of his own choice as well. [11] In fact, in the course of the *Expositio,* Cassiodorus quoted or

10. Another Psalm chosen at random, number 109, on which Augustine discourses at much greater length than Cassiodorus, reveals three identical proof texts in their treatments of verse one, six for verse three, and one each for verses five, six, and seven.

11. For example, in his treatment of Psalm 109.3 (see the preceding note), Cassiodorus used six texts already used by Augustine and three more of his own; in 109.4, he used seven texts, none cited by Augustine.

alluded to passages from nearly every book of the Bible. The most obvious implication of this wide-ranging use of scripture is the familiarity that Cassiodorus must have possessed to make this kind of rapid and easy allusion. To the period culminating in the composition of this commentary, we must attribute a certain amount of time spent studying the scriptures directly and intensively, in a way that made these parallels recall themselves to Cassiodorus' mind as he needed them.[12]

Cassiodorus' other principal patristic source besides Augustine was Jerome, especially the treatise on Hebrew names; but letters, treatises on the Psalms, and scattered other commentaries of Jerome were apparently used as well. Other patristic figures like Hilary of Poitiers, Prosper of Aquitaine, Cyprian, his old friend Dionysius Exiguus, his contemporary and acquaintance Primasius of Hadrumetum, even Pelagius, Leo the Great, and the decrees of the Council of Chalcedon are more and less demonstrably present.

Since Cassiodorus was interested in secular *artes* and *disciplinae* as they appear in the Psalms, and since he was forever mentioning the technical terms for this and that rhetorical figure, a certain number of secular authors appear as well, often (to be sure) at second hand. Vergil is quoted half a dozen times, and Cicero about as often; their presence is not surprising, but that of Macrobius, quoted by name three times, is at least tantalizing. In truth, however, the number of other authors cited is not great, nor are the quotations weighty;[13] nevertheless, the presence of the diverse batch of authors who can be found here, and the diversity of works cited for the more frequently named, evinces wide learning at least, and possibly access to a good library at the time of composition.

The most interesting citations in the work are the ones that

12. The role of memory in scripture study at this time was still great; Augustine held (*De doct. christ.* 2.8.12–2.9.14) that all scripture study should begin with intensive study and memorization of the text.

13. Professor Halporn advises me, however, that Cassiodorus made considerable use, undetected by Adriaen, of Latin grammarians and rhetoricians, as well as more use of Marius Victorinus and possibly of Pelagius on Paul.

give us just a hint of the circumstances surrounding its composition. There are three authors quoted whose works would not have been widely disseminated in the west at this time, even in translation: Athanasius, Cyril of Alexandria, and John Chrysostom. There are only brief citations from their works, but nevertheless it is clear that Cassiodorus had direct access to them. We do not see all the same works quoted later on in works from the period at Squillace (although Cassiodorus will be active in getting Chrysostom's homilies on Hebrews translated). Athanasius is quoted, both times from his letter to Marcellinus on the virtues of the Psalms, in the last chapter but one of the Preface to the whole work and in the last commentary on the last Psalm.[14] Cyril of Alexandria's letters are quoted twice, once from the Latin version of Marius Mercator, and once in a Latin version not identifiable with any surviving text (*Ex. Ps.* 21.70–72, 16.311–315). Finally, Chrysostom is quoted four times, but always in versions identifiable with translations in other Latin authors (i.e., Cassian, Leo the Great, and an anonymous manuscript version surviving from the seventh/ eighth centuries). Two things need to be said about this evidence. First, it proves nothing, since even if equivalent versions do not survive from some quotations, they could easily have existed at the time of Cassiodorus' writing, and he could have had access to them anywhere in the Mediterranean world. Second, however, despite the obvious focus on Augustine and Jerome, and despite the probability that Cassiodorus was associating mainly with other Latins in Constantinople, nevertheless the use of these Greek authors gives a hint of the atmosphere in which the work was composed. The possibility that they establish is further augmented by the dedication to Vigilius (who must have been in Constantinople when the work was completed) and the citation of Facundus of Hermiane. There can be no doubt that Cassiodorus spent some time at

14. *Ex. Ps.*, praef. 16.17–29; *Ex. Ps.* 150.189–191; if the commentary was in fact written in the order we now have, the last lines of the last comment might well have been written very shortly before the preface. Athanasius' epistle was available at the Vivarium: *Inst.* 1.4.3.

Constantinople; what remains to be certified is whether he spent the entire decade of the 540's there, composing the *Expositio* there, or whether he worked on it in Italy (presumably at Squillace) and brought it along, nine-tenths finished, to complete and hand to Vigilius at Constantinople. The combination of circumstantial evidence from the last chapter and this one add up to a strong probability in favor of the hypothesis of a longer stay, but certainty is still out of reach. Cassiodorus' Christological preoccupations in this commentary will offer a little more help later on in this chapter, but they are still not conclusive.

In this welter of unproved possibilities, there is one thread that leads to a fairly firm conclusion. However one reads the evidence, two facts come out in parallel to one another: that Cassiodorus did spend time in Constantinople in his middle years, and that his works do not show a strong influence of Greek thought. This is strong evidence for arguing that Cassiodorus did not in fact possess particularly useful facility with the Greek language. This impression can be confirmed by the effusive praise that he had in later years for those who could handle both Greek and Latin fluently (e.g., *Inst.* 1.23.2); moreover, in spite of the extensive program of translations from the Greek that he instituted at the Vivarium, there is no evidence that he ever worked as a translator himself. Quite to the contrary, we are repeatedly told the names of the actual translators who did the work; Cassiodorus' desire to see important texts brought over from Greek into Latin may very well be connected with his own inadequacy.

The *Expositio Psalmorum* depended for much of its interpretative doctrine on Augustine, but it was in fact a completely original work, almost unique in its formal approach to the text and certainly unique in the goals it sought to achieve in the study of scripture. As we examine the individuality of this work, we will begin to be able to grasp its general purposes a little more clearly; those purposes will shed some light on Cassiodorus' own actions at this period.

Cassiodorus' commentary certainly cannot be attacked by the common modern canard that medieval exegesis is disorderly, rambling on eternally on trivial texts; a quite contrary impression is derived merely from inspecting a page or two of the work. For every Psalm there is a clear layout of the material in an introductory paragraph on the *titulus* (the short attribution of the Psalm to an author or, as Cassiodorus would have it, cantor, with other brief identifying remarks), a section entitled *divisio psalmi* setting out the Psalm's different sections according to content, then a verse-by-verse exposition of the text, and finally a paragraph of *conclusio,* summarizing the important points of the exegesis and frequently discoursing on the symbolism of the Psalm's ordinal number. This external regularity is not merely superficial, but is an indication of the underlying principles of Cassiodorian exegesis.

In this vein, one important feature of the *Expositio Psalmorum* is the long preface, with an introductory section, then seventeen chapters of methodological and technical remarks, and a concluding list of the "chapters" into which the entire Psalter can be divided. From the point of view of the modern reader, this division of Psalms by allegorical subject matter is the heart of the most alien feature of the entire work. In fact, the principle behind the practice is a simple and obvious one. In the first chapter of the preface, "De prophetia," Cassiodorus defines prophecy as "a divine pronouncement predicting the outcome of events through the words and deeds of men with unshakable accuracy" (*Ex. Ps.,* praef. 1.1–2). By this definition, David, the author of every Psalm, was himself a great prophet, "filled with the breath of heaven" (*Ex. Ps.,* praef. 1.20). Therefore, "we see clearly that every Psalm is spoken prophetically through the Holy Spirit" (*Ex. Ps.,* praef. 1.24–25). Every Psalm can thus be interpreted allegorically to refer to the truths of the Christian faith. The reality of the allegorical nature of the Psalms in Cassiodorus' mind leads directly to his classification of the Psalms by subject matter. By observation, Cassiodorus determined the major subjects under which his interpretations of the Psalms could be summarized; he gives a list of them at the end of the preface, where they total, oddly enough, to just twelve:

1. the carnal life of the Lord;
2. the nature of His deity;
3. the multiplied peoples who tried to destroy Him;
4. that the Jews should cease their evil ways;
5. Christ crying out to the Father in the passion, and being resurrected from the dead;
6. penitential Psalms;
7. the prayers of Christ, chiefly in His human nature;
8. parables, tropes, and allegories, telling the story of the life of Christ;
9. Psalms beginning with the exclamation *Alleluia;*
10. "gradual" Psalms, fifteen in sequence;
11. the praises of the Trinity;
12. seven Psalms of exultation at the very end.[15]

After enumerating these headings, Cassiodorus then failed to give coherent lists of the individual Psalms that come under each category. Instead, therefore, of an index at the beginning by which we could be instructed to flip to, say, the seven penitential Psalms, our information regarding the assignment of the Psalms to given chapter headings must be garnered from scattered remarks throughout the commentary.

There is, however, good and adequate reason for this reticence about publishing complete lists of which Psalms come under which headings. First, the list of the twelve subjects is somewhat arbitrarily chosen in order to fill up the favored number twelve; the eighth category duplicates in not altogether obvious ways the first and second, while the eleventh covers part of the same ground as the second as well. Not every Psalm, moreover, fits one and only one category exactly; some useful categories are not exactly subjects (e.g., largely formal categories like prayers of David or penitential Psalms—and Psalm 101, for example, fits both these categories), while other subcategories develop as part of broader ones (e.g., poems prophesying the first coming of Christ as a subcategory of

15. *Ex. Ps.,* praef., "Ordo Dicendorum," 1–51. (The words "Ordo Dicendorum" were inserted in the *editio princeps;* MSS give "Prolegomena.")

those prophesying the first and second comings; or poems treating the passion and resurrection *brevius,* and those treating these subjects *latius).* Finally, there are the so-called alphabetic Psalms (with stanzas identified by the letters in the Hebrew alphabet), seven in number, but overlapping at least three other categories (*Alleluia, laudes,* and the carnal life of Christ). There is special allegorical significance assigned to the alphabetic Psalms in addition to their formal virtue; for there are four such Psalms styled "imperfect" (having fewer stanzas than there are letters in the whole Hebrew alphabet) that Cassiodorus takes to represent the church on earth, which is almost, but not quite, perfect. The three "perfect" alphabetic Psalms, having just as many stanzas as the alphabet has letters, describe the acts and lives of individuals who have in fact achieved the perfection toward which the church is striving.

Revealingly, it is the explicit, formal sort of category that comes nearest to puzzling Cassiodorus. Speaking of the twenty *Alleluia* Psalms (which we have seen overlap other categories as well), he says that their "even number perhaps represents the glory of Old and New Testaments, so that the power of the Creator should be praised always and everywhere. At least we have found no better reason why *Alleluia* is placed on just these Psalms" (*Ex. Ps.* 104.38–42). In contrast to that, the alphabetic Psalms found an exact interpretation: "the imperfect alphabet Psalms represent *Ecclesia,* which still flourishes here and has not yet been purified by the weeding out of the unjust; the perfect alphabet Psalms signify the heavenly Jerusalem, where the assembly of the perfect will be completed with the addition of saintly men" (*Ex. Ps.* 144.39–42).

For Psalms categorized strictly by subject matter, Cassiodorus' typical treatment can be seen in the *conclusio* for Psalm 108, the fifth of the Psalms to treat the passion of Christ at length (Psalms 21, 34, 54, and 68 are the others). These Psalms, he says, have four things in common: they are all spoken in the person of Christ, they describe the events of the passion (allegorically), they agree in detail with the Gospel (after they have been allegorized), and they end with exultant hope for the faithful (they look forward to the resurrection). In addition to these Psalms, there are as many as six (Cassiodorus' list is not complete or coherent) that deal more briefly with the same subject (*Ex. Ps.* 108.491–511).

One obvious formal category does not appeal to Cassiodorus as such: Psalms joined together by identity of text. For example, Psalm 13 has virtually the same text as Psalm 52 except for an interpolation; but Cassiodorus' interpretation resolutely casts the former as referring to the first coming of Christ and the rebuking of the Jewish people, while the latter is taken as referring to the second coming and the rebuking of sinners in the world. Similarly, Psalm 107 is a cento of sections from two earlier Psalms (56.8–12 and 59.6–14), but it bears a different *titulus* from either of the others and hence a different Cassiodorian interpretation. It cannot, however, be ascertained which came first: the allegorizations of the Psalms or the subject headings under which they were grouped.

The other principal division of the entire collection of the Psalms is a less functional one, introduced more for contemplation of the division itself than for any assistance it affords in understanding individual Psalms. For Cassiodorus breaks the entire commentary in two parts, making the first seventy Psalms a figure of the Old Testament and the last eighty of the New. He attributes this division to *patres nostri* (*Ex. Ps.* 70.494). He abandons this division for practical purposes, however, since by his own testimony and that of the manuscript tradition itself the commentary was in practice bound in three volumes, with fifty Psalms in each. But the figurative significance of the division by Testaments is insisted upon, and a brief new preface comes before Psalm 71. The principle remains clear, however, that the entire Psalter is to be referred to the content of the New Testament in particular by way of prophecy; thus this book of scripture, the first taken up by "tyros beginning the study of Holy Scripture" (*Ex. Ps.*, praef. 16.42), becomes a compendium of the central doctrines of the Christian faith.[16]

16. Cf. Jerome, *Ep.* 107.12, "Discat primo Psalterium. . . ."

Not only does this method provide a way to teach the truths of the faith, but it also fills the entire Psalter with abiding meaning for the student who learns its content in this way to begin with.

The highly formal, organized way in which Cassiodorus goes about the practice of his exegesis, as we have already indicated, is compatible with the didactic purpose of the whole work. Each Psalm is treated in the same way, with an interpretation divided into four clearly visible parts: *titulus, divisio, expositio, conclusio.*

The attention Cassiodorus gives to the *tituli,* the short identifying remarks given at the beginning of each (but not quite every) Psalm is an important part of his exegetical practice, termed by Schlieben the prosopographical approach.[17] Cassiodorus insists repeatedly that David and only David can be taken as the author of all 150 Psalms. Once he has assumed that the other names that appear in the *tituli* are not those of their authors, he is entitled to make use of these names, with their historical and etymological associations, to enlighten and organize his own exposition. To return to Psalm 81, for example, we recall that there the *titulus* is given as "Psalmus Asaph." Cassiodorus followed Augustine in interpreting Asaph's name as representing the synagogue (as opposed to the church). What is characteristic in Cassiodorus' approach in this Psalm is that he is dependent for the idea on prior tradition but independent in the importance he attributes to the matter. He reaches down into Augustine's discussion of the first verse, which mentions the ideas of the synagogue, to drag the etymologies of *synagoga* and *ecclesia* up into his treatment of the *titulus* alone, where Augustine dismissed the *titulus* in a single sentence (as he did with virtually every Psalm).

Significant names, however, are not the only subject that attracts Cassiodorus' interest in the treatments of *tituli.*[18] Every single word that appears in the rubric is grist for Cassiodorus'

17. Schlieben, *Cassiodors Psalmenexegese* (1970), 92.

18. For most of his name-interpretations, e.g., the "sons of Core," Cassiodorus followed the received opinion of the fathers as given in Augustine, with help from Jerome.

interpretative mill; in fact, much of the explanatory material
contained in the preface to the entire collection is intended to
resolve some of these difficulties once and for all so that Cassiodorus can then refer back to them as they come up, rather
than treat them over again time after time. For example, a separate chapter (the third in the preface) is set aside for the common inscription "In finem" found at the beginning of many
Psalms in the Latin versions. Augustine's practice was to pass
over this phrase briefly, usually citing Paul: "for the end [*finis*]
of the Law is Christ, unto justice for every believer" (Rom.
10.4).[19] Cassiodorus finds it more efficient to remove this discussion to a separate chapter of the preface, wherein he makes
more explicit the ideas contained in these and other throwaway
lines of Augustine. First he states that we can speak of a *finis* in
two ways, the end of something in the ordinary sense (as of
money when it has been spent) and "the perfect and everlasting
goal [*finis*] we are seeking (*Ex. Ps.,* praef. 3.9–10). This end
and fullness of the Law, he goes on, is Christ the Lord, and
then he quotes the passage from Paul himself: Christ is the true
end of all things that men seek. "When we reach Him we shall
seek nothing further, but enjoy perfect gladness abiding in this
consummation of happiness [*in ipso beatitudinis fine*]; the love
of this happiness grows as our understanding is illuminated by
the Lord. So as often as you find 'in finem' in the *tituli* of the
Psalms, then turn your mind to the Lord and Savior, who is an
end without end [*finis sine fine*] and the complete perfection of
all good things" (*Ex. Ps.,* praef. 3.12–18).

The last word on the *tituli* also requires a separate chapter of
the preface, "De unita inscriptione titulorum," which tells us
that the *tituli* "hang before the portals of the Psalms like sacred
veils through which, if you peer through the delicate fabric,
you can easily make out the inner secrets of the Psalms. Who
could think all this variety of names superfluous where we
know it is shameful to believe the Holy Scriptures contain anything useless?" (*Ex. Ps.,* praef. 10.20–25). Thus these mysteri-

19. Cf. *Enarr. in Psal.* 4.1, 139.3, and often elsewhere.

ous words, so laboriously explained at such length, are in fact keys to the spiritual understanding of scripture, providing the hints that we need to perfectly understand the superficially simpler content of the Psalms themselves.

Cassiodorus presents a summary outline of his treatment of the Psalms in the fourteenth chapter of his preface. First, he promises, the *tituli* will be explained. Second, each Psalm is to be divided up into sections, "lest any unnoticed change of subjects or speakers should trouble our understanding" (*Ex. Ps.*, praef. 14.5–7). Third, Cassiodorus will attempt to unfold the "meaning of the Psalm, partly according to the spiritual interpretations, partly according to the historical content, partly according to the mystical sense, analyzing the subtleties of things and words as far as possible" (*Ex. Ps.*, praef. 14.7–11). Fourth, he will attempt to elaborate the *virtus* of the Psalm, its *inspiratio divina*, "by which the divine meaning is opened up for us, drawing us back from immorality and persuading us to live uprightly by the words of the psalmist David" (*Ex. Ps.*, praef. 14.14–16). Fifth, he will discuss the ordering of the numbering of the Psalms, i.e., interpret the numbers according to mystical principles; he confesses that this will cause some difficulty, since not every Psalm admits such treatment. Finally, "in the *conclusiones* we will briefly summarize the whole Psalm or perhaps say a few words against despicable heresies" (*Ex. Ps.*, praef. 14.23–25).

The notion of the explicit *divisio* furnished for every Psalm (except Psalm 116, which has only two verses) is a Cassiodorian innovation resulting from his passion for formal order and the imposition of a visible logical skeleton on the work from outside.[20] Cassiodorus alludes to his own innovation in the conclusion to his treatment of Psalm 106: "I see this Psalm was divided in sections by the most learned *pater* Augustine, who says he believed he was thus expounding it to his audience in an

---

20. Hahner, *Cassiodors Psalmenkommentar* (1973), 65–96, treats this subject more fully.

unprecedented way. We imitate him as best we can, dividing all the Psalms in this way, showing in our comments that a practice authorized by so great a *pater* offers considerable assistance in understanding the Psalms" (*Ex. Ps.* 106.518–524). In fact, however, this appeal to Augustine's authority is strained. First, the very generality of Cassiodorus' practice is directly at variance with Augustine's more easygoing interpretations. But second, in the case of this very Psalm, Cassiodorus' own divisions differ from Augustine's. Augustine's treatment is nowhere near as enslaved to external form as is that of Cassiodorus.

The function of the *divisio* for the commentary on each Psalm is central to the sense of the exposition. The *divisio* begins with a summary of the Psalm's nature, which establishes the *persona* of the speaker of the entire Psalm, whether one individual or several (e.g., *Ex. Ps.* 81.17–19). In complex cases, the several voices may be those of the prophet himself, the Lord, or unfaithful men; moreover, the prophet himself may be addressing first the Lord in prayer, then his enemies in rebuke, then his fellow believers in thanksgiving for support, then the Lord again. In any event, the purpose is to represent before the student's eyes a precise understanding of who, according to a spiritual understanding of the Psalm, is speaking to whom at every point through the Psalm.

Having established the identity of the speaker, the exegete divides the content of his address into sections. Cassiodorus does not give specific verse numbers for division of the Psalms into sections; his concern rather is to lay out a general picture of the interpretation he is going to give, the framework onto which the individual verses will be stretched and shrunk to fit. The actual divisions in the text will not be noticed until they come up in the course of the detailed exposition (but they are never left unspecified).

The principles behind the division of the Psalms are more exegetical than formal, but one strictly technical point intervenes. Many Psalms are marked by *diapsalmata,* which Cassiodorus rightly recognizes as having been originally indicators of pauses in the performance of the Psalm.[21] Whenever these are available to him, he will make use of them to identify a point of division; in practice, this is usually successful, since they were originally inserted to indicate some break in the train of thought and direction of the Psalm, which is precisely what Cassiodorus wants to use them for.

The most significant departure from Augustinian practice in Cassiodorus, when all the trivial differences of interpretation are counted up, is reserved for the *conclusio*. The *conclusiones* to Cassiodorian interpretations are important sources, to be discussed below, for Cassiodorus' own views as distinct from Augustine's, since these passages are entirely original with Cassiodorus in every case. In Psalm 81, for example, a strongly Christ-centered Psalm from the exegete's point of view, the appeal of Cassiodorus' *conclusio* is to the Jews to come and open their ears to the true good news. But, more than that, Cassiodorus directs his words to those "who are boiling over with the pestilential breath of Nestorius and Eutychius" (*Ex. Ps.* 81.153).[22] "The error of believing in two natures divided according to two *personae* in Christ is very like that of believing in only one mixed nature, howbeit only in a single person" (*Ex. Ps.* 81.157–159).[23] After quoting a verse of Sedulius' *Carmen paschale* to the Nestorians thus refuted, he turns to the Eutychians, comparing them subtly to doubting Thomas. "Why do you fly," he asks them, "from confessing what our *patres* agreed upon by a revelation of the Holy Spirit? If you will not believe in two natures unconfused, unchangeable, undivided, and inseparable, say 'two substances' or 'two

21. Hilary of Poitiers seems to be his source for this information (Schlieben, *Cassiodors Psalmenexegese* [1970], 26), which he summarizes in the seventh chapter of the preface and again at *Ex. Ps.* 9.307–313, where he alludes explicitly back to the treatment in the preface.

22. I.e., both Nestorians and Monophysites; the rebuke of such heresy is a very common subject of *conclusiones* (see *Ex. Ps.*, Praef. 14.23–25).

23. *Ex. Ps.* 81.157–159: "Talis enim error est duas naturas divisas secundum duas personas in Christo Domino profiteri, qualis unam confusam credere, quamvis in unitate personae."

forms' . . . . Beware of shrinking from the healing poultice only
to prepare eternal ruin for yourselves" (*Ex. Ps.* 81.175–182).

We have already seen in Chapter 4, and we will see again in
more detail in Chapter 6, that one of Cassiodorus' chief concerns when writing as a Christian intellectual was the relationship between Christian and secular learning. This concern expressed itself in a remarkable way throughout the *Expositio
Psalmorum* and must become one of our chief objects of study.
Next to Cassiodorus' strictly exegetical principles and practices,
the attitude he held towards the secular disciplines is the most
obvious feature of his exegesis and one in which his contribution is unique and substantial. It is important, however, not to
allow mere idiosyncracy to become in and of itself a criterion
of significance; despite his fascination with the secular sciences,
Cassiodorus in this work is still primarily a Christian theologian expounding scripture, and it is to his principles in that field
that we must look first.

In the preface to the *Expositio,* Cassiodorus promised to
interpret the sense of the Psalms, "partly according to their
spiritual interpretation, partly according to their historical content, partly according to the mystical sense" (*Ex. Ps.*, praef.
14.3). This statement, covering three of the four senses of scripture traditionally listed, gives a false impression of the multipli-
cation of distinctions.[24] Although, for example, the mystical
sense of scripture is usually that which deals with eschatology,
while the spiritual sense is more generally that which seeks the
first allegorical meaning behind the literal one, the terms are by
no means mutually exclusive and can even be redundant.[25] In
fact, in Cassiodorus, redundant is what they are. Moreover, the
expression of interest in the historical sense here is little more
than perfunctory. For the *Expositio Psalmorum* is as resolutely
and monolithically allegorical a commentary as ever was

24. On Cassiodorus' terms for the senses of scriptural interpretation, see
Hahner, *Cassiodors Psalmenkommentar* (1973), 28–65.
25. Lubac, *Exégèse Médiévale,* 1.129–169, catalogues the various ways of listing the senses and their implications.

written. As can be judged by the list of "chapters" into which Cassiodorus divided the Psalms according to their content—the content imposed upon them by the allegorist—the entire Psalter is made an instrument for expressing and seeing expressed the truths of Christian revelation. Scant attention is paid to the historical background, even of the most obviously literal Psalms.

Psalm 17, to take the most literal case, is a verbatim repetition of a passage (a prayer of thanksgiving by David) at II Samuel 22.1–51; Cassiodorus merely furnishes the cross-reference, without attempting to place the piece in any of its historical context. He notes the "in finem" of the *titulus* and thus the reference to Christ; the use of the term *canticum* is meant, he goes on, to call our mind from the story of David to the celestial kingdom, with clear parallels to the resurrection of Christ. The division of the Psalm into section leaves only one short section for the prophet to give his thanks (the first four verses); the next three sections are placed in the *personae* of the church and the Lord Himself, and any possible reference to David is obliterated. In the *conclusio,* Cassiodorus' chief concern is to excuse the unusual variety of persons represented as speaking in this Psalm; the most important thing, he argues, is to notice that the Lord Himself did not disdain to mix his words with those of the prophet and the church, a figure for the generosity with which he undertook "to assume the abasement of incarnation" (*Ex. Ps.* 17.740–741).[26]

One Psalm in which Cassiodorus does make a serious professed attempt to observe the "literal" sense is a curious exception testing the rule. Psalm 103, a hymn of praise to God the creator, seems to Cassiodorus to be making explicit certain things implied in the Genesis account of creation. "Thus we have explained this Psalm *ad litteram* where appropriate; but where it could increase our knowledge of the faith we have interpreted allegorically [*spiritali intellectu*] as the ancients did"

26. A similar abandonment of the obvious historical reference of a Psalm takes place in the first lines of Cassiodorus' treatment of Psalm 95.

(*Ex. Ps.* 103.11–13).[27] Moreover, he tells us, Augustine has treated this Psalm fully and ought to be followed. When it comes time, however, to interpret the verses of the Psalm, the criterion for judging whether a given passage is to be taken literally or allegorically is fidelity to and compatibility with the Genesis account. Thus the verse "Qui tegis aquis superiora eius, Qui ponis nubem ascensum tuum, Qui ambulas super pennas ventorum" (Ps. 103.3) is to be taken *ad litteram,* "since the Lord climbs to heaven after the resurrection with the apostles looking on" (*Ex. Ps.* 103.104–106), and Cassiodorus quotes the relevant passage of Acts. But a later verse poses problems: "Qui fundasti terram super stabilitatem suam, non inclinabitur in saeculum saeculi" (Ps. 103.5). "It seems this verse cannot be taken *ad litteram;* for where we read that earth will be transformed [cf. Apoc. 21.1], how can it be that it will 'not be shaken through all ages'? But we recognize in this immutable *terra* the stability of the church" (*Ex. Ps.* 103.146–150). Similarly the sixth verse is not to be taken *ad litteram* (though Cassiodorus knows there are some who would like to do so).

That for Cassiodorus the literal sense of scripture includes what might more properly be termed allegorical readings is thus obvious in a number of cases. For example, commenting on the phrase "in mari viae tuae" (Ps. 76.20), Cassiodorus has already asserted that this section of the Psalm recounts the miracles of the Lord. That in itself is an allegorical interpretation, but within that framework his interpretation of this specific verse divides again into literal and allegorical. "If you take this literally, 'through the sea was His way' when He walked on the water and called Peter to come to Him. But 'through the sea was His way' is better understood of the thoughts of men, which roll and toss like a treacherous sea, but where Christ finds a way nonetheless, when He subjects them to Himself with great mercy" (*Ex. Ps.* 76.396–403). A consistent view of this exegesis would hold that the reference to

27. On Cassiodorus' varied terms for introducing and describing allegorical interpretations, see Hahner, *Cassiodors Psalmenkommentar* (1973), 132–165.

Christ's walking on the water was the allegorical interpretation, and the reference to the thoughts of men and Christ's action in them the moral signification. Cassiodorus is not, however, sophisticated enough in the practice of these subtleties of exegesis to make the distinction between literal and allegorical at this point. There is nothing surprising in this: even the subtlest of the analysts of the exegetical levels did not always in practice preserve exactly the distinction between the several levels, and they could commonly think of their interpretations on the simplest level of literal versus spiritual senses; Augustine's highly influential handbook *De doctrina christiana* confines itself to a twofold distinction of senses.

We have seen enough now to begin to understand the workings of Cassiodorus' mind in coming towards spiritual interpretations of the Psalms. Beginning with the assumption that Christ is at the center of so many of the Psalms (for fifty-one of the first eighty Psalms begin with the tag "in finem," and thirty-five of the last seventy are either "gradual" Psalms or *Alleluias,* all of which are given specifically Christological references in the preface), Cassiodorus did not feel that he was unjustified in interpreting the Psalter as a handbook of Christian doctrine. Obviously, Psalms originally referring to events in the life of David could be reinterpreted for application to Christ very easily according to standard ideas about typology; moreover, many Psalms of a more general nature (prayers to God, praises of God, etc.) could be read in a specifically Christian sense very easily indeed. Once that stage had been reached in the understanding of the Psalms as units, the interpretation of individual verses was no tremendously difficult task. Where the interpretation flowed naturally from the sense assigned to the Psalm as a whole, well and good; where it did not, the law of spiritual interpretation could be invoked and difficulties would evanesce.

It would be wrong, however, to see in Cassiodorus' practice, or that of any of the *patres,* a deliberate obscurantism, exploiting the notion of spiritual interpretation to wash away difficulties without facing up to them. The entire problem with Psalm

103.5 is of Cassiodorus' own creation, for example, since it was his own decision to interpret the Psalm as a gloss on Genesis. If the whole Psalm were taken either more or less allegorically to begin with, the problem need never have arisen. Furthermore, it is wrong to assume that the interpretation retailed by a given patristic commentator of a given passage of scripture is intended always and without exception to be the one and only acceptable reading of the passage. The purpose of expounding the Psalter, for example, is not to establish what Christian doctrine is so much as to teach it and—even more important—to make the Psalter come to life with contemplation of things seen through, rather than in, the words on the page. To read the Psalms, for example, as a document of Jewish liturgical piety, or even simply as inspiring religious poetry, still confining oneself to the simplest sense of the text at hand, inevitably becomes a tedious procedure if often repeated. The central position of the Psalter in the life of the medieval church, and in monastic culture especially, indicates that, quite to the contrary, it never did become a boring round of repeated platitudes. For insofar as a medieval reader of the Psalter had already embedded in his mind remarks of the sort that Cassiodorus makes about every Psalm, and insofar as the Psalms themselves had been transformed from ordinary verse into magnifying glasses through which all sorts of wondrous things became more visible than before from a new light, the words of the Psalms became living teachers of infinite resource. The decision, then, to overlook minor verbal inconsistencies that come up in the course of, and often only as a result of, the allegorical practice, is not an effort to cover up difficulties in the definition of the truths of Christianity and their support in scripture, but rather only a convenience for the reader, a device for augmenting the reader's ability to make profitable use of the scriptures as a support for contemplation and liturgy.

What sets Cassiodorus' commentary apart from other allegorical interpretations of the Psalms, however, is not any strictly theological feature, but rather a pedagogic one. Cassiodorus is visibly interested not only in the spiritual benefits to be derived from an enlightened reading of the Psalms, but also in the didactic benefits. He has made of the Psalter a textbook in the liberal arts. The reason for this is quite simple: to enable readers to draw from the scripture a knowledge of these things, in order to enable them to go back to the same and other scriptural texts better capable of making their own analysis. This exaltation of the Psalter as textbook is based on a fundamental theory about the nature of the liberal arts that, though it goes back to Clement of Alexandria, is never so fully worked out and so consistently presented as in Cassiodorus.[28]

For Cassiodorus believed that the arts of secular learning, the trivium and quadrivium, had themselves a scriptural origin. His interpretation of Psalm 18.5 ("Their voice resounds through all the earth, and their words to the ends of the earth") is that the teachings of the Bible were known to all men throughout the world. The genesis of the secular arts and sciences he explains this way: "First we must recognize that the omnipotence of the Lord has so enriched its eloquence with many *artes* and *disciplinae* that it both shines marvelously in the eyes of those who study it and plants well-watered seeds of other disciplines. Thus we find in Holy Scripture the things which teachers of secular literature [*magistri saecularium litterarum*] have transplanted to their own books. Orators speak, for example, of the 'concessive deprecative' mode of speaking, when a defendant does not defend what he has done but begs that he be forgiven; before earthly judges this is a feeble tactic, but before the judgment seat of God it is invincibly strong, since faithful confession alone can vindicate what no argument could defend" (*Ex. Ps.* 6.94–107).[29]

28. E. R. Curtius, *European Literature and the Latin Middle Ages* (1953), 41.

29. See also *Ex. Ps.*, praef. 15.45–76; *Inst.*, praef. 6; *Inst.* 1.4.2. Cassiodorus' statement of this theory forces him to abandon the traditional patristic use of Romans 1.20 as a general theory of the availability of divine knowledge to the pagans. That passage, speaking of the invisible things of God being visible through the things that are made, never appears in the *Expositio Psalmorum*; it would, one sees, contradict Cassiodorus' belief that the scriptures themselves were known to all men. (Augustine does recommend the study of the Bible as a repository of rhetorical figures: *De doct. christ.* 4.2 and 4.20.) See also J.-M. Courtès, *Revue des études latines,* 42(1964), 361–375.

It is precisely this "fidelis confessio" that, Cassiodorus argues, is illustrated by Psalm 6.2, the passage being expounded at this point. Briefly put, this idea, which contains all that Cassiodorus thought on the relation of secular and sacred learning, is that the secular *magistri* plagiarized their material from the sacred scripture, where the seeds of their discipline had been hidden by God. The Cassiodorian scheme for expounding scripture is to bypass the secular *doctores* entirely, plucking out the seeds himself and presenting them directly to the student in the commentary on the sacred text.

Before and after Cassiodorus, Christian authors found themselves frequently in positions where they felt they had to explain away somehow their use of the pagan-tainted liberal arts in the study of scripture. Jerome's *Ciceronianus* dream, Augustine's metaphor of the Egyptian gold, and Gregory's oft-misinterpreted refusal to be bound by the rules of Donatus, are all efforts at establishing some kind of harmony between sacred and secular intellectual life.[30] One recalls as a closer forerunner of Cassiodorus the efforts of Apollinaris of Laodicea and his son in the fourth century, when Julian forbade Christians to teach the pagan classics; their rewriting of the scriptures into a Homeric epic, Euripidean tragedies, Menandrian comedies, Pindaric odes, and Platonic dialogues was an effort to make of the scriptures precisely the thing Cassiodorus said they already were. Moreover, Cassiodorus' notion of the hiddenness of the *artes* in scripture more than accounted for the apparently superficial barbarity (i.e., nonconformity to secular rules) of biblical eloquence.

The practice of this exegetical theory in Cassiodorus is persistent and intentionally overwhelming. Rare is the verse of the Psalter that is not noted to contain some obscure form of syllogism, some recondite rhetorical figure, or some one of the seemingly endless *species definitionis* that Cassiodorus is adept at

---

30. Curtius, *op. cit.*, 448. Lubac, *Exégèse Médiévale,* 3.53–77, has once and (one hopes) for all removed clouds of misunderstanding from Gregory's passage in particular. In general, however, it should be noted that modern scholars agonize over medieval attitudes towards the classics more than the medieval authors themselves ever did.

identifying. Moreover, Cassiodorus provided marginal nota-
tions to enable the student to pursue these rhetorical rules
throughout the work. In all important early manuscripts of the
commentary there is prefixed a list of standardized marginal
notes that then reappear throughout the work, singling out
rhetorical figures, etymologies, etymologies of Hebrew names,
necessary dogmas, and (most common) *idiomata,* that is,
uniquely scriptural figures of speech.[31] Thus the interpretation
of Psalm 16.8 ("Guard me as the pupil of your eye, hide me in
the shadow of your wings") presents the following information: (1) "By the figure *icon,* in Latin called *imaginatio,* he com-
pares himself to the pupil of the eye of the Lord." (2) "*Pupilla* is
derived from the notion of smallness, as *pusilla.*" (3) (After the
final clause:) "Here is introduced the figure which is called
parabole in Greek, *comparatio* in Latin, since it joins unlike things
in a sort of connection" (*Ex. Ps.* 16.157–169). Certainly it is
unusual for a single verse to offer two *schemata* and one
etymology for Cassiodorus' pleasure, but his treatment of them
here is characteristic.[32] Note especially the bilingual designation
of the figures identified; this affectation is maintained in virtually every case where they are mentioned.

31. The marginal signs are printed in the *editio princeps* and in Adriaen's
edition; Professor Halporn advises me that they appear in all the best early
MSS, a point on which Adriaen is misleading; he also points out their possible
derivation from scholiastic tradition. The complete list of Cassiodorus' signs is
as follows:

PP *idiomata,* i.e., *propriae locutiones* of scripture

ℛ necessary dogmas	TOP *topoi*
P definitions	SYL syllogisms
SCHE *schemata*	AR arithmetic
ET etymologies	GEO geometry
RP interpretations of names	M music
RT rhetoric	* astronomy

32. Many of Cassiodorus' etymologies come from Varro, whether directly
or by an intermediary. See G. Goetz, *Berliner Philologische Wochenschrift,* 30(1910),
1367–1368, and the dissertation that note inspired, H. Erdbrügger, *Cassiodorus
unde etymologias in Psalterii commentario prolatas petivisse putandus sit* (1912).
Erdbrügger examines 160 etymologies, of which 55 come from identifiable
sources (or analogues), of which 41 are Varronian.

The special idioms of scripture are those things therein that seem to go against the rules of secular rhetoric or that are merely unusual in common parlance and unusually frequent in scripture;[33] a few lines beyond the examples quoted in the last paragraph, we find "He uses *nunc* to put the present tense where you would expect the future, a common practice with the prophets" (*Ex. Ps.* 16.198–199) marked with the marginal note P̂P. In the very next paragraph the mark reappears next to: "We refer the word *leo* now to the devil, now to Christ. This mannerism is to be considered one of the *propria sanctae scripturae*—here obviously it refers to the devil" (*Ex. Ps.* 16.208–211—cf. *Inst.* 1.15.4). This, too, is a response to the older criticisms of scripture's inattention to the proprieties of grammar and style; where, for example, the Old Testament frequently uses the plural of *sanguis,* as in the phrase *viri sanguinum* (e.g., Ps. 54.24), Cassiodorus had to explain that this is correct and not to be tampered with, precisely because it is the practice of scripture.

Obviously, all of this material transforming an allegorical commentary into a commentary *cum* textbook is uniquely Cassiodorian, departing completely from the homiletic form of Augustine's *Enarrationes.* Where Augustine would pursue at length possible alternate figurative meanings of a given line, Cassiodorus would cut short after the first to tell you what the Greek and Latin terms are for this figure as he interprets it. On the one hand, this is not the most orderly way to give instruction in figures of speech; but on the other, the Psalter is the most familiar text of scripture, and to the extent that it can be made the mnemonic peg for dozens and dozens of these definitions it becomes a recurring reminder of the substance of the education in the liberal arts that Cassiodorus had in mind. The Augustinian element of Cassiodorian exegesis is chiefly the allegorical interpretation; the Cassiodorian element is chiefly the regularization of form and the addition of the didactic material about the *artes.*

33. These *propria genera locutionum* are a common Augustinian notion (e.g., *De vera religione* 50.99), which Cassiodorus treated again at *Inst.* 1.15.

Because Cassiodorus' theory eliminated any fundamental conflict between sacred and secular literatures, he could use secular sources without any of the self-conscious histrionics of other Christian authors. But it is not possible to go, as Schlieben does, from this lack of polemic against "worldly men" to a general concept of "Cassiodorus' Christian humanism."[34] Implicit in Cassiodorus' theory, far from any approval of an enthusiasm for the secular classics in themselves, is a far more thoroughgoing disdain for classical literature; rather than acknowledge that the Bible is less rhetorically eloquent than secular texts, Cassiodorus insisted that the Bible, as source of all rules of eloquence, is absolutely superior on literary as well as theological grounds to anything the secular authors have to offer. Moreover, the secular authors whom he did make frequent use of, both in the Psalm commentary and in later works, were not the great literary classics at all, but rather textbooks and handbooks of the rules that, by his theory, secular *magistri* had deduced from scripture. In establishing this notion, Cassiodorus was so far from embracing the classics that he could abandon them altogether as merely redundant to what is already present in scripture. At all times for Cassiodorus, the secular sciences only serve to lead men back into scripture.

After the exposition proper of each Psalm, in which the Augustinian and Cassiodorian elements are fused to produce an exegetical and pedagogical interpretation, each short treatise is capped with a paragraph (sometimes running a page or more) of *conclusio*. In the preface, Cassiodorus indicated that this would be the place to demonstrate the Psalm's *virtus*, its *inspiratio divina*, and to give an account of the Psalm's number, where possible. The first of these purposes is always achieved.

The typical *conclusio* is little more than a summary of the exegetical doctrine propounded in the body of the exposition. It is not so schematic as the *divisio*, but it frequently repeats much of the same material. In the course of the whole commentary, however, there is a noticeable development in the nature of

34. Schlieben, *Cassiodors Psalmenexegese* (1970), 170, 222.

these final paragraphs. The first examples are the most schematic; see, for example, the *conclusio* of the commentary on Psalm
7, which repeats the sections of the Psalm ("prima parte . . .
secunda parte . . . tertia parte") in praising its eloquence. This
résumé is followed by a brief prayerful apostrophe to God,
ending "Who indeed could avoid suffering from the justice
of God without the prior assistance of his mercy?" (*Ex. Ps.*
7.362–378). Then the paragraph concludes with two sentences
on the significance of the number seven.

By contrast, the later *conclusiones,* while not always ignoring
the same threefold pattern (summary, prayer, number), show a
definite trend toward the emphasis of the prayerful content at
the expense of the other elements.[35] In part this is a function of
the lessening significance of number symbolism when the
numbers become unwieldy, and in part it reflects a recognition
of the superfluity of an explicit rehash of the Psalm's contents.
Nevertheless, the importance of the prayerful content is growing apace of its own accord.[36] By Psalm 139, for example, the
whole paragraph is a unity, starting from the Psalm's *virtus* (expressed in exclamations more and more breathless as we near
the end of the Psalter) and turning rapidly into direct prayer:
"How salutary, how sweet are these words of the holy mother!
She has prayed that we might avoid the temptations of the
devil by which she knows us to have been violently beset. To
the ones so freed she promises that they will see the face of
God, that we might fear no toils and sadness, we to whom such
a boon is promised. Grant, Lord, that you might show by the
splendor of your mercy how desirable you are to your servants.
The sins we have ourselves righteously rebuked will not
obstruct us. We confess our sins, that we might placate you; for
you are the only judge who grants forgiveness to the confessed

35. I say "later" on the assumption, which this development of the *conclusiones* tends to support but does not prove, that the treatises in *Ex. Ps.* were
written in the numerical order of the Psalms themselves.

36. These prayerful conclusions were useful independently as well, for devotional purposes, as shown by H. Ashworth, *Bulletin of the John Rylands Library,* 45 (1962–1963), 287–304.

offender; and since nothing escapes your knowledge, you still require us to acknowledge publicly what you know far more surely" (*Ex. Ps.* 139.226–236). The function of this kind of conclusion is not simply intepretative or didactic, as is the case with the expositions proper. Instead, such sentiments, so vividly worded, have the function of calling the reader back from a too-studious approach to the Psalm merely as a document of doctrine and the rhetorical arts. The *conclusio* serves to make vivid again the profoundly spiritual nature of the experience towards which the study of the Psalm is meant to lead. Having taken the Psalm out of its context, examined it from every side, and presented it to the student with all its rivets undone and seams unzipped, the commentator is here putting the whole thing back together again, synthesizing his own analytical labors into the text of the word of God, always for the purpose of intensifying the devotional experience that the Psalm's student is meant to undergo.

To modern sensitivities, Cassiodorus' speculations in so many of these *conclusiones* about the significance of numbers strike a discordant note. We find such ideas superstitious and are prone to treat them as amusing primitive aberrations. Nevertheless, they do perform a useful function. Note first that Cassiodorus does not intrude discussion of them at the very beginning of each exposition, where they might function (as the *tituli* do) as arbiters of the exposition to follow, sources for the particular line of interpretation to be taken. Instead, by saving them for the very end of the whole discussion of the Psalm, after even prayerful summation, Cassiodorus manages to use these discussions to serve the broader purpose of putting the interpretation of a given Psalm in a wider context of Christian thought and experience, summoned up at random by the chance associations of the numbers. Thus the interpretation of Psalm 12 deals chiefly with man's search for God through faith; the *conclusio* presents a seemingly random assortment of associations of the number: "The number twelve reminds us of the twelve apostles who, in perfect obedience to His commands, loved the Lord above all things and loved their neighbors as themselves in *caritas,* so that it is fitting that this Psalm has granted such wisdom to us as is known to be dedicated to the number twelve and thus to the apostles. We know also that the Hebrew people were divided into twelve tribes; the Lord promised twelve thrones at the Last Judgment to the apostles; and the year itself is divided into twelve months. But the diligent reader can find many more such things for himself, by which he will recognize that this number is replete with many *mysteria*" (*Ex. Ps.* 12.130–140). In this randomness, it seems more than merely coincidental that one sees summarized the whole life of the people of God, from the Old Testament to the New Testament, through the mundane revolution of the year to the Last Judgment at the end of all things. This is the truest full context in which the search for God in faith takes place, and it is to this context that the remarks on the number twelve draw the reader.

The use of number symbolism, moreover, is not absolutely central to Cassiodorus' commentary, however much he enjoyed such considerations. The first eighteen Psalms are all concluded with discussions of their particular numbers; but when Cassiodorus got to Psalm 19, the system broke down: "The significance of this particular number escapes us, but perhaps it can be interpreted as the sum of its parts" (*Ex. Ps.* 19.160–162). Instead of telling us about the number 19, Cassiodorus was forced to recall the significance of twelve (the apostles) and seven (the first week of creation), thus making the Psalm a summary of Old and New Testament truths over again. This kind of analysis by subdivision is clearly not as direct and successful as the simpler kind and leads to a greater repetitiousness. Thus Cassiodorus began to retract from giving a numerical analysis of every Psalm; Psalm 29, for example, has its number go unnoticed, while Psalm 30 (Joseph's years in Egypt, Christ's age at baptism) is more pliable. On occasion, Cassiodorus will return to the subdivision technique, as in Psalm 112, which is made a reprise of earlier considerations on the number 12, slightly expanded, designed especially to make the Psalm into an image of eternal beatitude. In general, however, the use of such symbolism declines, revived only for the more obvious numbers. Thus the technique is not a central one to Cassiodorus' style of interpretation, but merely a useful device for calling in echoes of the doctrine and faith into which individual interpretations are fitted.

We have thus completed a survey of the mechanics of Cassiodorus' exegesis in the *Expositio Psalmorum*. Despite the importance of such considerations and the considerable influence that such form has on content, it is both possible and necessary to dissociate from the running stream of exegesis at least some of the more significant of the discernible theological preoccupations that guided the writer's pen. We have been analyzing the work hitherto on a deductive basis, from externals to their implications. Now our attention reverses its path, working inferentially back from scattered hints in the text to broader ideas that can be concluded to lie behind the words on the page.

We have already seen hints of the predominant theological issue that concerned Cassiodorus: Christology. Schlieben noted this, only to remark that the Christology expressed was thoroughly orthodox according to the Chalcedonian definition;[37] but Schlieben was assuming that the commentary was written in Italy only for local consumption, and that its dedication to Pope Vigilius at Constantinople was merely an accident of fate, as Cassiodorus happened to be in the east at that time. Such a bland explanation of Cassiodorus' Christology does not, however, adequately lay bare the facts of the case.

For merely to say that Christology is a central concern for Cassiodorus and that his Christology is orthodox Chalcedonian does not begin to do justice to the frequency and the fervor with which the doctrines of Chalcedon are set forth. As early as the second Psalm is interpreted as teaching the doctrine of the two natures of Christ united in one person, concluding that "this doctrine Pope Leo together with the holy Chalcedonian synod decreed and ordained, that whoever wishes to be a

37. Schlieben, *Cassiodors Psalmenexegese* (1970), 183.

catholic [*quicumque se vult esse catholicum*] should preach one Christ, a perfect union in and of two natures" (*Ex. Ps.* 2.399–403).[38] The comments on Psalm 8 again already speak of the two natures of Christ and refer the reader, in the *conclusio,* to another seven comments that treat the subject at length (Psalms 2, 20, 71, 81, 107, 109, 138). But these Psalms are not the only ones that excite Christological reflections; such remarks are everywhere, becoming a refrain every few pages. The formula appears, for example, in response to the phrase "non erit in te deus recens" (Ps. 80.10): "Wherefore our *patres* have preferred, by a marvelous and holy device, to believe and preach two natures united and perfect, abiding in one Lord Christ; so that the diseased and fetid belchings of the heretics might be shut up like a pestiferous mouth by their saving remedy" (*Ex. Ps.* 80.209–213).[39] It is not in connection with one of the substantial treatments of the subject that Cassiodorus is moved to quote for us the Latin translation of the decree of Chalcedon; the quotation occurs in the abnormally long explanation of the *titulus* of Psalm 58, arising out of general considerations upon the phrase "in finem." The Nestorian heresy is mentioned expressly in an introduction to the long quotation of the essential features of the Chalcedonian decree, including the statement of the *homoousios* doctrine, the legitimacy of the term *Theotokos* for Mary, and the four famous Chalcedonian adjectives, rendered here as "sine confusione, sine conversione, sine divisione et sine separatione" (*Ex. Ps.* 58.41–42).[40] To this full statement of the orthodox doctrine, Cassiodorus adds: "A holy faith, inviolable truth, a preaching eagerly to be embraced, which the catholic church professes throughout the whole world through the grace of the Holy Spirit" (*Ex. Ps.* 58.48–50).

Other heresies than the Nestorian are rebuked in these Christological remarks, chiefly the Eutychian (i.e., Monophysite), but also including the Arian and even Sabellian. To revert to

38. Note the foreshadowing of the first words of the Athanasian Creed.

39. The *chi-rho* appears in the margin for a "dogma valde necessarium."

40. At *Ex. Ps.* 81.175–182, the same adjectives are rendered "inconfusas, immutabiles, indivisas, inseparatas."

the example of Psalm 81, the *conclusio* there, which is unusually long for so short a subject text, attacks Nestorians and Eutychians for almost forty lines, based loosely on the Psalm's first verse ("Deus stetit in synagoga deorum"). This is, of course, one of the Psalms identified as an extended treatment of the subject; such discussion in the *conclusiones* of the commentaries on these Psalms is the rule. As already shown, these longer disputations form only the tip of the Christological iceberg; one simply does not hear of Christ in the *Expositio,* it often seems, without having "duae naturae" and "una persona" thrown in immediately, lest we should risk forgetting orthodox doctrine (e.g., *Ex. Ps.* 109.331–334).

It is worth examining further, therefore, the circumstances of the composition of the *Expositio Psalmorum,* to determine just what sort of role this fixation on the Chalcedonian definitions played in Cassiodorus' thought. If we are right in concluding that the *Expositio* was written in Constantinople through the 540's, we can begin by examining the theological conditions that prevailed there in the years when Justinian was at his best. The Council of Chalcedon was already gone from living memory after the lapse of a century.[41] Eutychius as well, the great rebel against the Chalcedonian doctrine, had long since passed from the stage, leaving his name for a sect. In the first years of the sixth century, under the leadership of such figures as Severus of Antioch (and with the support of the writings of the pseudo-Dionysius, who seems to have lived in this milieu), the first institutionalizing of the Monophysite movement occurred. This quickly became a more serious problem than ever for the Constantinopolitan emperors, who were committed externally to maintaining the Chalcedonian definition (the *Henotikon* had not succeeded in extricating them from that, especially after Justin ended the Acacian schism and reconciled east and west again for a time), but who were watching more and more of their own subjects in the east abandon the complex formulas of the council.

41. See W. H. C. Frend, *The Rise of the Monophysite Movement* (1972), for a coherent account of the development of the theological pressures that Justinian felt.

In this developing crisis, we witness the playing out of the drama of the Three Chapters controversy. The decree originally issued by Justinian in 543 declared anathema on writings of three figures of the last century, Theodore of Mopsuestia, Theodoret of Cyrrhus, and Ibas of Edessa, all of whom were at least of the Antiochene school if not in fact forthrightly Nestorian. The purpose of the edict was to attempt to win support from the right wing of the church, the Eutychians, by seeming to condemn writers of the left. There was, however, a backlash, particularly among westerners, whose terminology on matters of Christology differed slightly but crucially, by a fluke of language and history, from the eastern. One can generalize that the edict condemning the three allegedly Nestorian writers was more or less accepted in the east and rejected in the west. Justinian, however, felt that he needed the approval of the pope for his theological adventure, an approval that proved difficult, but not impossible, to obtain. It was to pressure Pope Vigilius into accepting the Three Chapters decree that the pope was summoned to Constantinople in the mid-540's. Justinian, who always got what he wanted, however high the price, kept Vigilius at court, variously humiliating and exploiting him, until 554, when he sent him off to Italy after the Pragmatic Sanction; Vigilius died en route. The crucial break had come, however, in April 548, when after much procrastination, Vigilius agreed to accept the decree in principle. We have already seen how some scholars have tried to date Cassiodorus' *Expositio* to some brief period between the publication of Facundus of Hermiane's defense of the writers in question and Vigilius' capitulation to Justinian (i.e., between February and April of 548).

Now let us consider Cassiodorus' theological position. On every page, all up and down the commentary that he wrote at Constantinople in the 540's, there is implicit and explicit in Cassiodorus the exact wording of the Chalcedonian Christology. But this is precisely the sort of thing that was in Justinian's interest not to remind people of any too loudly. Particularly the notion about one person *in* two natures as well as *of* two natures, which Cassiodorus never fails to mention, was a sticking point at a time when the establishment at Constantinople was attempting to anathematize writers who were, at most, marginally Nestorian in their theology (and who might have been expected to emphasize the duality at the expense of the personal unity). The emphasis of Constantinopolitan theology at this time, for many reasons, was on the *una persona*. The possibility therefore arises that, whatever its other purposes were, the *Expositio Psalmorum* was written at least in part as a tract in favor of the traditional definition (and in favor of the historical fact that the writers condemned by the Three Chapters decree had died in the peace of the church, uncondemned by that very council of Chalcedon as well) and against the revisionist tendencies of Justinian. Looked at in this way, there is nothing at all surprising about the quotation from Facundus of Hermiane, and the dedication to Vigilius makes all the more sense for bringing the work to the attention of one westerner on whose opinion much depended.

Whether the commentary was completed before Vigilius' decision of April 548 is not an altogether closed question. The only indication we have that Cassiodorus ever accepted the decree for himself, even as a *pro forma* matter, is the letter of Vigilius excommunicating two diehard opponents of the decree and mentioning Cassiodorus as someone who had been an envoy between Vigilius and the opponents. Although this seems to indicate that Cassiodorus was publicly seen to conform with the decree, it also demonstrates that he was someone whom Vigilius thought would have influence with opponents of the decree. Cassiodorus, at least, was not excommunicated, even if he was still talking to people who were.

Beyond the immediate situation in Constantinople, however, we must look to the later life of Cassiodorus to give us a clue here. After Vigilius' death, the anathema against the three authors did not receive wide or immediate acceptance in Italy. As late as the end of the sixth century, the Irishman Columbanus came to settle at Bobbio, only to find himself in the midst of a controversy still raging among the orthodox. The Lombards, particularly, found the writings of the Three Chapters authors a useful bridge between Arianism and Catholicism, for making

Christ seem more human; Columbanus wrote in 613 to Pope Boniface IV that the Lombard king Agilulf, still an Arian, had been reported saying that if the Catholics could make up their mind just what was the orthodox doctrine, he would be happy to believe it.[42] In Cassiodorus' own case, two arguments, one *ex silentio,* need consideration.

First, he never discusses the decree of the Three Chapters, nor does he include the Council of Constantinople of 553 in his list of accepted synods (*Inst.* 1.11). If he wrote the *Expositio Psalmorum* when and where he seems to have done, it would be remarkable indeed to have said so much about Christology without mentioning the Three Chapters, unless the purpose was specifically to ignore the embarrassing decree. More positively, however, there is the indisputable fact that when Cassiodorus came to compile a Latin ecclesiastical history to serve as a continuation of Rufinus' translation of Eusebius, one of the three authors whose works he admitted for inclusion of excerpts in the new *Historia ecclesiastica tripartita* was Theodoret of Cyrrhus, one of the targets of the Three Chapters edict.

It is not therefore likely that Cassiodorus ever enthusiastically embraced the edict against Theodore, Ibas, and Theodoret. It is apparent that, on the other hand, he made his peace with the authorities, at least while he was at Constantinople and in the vicinity of great powers, civil and ecclesiastical. Moreover, he did so at a time when others were making a stand on grounds of conscience and fidelity to the earlier councils. The outcome of this inquiry, finally, demonstrates conclusively that we cannot date the *Expositio Psalmorum* at all precisely by reference to this dispute. If it were published before the decree of Vigilius in April 548, one might indeed have expected to see some explicit appeal to the pope; if published after that time, one might very well expect not to see any explicit discussion of the issue (for that would be dangerous), but instead a continuous barrage of arguments in favor of the full version of the Chalcedonian definition in an attempt to get Vi-

42. Columbanus, *Ep.* 5.9 (ed. G. S. M. Walker [1957], 44, lines 25–28).

gilius to repudiate his earlier capitulation. Moreover, the work, obviously composed over a long period, would reflect throughout the atmosphere of Constantinople in the 540's and Cassiodorus' position therein. Thus, the only conclusion we can come to about dating for this work is that it seems to have been begun sometime in the early 540's (and recall the statement at the very beginning of the *Expositio* that puts Cassiodorus' study of the Psalter back to his last days at Ravenna) and completed sometime after Facundus' treatise was published, and very possibly after Vigilius' first decree. Since we have tentatively argued that Cassiodorus remained in Constantinople until about 554, plenty of time remained for him to complete and publish the work during that interlude. Finally, this pattern of Christological preoccupation adds measurably to the probability of our hypothesis for a long stay in Constantinople by Cassiodorus.

If one purpose of the work, however, was to establish the position of orthodox Christology, we have already postponed almost too long a discussion of what seems to have been the dominant purpose of the entire work, namely the introduction of the Psalter to a specifically monastic audience. From early in the church's history, the Psalter had been the specifically monastic book of the Bible, and the recital of the Psalter was an important part of the monastic liturgy, usually meant to be done in full at least once each week. At the same time, the Psalter was the first book to which Christian youths were introduced when they were taught (usually under a monastic aegis) to read. Jerome specifically named the Psalter as the first book that one should read when taking up the study of scripture (followed by Proverbs, Ecclesiastes, and Job, then the Gospels, Acts, and Epistles, and then back to the Old Testament for the Prophets, etc.).[43] By the time of Benedict, the

43. Jerome, *Ep.* 107.12. *Ex. Ps.*, praef. 16.39–43: "Non enim tirones incohant a Genesi, non ab apostolo, non inter ipsa initia auctoritas evangelica sancta pulsatur; sed, licet psalterium quartus codex sit auctoritatis divinae, primum tamen tirones incohantes scripturas sanctas, inde legendi faciunt decenter initium." This mention of the "fourth codex" probably identifies this passage as an insertion made at Squillace; cf. *Inst.* 1.4.

practice of reciting the entire Psalter once around in the course
of a week could be codified into a regular routine (*Reg. Ben.*
18). It is not too much to argue that in the early church the
Psalter was a specifically monastic book in more ways than
one.

All this is represented in Cassiodorus; indeed, the strongest
reason for scholars to believe that the commentary was written
when Cassiodorus was already in his monastery was precisely
the monasticity of the whole enterprise (though that does not
account for the explicit statement of the origin of Cassiodorus'
interest while he was still at Ravenna).[44] The particular role of
the Psalms in the monastic life is luminously summarized in
Cassiodorus' remarkable quotation from Athanasius' letter to
Marcellinus on the Psalms: "Whoever recites the words of a
Psalm chants them as if they were his own, and each reciter
sings them through as though they had been written by him
and not someone else and not as if they referred to someone
else; but speaking as if about himself, so the reciter utters these
words and utters these sentiments to God as written in the
Psalm but as coming directly from himself" (*Ex. Ps.*, praef.
16.31–37—cf. *PG* 27.24A).[45] This is the entire purpose of Cassiodorus' commentary, the desire to make the Psalter come to
life in the student's hands in such a way that he has it for his
own possession forever after. For such a student-monk, the
duty of the liturgical office thus becomes less and less a formal
routine and more and more a personal encounter with God in a
way that allows the suppliant to pray with words that are at
once those of God's prophets and of the suppliant himself giving those words back to God.

There are specific references throughout the commentary,
but only few and scattered ones, directly to the community at

44. The two mentions of the canonical hours in Cassiodorus (*Ex. Ps.*, praef.
77–82 and *Ex. Ps.* 118.3045–3048) are confused by manuscript interpolations
and a mass of scholarship, of which chiefly see G. Morin, *Rev. Ben.*, 43(1931),
145–152, and M. J. Cappuyns (completely off the mark), *RTAM,* 15(1948),
209–268.

45. This principle is put into practice, vividly and explicitly, by Augustine
in his *Confessions,* 9.4.8–11.

Squillace. This is not in itself proof that the work was originally composed at Squillace, or even that it was meant for that
monastery. By contrast, we have seen that the indications are
that the Vivarium's library did not contain the whole of Augustine's commentary, when the whole of Cassiodorus' work
reeks of direct contact with the Augustinian model. There is
every possibility that the work of Cassiodorus was carried out
with some monastic intention in mind; since, moreover, it does
not seem likely that he was already mured up in a monastic
establishment in Constantinople, the connection to the enterprise back at Squillace seems more than possible. But again,
such possibility must be carefully circumscribed, and one must
not assume that this means that Cassiodorus had actually visited the community at Squillace, if it already existed, at any
recent time prior to the composition of the *Expositio Psalmorum*.
But this is a matter that will occupy us further in the next
chapter.

We can, for the moment, do little better to conclude this
study of the *Expositio* than to look at the way Cassiodorus
ended the work himself. The *conclusio* of the commentary on
Psalm 150 became the conclusion of the whole work by the
device of expanding the comments on the Psalm's number to
refer to the significance of the whole number of Psalms. The
theory about the Psalter representing all of scripture (seventy
Psalms for the Old Testament, eighty for the New) is repeated,
and this one book is called a "caeleste armarium scripturarum
divinarum" (*Ex. Ps.* 150.179), containing within its scope all of
Genesis, the Prophets, the Gospels, and the message of the
Apostles. Other aspects of the commentary are recalled, with
an emphasis on the technical features that Cassiodorus has been
at the most pains to explain for beginners, e.g., the nature of
the *tituli,* the reason for inserting letters of the Hebrew alphabet
at the head of stanzas in some Psalms, and the reason for the
name *unifines* being applied (only by Cassiodorus among the
church fathers) to Psalms all of whose verses have the same
ending. With prayers for the readers' benevolence, then, Cassiodorus concludes: "But now we must convert our hearts to

the Lord to whom all thought and deed should tend" (*Ex. Ps.* 150.246–248).[46] Then follows the last *oratio*.

The achievement of Cassiodorus in writing the *Expositio Psalmorum* has received mixed reviews over the years. The work's editor, Adriaen, spoke of the work's "overall arrangement of the material, redolent of enormous erudition rather than true wisdom."[47] Schlieben enthusiastically called it "a synthesis of unprecedented intensity."[48] Both views are extreme. The purpose that Cassiodorus set out to achieve was a limited one: to make of Augustine's treatise a textbook of sacred and secular learning and an introduction to the spiritual life and liturgy of monasticism. Once again, his protestations of mediocrity must be taken into account as sincere indications of a modesty of ambition. He was not seeking to scale new theological heights, to bring to bear hitherto unknown lore to make the work in some way completely his own overpowering contribution to the history of interpretation. If his limited aspirations are understood and accepted as legitimate, as I think they should be, we can better understand the diligent, methodical, and self-effacing activity that preoccupied Cassiodorus during his years at Constantinople.

Whatever the work's faults, it was a success in medieval terms, which is to say that it found acceptance across the centuries as a useful introduction to the Psalter for generations of monks entering upon the Psalm-centered life of medieval monastic communities. We have seen throughout this chapter that the details of Cassiodorus' method were carefully and often quite subtly thought through to make the work precisely useful

---

46. There is a faint echo in this sentence of Romans 13.11, the beginning of the passage that Augustine picked up in the garden at Milan at the moment of his "conversion" (*Conf.* 8.12.29). There is a further parallel to Augustine in that in the corresponding position at the end of the *Enarrationes* there is a paragraph headed, "Sancti Aurelii Augustini Oratio quam post singulos sermones atque tractatus dicere consuevit," and which begins with the phrase, "Conversi ad Dominum Deum Patrem omnipotentem. . . ."

47. Adriaen in *CCSL* 96.v.

48. Schlieben, *Cassiodors Psalmenexegese* (1970), 242.

on just this narrow basis. Read hastily, analytically, and skeptically, as moderns are wont to do, the work leaves much to be desired. But we have not read it on Cassiodorus' own terms until we have used it for its original purpose. That would require, in the end, a monastic dedication to the study of the Psalter on the part of the modern scholar; each Psalm would have to be recited at least once a week all through the period of study. In turn, each Psalm studied separately would have to be read slowly and prayerfully, then gone through with the text in one hand (or preferably committed to memory) and the commentary in the other; the process of study would have to continue until virtually everything in the commentary has been absorbed by the student and mnemonically keyed to the individual verses of scripture, so that when the verses are recited again the whole phalanx of Cassiodorian erudition springs up in support of the content of the sacred text. It is in fact unlikely that any modern scholar outside a monastery would ever undertake such a devoted study of this work; but merely to reconstruct the possibility of such a study in the imagination affords a better idea of what the work was and what it meant to its intended audience. In that context it was neither pedantic nor brilliant, but only a shrewd, self-effacing propaedeutic to the most central text in the reader's life.

6

Vivarium

A trick of the evidence exaggerates the way in which Italy seems to have changed during Cassiodorus' absence; but an exaggeration is not always a falsification. Cassiodorus himself is the chief source for our knowledge of life in Italy, seen from the inside, throughout these years. Until he departed for the east, his perspective was the same as that of the ruling power—it was centered on Ravenna. Even after his retirement, apparently, he remained at the center of Gothic affairs, watching Gothic Italy being crumpled in the hand of Byzantine might. He was gone, most probably, for almost fifteen years, the very years of his life when he passed to the threshold of old age. When he returned to Italy, he was no longer a great man, nor did he any longer associate with such. It is chance, but symbolic chance, that his retirement retreat was situated very nearly as far as it was possible to get from Ravenna without leaving Italy. Now he was on the periphery.

The Goths are as good as vanished from our story. There was an exarch at Ravenna, and insofar as there was government in Italy it was Byzantine. The Lombards were at most a distant rumor; they did not enter Italy until 568 and never penetrated as far as Squillace. In fact, Cassiodorus' homeland remained in Byzantine hands until the Normans arrived in the eleventh century. But for our purposes, even the Byzantine rulers did not exist. Politics, government, armies, all became distant memories, forgotten in the cloister of the Vivarium. This is, I say, deceptive. Merely because the central character of our limited story has disappeared into the monastic life in a remote corner of the continent does not mean that the whole world is somehow colored by this act.

Cassiodorus was about sixty-five years old when he returned to Italy. He had had no special revelation of the kindly fate that would give him almost thirty years of life in retirement at the home of his youth. At the same time, he did not think it worthwhile to withdraw from life completely. To the contrary, the activity that he began then was surely demanding and intellectually rigorous. Because it was prolonged by a kindly fate, he became a symbol of one easy opposition of ancient and medieval qualities; and the symbol would be valueless if it did not in some way reflect the realities of the world in which he lived. At the same time, nothing had changed. One elderly politician, out of office for many years and exiled, had returned home to a monastery he had founded, to settle down to collecting books. There is nothing remarkable about this, for retirement to family estates and indulgence in literary pastimes was a common decision for Roman aristocrats at all periods.

Both of Cassiodorus' passions in old age, Christian intellectual culture and the specifically religious life, were furthermore the fruit of developments that had been building throughout his life. When he finally got back to Italy, twenty years had passed since his first effort to found a school of Christian learning, and fifteen years had passed since his first published treatise on a theological subject. There is nothing anywhere here of a man in a hurry, of frenetic activity; rather, there is the slow, measured working out of an obsession that had been fostered in the very busiest days of his secular career and that did not finally achieve realization until he at last got himself away from the vicinity of the great and the powerful and back to the land of his birth on the coast of the Ionian Sea.

Cassiodorus did not, however, take the steps that he did out of touch with the rest of his age. If the institution he founded, at first glance an unseemly hybrid of ancient traditions of rhetoric and "modern" ideas about ascetic life, was a unique place unduplicated by his contemporaries or by following generations, it is nevertheless at least better, if not fully, understood in terms of other institutions in sixth-century Italy, chiefly the schools of Rome and the monastery at Monte Cassino.

In 529, the very year in which we are told that Benedict founded Monte Cassino, Justinian closed the Academy at Athens.[1] There is another facile opposition of ancient and medieval here that obscures as much as it illuminates reality. But Athens with its pagan sentiments had already been by-passed; for if Constantinople was the new Rome, it was as well a new capital of Greek culture replacing Athens, supported by Antioch and Alexandria. The last shreds of nostalgia, which had kept the Hellenistic world harking back to Athens as the fountain of their teaching, had blown away, leaving behind a new intellectual map of the Mediterranean. As we shall see below, moreover, for Cassiodorus the life of the mind was something to be pursued in the Latin language, with whatever (limited) support could be brought over from the Greek world within the narrow restraints imposed by the growing division between Greek and Latin lands in the Mediterranean.

Thus it was the schools of Rome that occupied Cassiodorus' mind as representatives of the old intellectual order; from the eastern world he heard only good news. Indeed, the strongest direct evidence for the survival of rhetorical schools in the ancient tradition is Cassiodorus' own opening remark in the *Institutiones* (however much it must be qualified by regard for the rhetorical point he was making): "When I saw secular studies being pursued with great fervor, so much so that a great mass of men believed such studies would bring them the wisdom of this world, I confess I was seriously perturbed that there should be no public professors of Holy Scripture, when worldly texts were the beneficiaries of a distinguished educational tradition" (*Inst.*, praef. 1). The clear import of this passage seems to be that there really were secular schools flourishing into Cassiodorus' own middle age. He went on immediately in his preface to speak of his collaboration with Agapetus in the 530's, now long forgotten by all but him. Whether some of Cassiodorus' concern was inflamed by seeing similar institutions of higher secular learning at Constantinople, we do not know; but

---

1. A. Cameron, *Cahiers d'histoire mondiale,* 10(1967), 653–673.

it is clear that this concern with the *magistri saeculares* and their excessive influence goes all the way back to the 530's. We saw in Chapter 4 how these worthies were made Cassiodorus' chief foils in the *De anima,* and we saw in Chapter 5 how by the late 540's Cassiodorus had developed a complex theory of the ultimate dependence of secular on sacred learning that would justify to himself and others his own distaste for the secular sciences.

For there must have been some conflict within Cassiodorus on these points. He was himself clearly one of the last completely rhetorical men, owing most of his intellectual formation and his career itself to his rhetorical training. It was as an orator that he came to Theoderic's attention, it was as a wordsmith that he was employed, and it was as a rhetorician that he pleaded the cause of the Gothic kingdom in the published works of his secular career. There was, therefore, a certain breach of *pietas* in his rebellion against secular rhetoric but a certain manifestation of *pietas* in the way he attempted to model his school of Christian learning on the secular schools. His theory may have been that secular rhetorical principles were derived from scripture; but nothing could be clearer than that his own Christian rhetorical principles were in fact derived from secular ones. If they were originally Christian, as he would claim, he had them only at second hand, after a filtering through the centuries of ancient pagan tradition.

There is, to be sure, evidence outside Cassiodorus' own assertion in the *Institutiones* for the existence of schools at Rome in this century. Gregory the Great himself, who later expressed impatience with the rules of Donatus, was born perhaps half a century after Cassiodorus and yet still received the old kind of education in the city of Rome. There are other cases, as well, scattered about the literary remains of the period, several in Cassiodorus' own works. For example, there was a quaestor appointed in about 534, following Cassiodorus' footsteps in office by a quarter century, who was specifically praised for having learned his eloquence at Rome, where it was specially cultivated (*Var.* 10.7.2: "Roma tradit eloquium"). From early in Cassiodorus' career, during the quaestorship, two letters survive directing patricians (Festus in one case, Symmachus in the other) to allow named individuals to return home to Sicily (the letters are almost identical in wording) while leaving their sons behind in Rome for educational purposes (*Var.* 1.39, 4.6). The most important evidence, however, is the letter in which Athalaric admonished the senate that he had heard that the "doctors of Roman eloquence" were disgruntled about shortages in their pay, "as the sum set aside for the schoolmasters seems to have been reduced" (*Var.* 9.21.1). These *doctores* were specifically said to be concerned with the training of *adulescentes*. The letter praised at length the liberal studies, particularly the trivium. The gist of the letter is that, in some undefined way, the responsibility of the senate to look after the support of these teachers continued, to see that they received the "remuneration fixed for their services" *(ibid.)*. Whether they were being fully subsidized or only partially is not clear; what *is* clear is that there were schools at Rome and that teachers were finding work.[2]

This conclusion is partially supported by what external testimony there is. Venantius Fortunatus, born between 530 and 540, claimed to have gone to school at Ravenna to learn both grammar and rhetoric (obviously in the years during or just after the war of reconquest). Gregory the Great is another principal case, while Benedict himself seems to have had at least some of the old education before devoting himself to ascetic pursuits.[3] Despite this relative scarcity of evidence, we are justified in concluding that so well-entrenched an institution was

2. See also the formula for the urban prefect at *Var.* 6.4, which I do not choose to make much of because of the unresolvable question of the traditional element in these *formulae*, perhaps making them evidence for affairs at an earlier date than their composition. *Var.* 6.4.6: "Advocati tibi militant eruditi, quando in illa patria difficile non est oratores implere, ubi magistros eloquentiae contingit semper audire." (An echo of Juvenal 1.1 and 1.30?) Justinian, *Pragmatic Sanction* (August 31, 554), authorized subsidy for *grammatici, oratores, medici,* and *iurisperiti;* but might not his knowledge of western affairs have been outdated?

3. R. R. Bolgar, *The Classical Heritage and Its Beneficiaries* (1954), 405, collected the evidence. See also F. Ermini, *Archivum Romanicum,* 18(1934), 143–154; and H.-I. Marrou, *A History of Education in Antiquity* (Eng. trans., 1964), 460.

not one that would disappear rapidly. It has been argued with some verisimilitude that Theoderic barred Goths from the schools of Rome; there is certainly no conclusive evidence of Gothic interest in Latin culture outside of Theoderic's own household.[4]

There is no reason to doubt the literal sense of Cassiodorus' own words nor the sincerity and purpose of his remarks about his endeavor with Pope Agapetus to found a school of Christian learning at Rome. As he put it, "Together with Pope Agapetus, I sought to raise funds to endow Christian schools with paid professors in the city of Rome, as we hear has long been done at Alexandria and now is reported being done by the Jews at Nisibis in Syria; from these Christian schools the soul could win eternal salvation while the tongues of the faithful were being trained in chaste and eloquent speech" (*Inst.*, praef. 1). Everything thus far in this chapter finds its place in this remarkable sentence. First, we note that Cassiodorus' interest, focused on Rome, was further inflamed by his knowledge of distant lands. We have already discussed his contact with the Nisibean experiment through the quaestor Junillus at Constantinople, where it would also have been easy to hear of the exegetical activities of the schools of Alexandria. Second, we see implicit confirmation of the apparent public support of teachers in the secular schools, since the plan is to provide support for them in Christian schools.

What else we know about Agapetus and his intellectual activities confirms the likelihood of his participation in such an enterprise. There survive today ruins of a library, attributed confidently to Agapetus, that is located west of the Caelian Hill in Rome, on the ancient *Clivus Scauri* (on the modern Via d. SS. Giovanni e Paolo) opposite a church of fifth-century origin.[5] An inscription from the sixth century, now destroyed, was preserved in an early manuscript collection at Einsiedeln and is worth quoting in full:

4. P. Riché, *Éducation et culture dans l'occident barbare* (1962), 100–104.

5. H.-I. Marrou, *MEFR,* 48(1931), 124–169. Agapetus' father was a priest of the church of John and Paul.

Sanctorum veneranda cohors sedet ordine [longo],
    Divinae legis mystica dicta docens.
Hos inter residens Agapetus iure sacerdos
    Codicibus pulchrum condidit arte locum.
Gratia par cunctis, sanctus labor omnibus unus;
    Dissona verba quidem sed tamen una fides.[6]

There can be no doubt that this preserves an authentic bit of the
original ornamentation of the library, probably connected with
some mural or fresco; the historical content of the inscription is
that Agapetus did indeed found a library. This would be completely in character with the enterprise that Cassiodorus described. From what we know of the area and the ecclesiastical
history of the sixth century, it is apparent that this library was one
that Gregory the Great knew; his own monastery was close by,
just up the Caelian Hill from where Agapetus' structure stood.
The likeliest possibility is that the contents of Agapetus' collection were removed to the Lateran by Gregory the Great.[7]

It is possible that we know one thing more about the history
of this library. In the *Institutiones,* Cassiodorus alludes in passing to a library at Rome; he speaks of a treatise *de musica* by
one Albinus, "which we recall having and reading carefully in a
library at Rome. If that copy has been carried off in the barbarian invasions [*gentili incursione*], you have a copy of Gaudentius here instead" (*Inst.* 2.5.10).[8] Not only did Cassiodorus
make specific reference to a library at Rome (to which he hoped
that his monks might yet gain access to retrieve a copy of the
work), but it was a library of whose fate Cassiodorus was ignorant. We have already seen very well how this could be, since

6. H.-I. Marrou, *MEFR,* 48(1931), 125: "The venerable band of holy men
sits in a row, teaching the mystical precepts of divine law. Sitting among them,
Agapetus, a priest by right, has founded an attractive repository for his books.
In grace he is the equal of all men, his holy labor excels them; disparate words
are used to express a single faith."

7. H.-I. Marrou, *MEFR,* 48(1931), 167.

8. Gaudentius is another writer on music, translated from the Greek at the
Vivarium.

Cassiodorus seems most probably to have gone from Ravenna to Squillace only via Constantinople. What is remarkable, however, is that Cassiodorus, the great collector and lover of books, would have abandoned such a library behind him, presumably when he went up to Ravenna in 533 to become prefect. There can be no proof one way or the other, but the likeliest explanation of this remarkable and uncharacteristic loss is that the library to which Cassiodorus refers is the one that he created for the institution for which Agapetus built the building.[9] It is apparent that the library of Agapetus was to be at least an adjunct to and perhaps the heart of the Christian university planned at Rome, in the way that the library was central to the enterprise at the Vivarium. One coincidence reinforces this hypothesis: the casual remark in the *Institutiones* speaks of the *gentilis incursio* by which the work may have been carried off; precisely the same circumstance is alleged at the beginning for the failure of the whole plan for the school: "My plan proved impossible of implementation on account of raging wars and upheaval in the Italian kingdom (for an affair peaceful by nature finds no place in turbulent times)" (*Inst.*, praef. 1). Since, moreover, Agapetus died in the midst of the war, in 536, while Cassiodorus was at Ravenna functioning as prefect, Cassiodorus may well have lost contact with the whole institution just at the moment when it was being dragged down by the undertow of war. In that context, more than any other, one can make sense of Cassiodorus' having lost track of the valuable book that he mentioned later in the *Institutiones*.

What the school in Rome would have been like is another unanswerable question. Clearly the secular schools themselves would be taken as some kind of competitive model, but the intellectual directions taken later at the Vivarium would no doubt have had a dominant role. Most tantalizing, however, is

9. Riché, *op. cit.*, 176, and Cappuyns, *DHGE*, 11(1949), 1389, oppose identifying Cassiodorus' Roman library with that of Agapetus. (But Cappuyns multiplied libraries beyond necessity, implying that there were two libraries at Squillace: Cassiodorus' private collection and that which the monastery possessed in its own right.) Courcelle, *LLW*, 334, accepts the identification.

the moot question whether the school was conceived as leading exclusively to the religious life (as medieval monastic schools would), or whether it was meant to be a training ground in direct competition with and imitation of the secular schools, leading to public life. The balance of probability (owing to the deliberate mention of competition) seems to incline slightly in favor of the latter thesis. Furthermore, when Cassiodorus established the Vivarium, one thing that he was clearly not doing was setting up shop in the forum of a great city. By the time the Gothic war had blown itself out in Italy, the model to be pursued was monastic rather than scholastic.

Despite the presence of some isolated centers of ecclesiastical learning in Italy, Cassiodorus' Vivarium was the most ambitious and important such enterprise of its time.[10] First, the Vivarium was at least some kind of success; the textbooks and texts composed and copied there found wide diffusion up and down Europe. The *Historia tripartita* and the Latin Josephus, particularly, were widely popular throughout the middle ages (because of their deliberately useful character) in a way that Eugippius' abridgment of Augustine (compiled at Naples in Cassiodorus' lifetime) was not. Second, there was a clarity of purpose at the Vivarium that was lacking elsewhere. Cassiodorus was not merely preparing convenient handbooks, for he was in his own eyes saving, preserving, expanding, and exalting his idea of Christian intellectual culture. Moreover, his enterprise was comprehensive, in the sense that it sought to provide a complete, well-rounded education for the Christian scholar, concerning itself with all the details of the educational advancement of everyone in the monastery, down to the least literate. In a way, the eccentricities of the Cassiodorian system can be taken as the indications of a firm unified purpose guiding a complex enterprise. Cassiodorus' institution was well-organized while other intellectual projects at the time seem randomly inspired.

If the Vivarium meant a departure on several fronts at the intellectual level, it was considerably less original and more

10. Riché, *op. cit.*, 201–203.

mimetic at the level of the precisely monastic features of the enterprise. For of course Cassiodorus' contemporary, Benedict, born in about the same decade as he, shaped the whole monastic future of the middle ages. The traditional date of the founding of Monte Cassino is 529, and Benedict's death is given as occurring in about 547. Thus the Benedictine enterprise flourished first in the years between Cassiodorus' term as *magister officiorum* and the middle of his stay in Constantinople. The first destruction and abandonment of Monte Cassino took place in 581, about the time of the likeliest date for Cassiodorus' own death. How far the odor of Benedict's repute had spread in his lifetime is questionable; and how widely his praises were sung after his death is debatable. The embarrassing truth is that, apart from Gregory's life of Benedict in the second book of his *Dialogi,* we know virtually nothing of the early history of the Benedictine movement.

What we do know is based chiefly on the *Regula* that is handed down in Benedict's name. It is too well known to need a summary of its contents, but certain aspects of its tone and tenor are worth remark. Benedictine monasticism strikes a *via media* in monastic customs. Although it recognizes, for example, the virtues of the anchoritic life, it prescribes the cenobitic, while scorning the wandering life of the gyrovagues. While it does not leave administration entirely to the discretion of the abbot but lays down written regulations for the life of the monastery, at the same time it does not go to the opposite extreme of attempting to define legalistically every detail of the monk's life. Until this time, western monasticism, exemplified by figures like Cassian in Gaul, had sought the two extremes. In Italy, the chief example of the legalistic style of monasticism is recorded in the anonymous *Regula Magistri*. Benedict is more precise about the order of saying the Psalms and the twelve grades of humility than about the order of seating in choir; his emphasis is on the spiritual life as supported by the minimum of necessary, continuing legislative authority. That his choice was an effective one is testified to by the most pragmatic of standards: it worked, it survived, it lives today.

When we mention the *Regula Magistri,* however, we address a subject that beclouds our knowledge of early Benedictinism by adding information that we do not know how to use. There has been an effort, moreover, in recent years to use the same document to confuse our knowledge of Cassiodorus. The problems are three in number:

1. There are substantial duplications of content between the *Regula Magistri* and the *Regula Benedicti.*
2. There is no surviving *Rule* as such of Cassiodorian monasticism.
3. There is not one mention of Benedict, nor one clear allusion to his *Regula,* anywhere in Cassiodorus.

Certain scholars have attempted to use this information to achieve two separate purposes: the establishment of the priority of Benedict's rule over that of the Master, and the subordination of Cassiodorus to Benedictine ideas. Neither attempt, however, is grounded in fact.

The literature on the question in recent years is vast and dismaying. The identification of Cassiodorus with the author of the *Regula Magistri* was first proposed by Dom Cappuyns and may now be said to have been thoroughly disposed of, most recently and most effectively by Dom David Knowles.[11] There is no purpose in recording again at length the tortuous arguments in favor of the identification and their meticulous refutations. I have no arguments to offer in favor of the identification, but I can propose two new ones against it. First, the con-

11. The identification of the Master and Cassiodorus was proposed by M. J. Cappuyns, *RTAM,* 15(1948), 209–268; followed by E. Franceschini, *Aevum,* 23(1949), 52–72; and by the same author, *Liber Floridus: Festschrift Paul Lehmann* (1950), 95–119; and by F. Vandenbroucke, *RTAM,* 16(1949), 186–226; and by the same author, *Rev. Ben.,* 62(1952), 216–273. The identification was opposed by H. Vanderhoven, *Scriptorium,* 3(1949), 246–254; C. Mohrmann, *Vigiliae Christianae,* 8(1954), 239–251; F. Masai, *Scriptorium,* 2(1948), 292–296; A. de Vogüé, in the introduction to his edition of the *Regula Magistri, SC* 105.9–270; and most convincingly by D. Knowles, in his *Great Historical Enterprises* (1963), 135–195. A bibliography on the broader question has appeared: B. Jaspert, *Subsidia Monastica,* 1(1971), 129–171.

siderable literary vanity of Cassiodorus, always giving lists of what he had written, signing his name over everything he wrote, even telling one where to find his works on the bookshelves of his library, would not, I am convinced, have allowed him to produce so extensive a work as the *Regula Magistri* without taking credit for it, both in the work itself and elsewhere. Second, there is a telltale sign lacking in the *Regula Magistri* that is characteristic of Cassiodorus' other works. After Cassiodorus' conversion to the monastic life, there is no work of his that does not have profusely scattered through its pages phrases like "Domino praestante," "Deo iuvante," and so on.[12] By contrast, the lexicon of the *Regula Magistri* shows such phrases appearing only twice in all the verbiage of that text.[13] After extensive contact with Cassiodorus' ecclesiastical prose style, I am convinced that this tag phrase, a defining characteristic of Cassiodorus' own newly emphasized humility, is in itself an acid test to Cassiodorian authorship, especially in a work as personal as a rule of life for his monks.

As to the matter of the duplications of content between Benedict and the Master, the truth is that Benedict was copying the Master and not the other way around. This is not in itself surprising, since the genius of Benedict lay in his temperance rather than in any originality of plan.[14] The difficulties in the textual transmission seem to have been fairly clearly solved by a stemma positing an archetypal version of the *Regula Magistri* that shortly became prevalent in two redactions, one of which leads to the present text of the parent rule, the other of which was used by Benedict.[15] With all this said, it can be freely ad-

12. For the *Institutiones,* where an index is available, I find sixty-four cases of such phrases using the key words *Deo, Domino,* or *Christo.* Such phrases are a literary stutter; it had appeared (less often) in the *Variae* and peeks through once or twice in the *Getica.*

13. A. de Vogüé, ed., *SC* 107, s.v. *Dominus, Deus, Christus.*

14. R. W. Southern, *Western Society and the Church in the Middle Ages* (1970), 221–223, provides the neatest and most concise epitome of the differences between Benedict's and the Master's approaches, with illuminating parallel citations.

15. This scheme appears in H. Vanderhoven, *Scriptorium,* 3(1949), 246–254.

mitted that there does seem to be a purely palaeographic connection between the *Regula Magistri* and the scriptorium of Cassiodorus.[16] This can be explained well and fully by assuming
that the text was one that found its way as easily to Squillace as
to Monte Cassino, that it was just one of the several "patrum
regulae" that Cassiodorus commended to his monks.[17] At any
rate, it should henceforth stand as proven that Cassiodorus did
not write the *Regula Magistri,* nor did he accord it a special place
of honor in his monastery.

But if we have a picture of monastic Italy in which Benedict
plays a central role, following somehow in the footsteps of the
shadowy Master, and if we now conclude that Cassiodorus did
not have direct contact with these movements, what then do
we make of Cassiodorian monasticism? That question can only
be approached by a consideration first of the historical data
about the foundation of the monasteries at Squillace.[18]

Here again we know nothing and presume too much. It
should be insisted first of all that we have no information about
the date or circumstances of the actual foundation of the Vivarium. The assumption of scholars has always been that the
foundation of the monasteries was directly connected with Cassiodorus' return to Squillace in retirement. Thus the issue of the
date of his retirement has been an important one, as well as the
question of his stay in Constantinople. The assumption has
been that if he went directly from Ravenna to Constantinople
he could not have founded the monastery until his return in the
550's. Thus the safer assumption has seemed to be that he returned to his estates in the 540's to found the monastery and
only then moved on to Constantinople; for this, however, it

16. P. Courcelle, *Revue des études anciennes,* 56(1954), 424–428.

17. *Inst.* 1.32.1; Cappuyns made much of the "patrum regulae," interpreting the phrase overliterally to refer exclusively to the *Regula Magistri.* But Cassiodorus' looseness of usage here is proven by his other two uses of that phrase:
Inst. 1.1.8 (the teachings of the church that Origen sometimes violated), and
Inst. 1.24.1 (the same general sense even less strictly applied).

18. We know the monastery was at Squillace with certainty only from Gregory the Great, *Epp.* 8.30, 8.32 (*MGH, Epp.* 2.32–35).

has been necessary to adduce the motive that Cassiodorus fled Calabria in the face of the approaching armies of the Goths. This is very dangerous, since it is known that at no time did those armies in fact ever reach Squillace.

The assumption of Cassiodorian presence at the creation of his own monasteries is further buttressed by the no less widely-accepted assumption that the first and express purpose of founding the monasteries was the intellectual enterprise undertaken there. Thus readers of the first pages of the *Institutiones* have read into the text something like this: "I, Cassiodorus, tried to found a school of Christian learning at Rome; war interfered, so I quit politics in disgust a couple of years later and came home here to found a monastic school instead." This is a tantalizing hypothesis, positing a fleshed-out image of Cassiodorus with which the reader can identify. But there is no shred of evidence for this whatever.

First, it must be stated that it is still perfectly credible that Cassiodorus did not found the monasteries at Squillace until about 554, upon his return from Constantinople. He was then in his middle sixties and still clearly vigorous. Furthermore, if the institution took root in buildings and facilities already present on the comparatively wealthy estates of the Cassiodori, relatively little bricks-and-mortar work would be required of the founder. But I believe there is another, likelier hypothesis. For this we must dissociate the monastic and intellectual enterprises somewhat in our minds.

The great patrician Liberius found time in the midst of his seventy years of public life in every corner of the Mediterranean to found a monastery on estates in Campania.[19] Indeed, to found a monastery took little investment of capital and needed only willing manpower. At least through the middle years of the sixth century, such manpower was apparently always forthcoming in Italy. Liberius died in his ninetieth year, having only just returned to Italy at last after the Pragmatic Sanction. Clearly his personal involvement in the administration of the

19. Gregory the Great, *Epp.* 9.162 and 9.164 (*MGH, Epp.* 2.162–164).

monastery was insignificant; the most that can be said is that he may have had it in mind to use the monastery as a refuge in that old age that he never took the time to have.[20]

Entering the realm of speculation, let us turn to Cassiodorus. Let us picture him as a man growing involved in the intellectual life of the church at Rome in the 530's, perhaps planning to move from a political to an educational career before many more years had passed, perhaps intending to remain in Rome for the rest of his life. Add then our assumption (only *ex silentio,* but relatively firm) that he never married and never had children. In this context it is certainly plausible to imagine him becoming concerned about the fate of his family's estates at Squillace, the more so because he had no heir to enjoy them. It is thus not difficult to imagine that at this stage of his career Cassiodorus took the initial step of establishing a monastic community on his own lands. Indeed, nothing at all prevents us from assuming that he founded such an institution very early in his career; if personal intervention was required, that could have taken place during one of his periods out of office, most probably during the time between his services to Athalaric (527–533). The purpose of such a foundation would be strictly monastic, in the way that the foundations of Benedict or the Master were monastic as against scholastic or cultural.

Where does this speculation get us, then? First, it gets the monastery established and running under independent leadership well before Cassiodorus ever goes near it to retire. Second, it throws new light on the direction that Cassiodorus' life was taking after his retirement, both while he was still at Ravenna and while he was in Constantinople. For if Cassiodorus at this

20. There is an allusion to the founding of monasteries on great estates: "*Passer* enim minuta et cautissima nimis avis est, monachorum significans parvitatem, qui in cedris Libani, id est in patrimonio potentium Christianorum velut in quibusdam ramis monasteria sibi quasi nidos aliquos aedificare monstrantur, eorumque roborum sustentati, velut passeres laudes Domini assidua voce fritinniunt" (*Ex. Ps.* 103.390–395). See also *Ex. Ps.* 103.410–412: "Sed magna est gloria illi arbori ubi nidus iste compingitur. Audiat enim a Domino se fuisse plantatum, qui tale continere noscitur institutum."

time had just seen the ruin of his plans for a school at Rome, was just beginning to see that his own political career had ended, and was finding himself half by chance, half by design, a *vir religiosus* now and no longer a *vir illustris,* this monastery already existing back at Squillace would have naturally come into his mind. Thus during the stay at Constantinople he would have begun to think more and more of returning directly to Squillace, to think more and more of transferring there, *mutatis mutandis,* the enterprise that he had thought to establish at Rome. How, then, does his activity at Constantinople appear to us?

First, we begin to understand his growing fascination with the Psalter that we saw starting already at Ravenna. For a man who had a house full of monks back in Squillace already chanting the daily office, and who was himself more and more drawn to the prospect of monastic retirement, the Psalter, the most specifically monastic book of the Bible, was the obvious object to study. Moreover, the particularly pedagogic way in which he chose to treat the Psalter was fully in harmony with an intention to prepare a textbook of the Psalter for a new monk to use in imbuing himself with the music of divine eloquence. Thus at last are explained the particularly monastic features of the commentary itself. Finally, if we choose to believe, as is plausible, that Cassiodorus was in Constantinople not entirely of his own accord, we understand better the nature of the delay and the heightening of the desire, while at the capital of culture, to make preparations for his return to the relative obscurity of Ionian shores.

Thus we reach firm ground for another speculation about Cassiodorus' activities at Constantinople. One of the remarkable things, indeed the most remarkable thing, about the Squillace enterprise is the comparative richness of the library. This is the more surprising since, as we have seen, Cassiodorus' earlier collection at Rome, whatever its institutional affiliation, had clearly not been transferred to Squillace. Nevertheless, within a very few years of Cassiodorus' return (the first draft of the *In-*

stitutiones can be confidently dated to about 562[21]), there was a bountiful library of scripture and scripture commentaries, histories and grammar books, miscellaneous useful guides (e.g., Columella), and the Greek works set for translation. To our picture of Cassiodorus, therefore, abiding impatiently in Constantinople, taking thought of the monastery to which he would return, attempting to salvage something of his notion of a school of Christian learning, we should add the likelihood of his becoming actively involved in the procurement of manuscripts for the library of that institution. He certainly must have picked up his copy of Junillus there, since the work had only just been composed. Other texts as well, particularly the Greek ones that would be translated at Squillace, could most readily have been obtained in Constantinople; there, moreover, would be the likeliest place to get the idea, from the abridgment made by Theodore the Lector, for a *Historia tripartita* and to collect the raw materials for it.

Thus in 554 we now picture, speculatively but plausibly, Cassiodorus returning to Italy (still accompanied by his steward?) with a trunkload or two of manuscripts, importing a healthy dose of Christian intellectual culture to the hitherto placid monastery. We need not assume that the state of learning at the monastery prior to Cassiodorus' arrival was as high as it became after the founder, hitherto a distant figure, a great man on the stage of politics, swirled in from the east with his load of books. Finally, we must not neglect the strong possibility that the bilingual scholars who did the actual work of translating for Cassiodorus—Mutianus, Bellator, Epiphanius, and perhaps no others—may have come back to Squillace with the monastery's founder, a core of professorial staff, perhaps enticed away from their former positions with promises of lifetime tenure, the scenic delights of Squillace, and the quiet, monastic life in a secluded region.

21. P. Lehmann, in his *Erforschung des Mittelalters* (1959), 2.41–55, dates the *Institutiones;* see further later in this chapter.

Some at least of this propaganda seems to have been true. "The site of the monastery of Vivarium conduces to making provision for travelers and the poor, since you have irrigated gardens and the nearby river Pellena full of fish—its waves threaten no danger, but neither is it despicable for its size. It flows into your precincts, channeled artificially where it is wanted, adequate to water your gardens and turn your mills. It is there when you want it and flows on when no longer needed; it exists to serve you, never too roisterous and bothersome nor yet again ever deficient. The sea lies all about you as well, accessible for fishing with fishponds [*vivaria*] to keep the caught fish alive. We have constructed them as pleasant receptacles, with the Lord's help, where a multitude of fish swim close by the cloister, in circumstances so like mountain caves that the fish never sense themselves constrained in any way, since they are free to seek their food and hide away in dark recesses. We have also had baths built to refresh weary bodies, where sparkling water for drinking and washing flows by. Thus it is that your monastery is sought by outsiders, rather than that you could justly long for other places. These are the delights of temporal things, as you know, not the things the faithful hope for in the future; these things shall pass away, but those shall abide without end. But placed here in the monastery, let us be in the power of those desires that will make us co-regents with Christ" (*Inst.* 1.29.1). The cloister becomes an image of paradise: an irresistible picture.

Numerous travelers over the years sought to establish the site of Cassiodorus' foundations, without much success.[22] The evidence had never received close and exacting scrutiny, however, until Pierre Courcelle undertook the study in the 1930's.[23]

22. The chief efforts were F. Lenormant, *La Grande-Grèce* (1881–1884), 2.329–447, on the whole history of Squillace, with particular attention to the Cassiodorian sites; and T. Hodgkin, *The Letters of Cassiodorus* (1886), 68–72, based on the researches of A. J. Evans at Hodgkin's behest.

23. See chiefly P. Courcelle, *MEFR*, 55(1938), 259–307, as modified by his article in *Actes du Ve congrès international d'archéologie chrétienne* (1957), 511–528.

His conclusions, based on textual, palaeographic, topographic, and archaeological evidence, have now won wide acceptance and even, by a stroke of luck, partial archaeological confirmation. Courcelle began principally with the text just quoted wherein Cassiodorus gave the closest description of the precise site of the Vivarium. To this he added the shorter passage a little further on in the *Institutiones* describing the hermitage monastery on the *mons Castellum,* which provided a happy retreat for the monks of the Vivarium when they sought anchoritic silence and solitude (*Inst.* 1.29.3). To these texts he juxtaposed (and this was the telling piece of evidence) manuscript illustrations from three ninth-century copies of the *Institutiones.* The similarity of these pictures, placed just before the chapter on the site of the monastery in the manuscripts, led Courcelle to believe that they were copies of an original, authentic depiction of the scene, stemming from a Vivarian archetype. These pieces of evidence together began to suggest the probability of identifying the center of the Vivarium with the present site of San Martino di Copanello, a small church now on private property; furthermore, the mention in the *Institutiones* that the hermitage on the mountain was located inside ancient walls led him to identify that site with the original location of Greek Σκυλλήτιον, long abandoned in the sixth century, on a mountain overlooking the shore, about half a mile from the Vivarium site. The site of the Vivarium is thus south of the Roman city along the coast, on the Punta di Staletti marked on modern maps just south of the Alessi river, with the hermitage on the site of modern Santa Maria de Vetere.[24]

All of this information Courcelle confirmed by a visit to the site in 1936. In the vicinity he found that the monks of the abbey of Gregory Thaumaturgus at Staletti (inland from the coast) claim to succeed Cassiodorus, but their site is no older than the seventeenth century. On the Vivarium site itself there stands a little nineteenth-century chapel built by a Garibaldian colonel near the traces of an earlier church known in the papal

24. See Courcelle, *MEFR,* 55(1938), 289, for an important map.

bulls of Eugene III (1151) and Alexander III (1178). Since the manuscript illuminations had specifically identified one of the monastery churches as dedicated to St. Martin, and since the cult of that saint is otherwise rare in southern Italy, Courcelle found his conclusion further supported. As corroboration, some decorated stones from the earlier church have come to rest in the museum at Catanzaro; they bear decorative forms identical to ones from the church of Saint Clement on the Caelian Hill in Rome, narrowly dated to the reign of Pope John II (532–535). Two obvious facts leap out of the page with this news: first, the library of Agapetus was in the same neighborhood of Rome; and second, the period 532–535 embraces Cassiodorus' last possible years in Rome before returning to Ravenna for the prefecture, and the period immediately precedes Agapetus' own pontificate. Thus there is further corroboration for at least the possibility of our suggestion that the establishment at Squillace dates to before Cassiodorus' prefecture, when he might have had the opportunity to direct the construction of the church, starting in Rome and perhaps visiting the site himself, perhaps in connection with the formal establishment of the monastic community. Thus it is likely that Cassiodorus took one decision in the early 530's, to spend the rest of his private life in Rome working on the school of Christian studies and to devote his estates at Squillace to monastic purposes; we have already sketched how his plans were changed by the forces of war and politics and how he would then have come to rest at the monastery at Squillace himself.

There are also on the present site three natural basins (10–12 meters long, 4–5 meters wide, 1 1/2–2 1/2 meters deep—about the size of a modest swimming pool today) communicating with the sea by narrow canals. These basins could easily be diked off from the sea to make permanent fishponds, in which the fish would not sense themselves captured.

The little church of Santa Maria de Vetere was convincingly identified by Courcelle with the church called the *Sancta Maria de veteri Squillatio*, known from the sixteenth century. One Marcellus Terracina, inspecting Basilian monasteries in the south of Italy for the Holy See, visited that church on October 11, 1551.[25] He saw it when it had only a few monks left suffering badly from the depredations of pirates. Working backward from that identification, Courcelle found the monastery recorded in a list of Basilian institutions of the fourteenth century; there are as well two Greek documents of September 1242 and June 1243, recording a land deal participated in by the abbot of the monastery τῆς Θεοτοκού του παλεού Σκυλλακός. Finally, there is a bull of Honorius III of May 26, 1219, which a seventeenth-century commentator explained by citing a tradition that the Basilian monastery succeeded one of Cassiodorus' foundations. In all likelihood, Courcelle concludes, the name change to the typically Greek invocation of the *Theotokos* came some time around the end of the seventh century, when Basilian monks took over.

Courcelle concluded his article in 1937 by urging the need for excavations on the site of San Martino. The tides of war washed away those plans, but not all was lost.[26] For in 1952, workmen beginning construction on a private summer house on the site uncovered a sarcophagus of considerable archaeological interest.[27] This object, associated with the ruins of the ancient church (a tidy structure with a foundation only 20 meters by 12 meters), and containing a few bones, seems to be contemporary with firmly datable sixth-century sarcophagi from Ravenna. Furthermore, there are two short Greek graffiti on the outside that indicate that the coffin's occupant was treated as a saint by local inhabitants. The irresistible conclusion (to which I subscribe) is that the coffin is that of Cassiodorus himself. The truly remarkable feature of the discovery is that it came after Courcelle's groundbreaking article, enabling the new find to be treated as corroborating evidence for the former con-

25. Courcelle, *MEFR*, 55(1938), 300.

26. Cf. J. Carcopino, *Souvenirs de sept ans, 1937–1944* (1953), 104–105, 120–121, for the story of the obstacles to formal excavation.

27. See Courcelle, *Actes du Vᵉ congrès . . .*, 511–515, evaluating and reviewing the information first published by G. Jacopi, ΠΕΠΡΑΓΜΕΝΑ ΤΟΥ Θ′ ΔΙΕΘΝΟΥΣ ΒΥΖΑΝΤΙΝΟΛΟΓΙΚΟΥ ΣΥΝΕΔΡΙΟΥ (1955), 1.201–205.

clusions and to be itself authenticated in part by them. Thus the happy sequence of events increases on all sides the probability for identifying the site and the sarcophagus.

Of what import is all this information for our knowledge of Cassiodorian monasticism? First, it gives us a notion of the size of the property owned by Cassiodorus and composing the establishment. Roughly half a mile lay between Castellum and Vivarium proper, then another kilometer or so up the coast lay another church associated with the monasteries (known from the manuscript illustrations). We know that there were agricultural laborers, perhaps regular tenant farmers, living on the land controlled by the monastery, and providing in part for its material needs (*Inst.* 1.32.3). But for all this expanse of rural country, there are indications that the monastic community itself was modest in size; the ruins described for the one church, apparently the central establishment, do not indicate a large body of monks. With space set aside for altars and processional and ritual space, a building 20 meters by 12 might conceivably have had room for as many as a hundred monks, so long as one assumes an interior austerity of plan to go alone with the apparent austerity of size. Such a building, however, would be more comfortable with only a quarter to a half that number of monks.

We possess one other piece of information about the monasteries of Cassiodorus that we could too easily overlook: they did not survive and thrive. We have already seen that the successor monastery established by Basilian monks took the most remote of the Cassiodorian sites for its own, and how even it was not safe from piracy in the later middle ages. We know nothing of the later history of the Vivarium and how it came to an end; yet we can at least conclude that it did not, at any rate, prove widely attractive, nor did it grow to great size, nor did it win wide influence over other monasteries. This is some kind of evidence for scarcity of recruits and hence perhaps a relatively small community.

Once we have appreciated, then, the attractions of the site and the comparative luxuries afforded by nature if not by the builder's art, what is more worthy of our consideration is the kind of life that Cassiodorus and his monks lived at Squillace. Unfortunately there has not been a shortage of scholarly energy trying to prove connections of monastic customs between Cassiodorus and Benedict. Before plunging once again into that fevered pool of speculation, it is well to review the Cassiodorian texts that tell us something specific.

First, we know that Cassiodorus recommended the writings of John Cassian. In the chapter in which he described the sites of the Vivarium and Castellum, he appended to the description of the first his only specific recommendation for readings on particularly monastic subjects: "Read diligently and heed willingly the precepts of Cassian, who wrote on the indoctrination [*de institutione*] of faithful monks and who set out at the beginning of his work the eight principal vices to be avoided" (*Inst.* 1.29.2). But, he went on to add, Cassian was not to be trusted on the question of free will, and Cassiodorus recommended prudence in reading him, with the help of an expurgated text that Cassiodorus himself had made. (And one Vivarian church was named for the monk of Tours, St. Martin.)

After that crucial chapter, there follow two in which Cassiodorus approved specific kinds of monastic activity, including the scriptorial (resuming some of his earlier arguments) and medical, with his usual bibliographical advice. Then there follows a much disputed chapter entitled "Commonitio Abbatis Congregationisque Monachorum" (*Inst.* 1.32). In this, Cassiodorus first urged the monks to follow the *patrum regulae* as much as their own superior's commands ("tam patrum regulas quam praeceptoris proprii iussa servate"), and then he urged two abbots, whose names are given as Chalcedonius and Gerontius (Greek names), to rule their flock (in the singular) wisely. Moreover, they should receive visitors "ante omnia," give alms, clothe the naked, and break bread for the hungry, "for he can truly be called consoled who himself consoles the wretched" (*Inst.* 1.32.1). The remainder of the chapter is general spiritual advice to the community and the abbots, including only one section on suggested readings: "And so read diligently the lives of the *patres,* the confessions of faithful souls, and the acts of martyrs, always mindful of future beatitude; to this end particularly see Jerome's letter to Chromatius and Heliodorus" (*Inst.* 1.32.3).[28] That is not much, in sum, to go on. What, then, do we know?

First, there is no mention in the *Institutiones,* a work obviously addressed to the coming generations of Vivarium monks (we believe it to have been given a last revision in Cassiodorus' very last years, since it mentions the *De orthographia,* written when he was ninety-two), of any specific monastic *Regula* to be followed to the letter. This is the strongest obstacle that proponents of Vivarian adherence to the *Regula Benedicti* or the *Regula Magistri* have to overcome.

In fact, no convincing case can be made that there had to have been a *Regula* as such for the community. Everything about Cassiodorus' idyllic description seems more in tune with a community run by an unwritten constitution, populated by a small number of well-disciplined individuals. That impression may not be correct, but it is the only shred of evidence we have. In particular, it seems to give the lie to the possibility that the legalistic and harsh code of administration set out by the *Regula Magistri* could ever have been intended by Cassiodorus for his monks to follow.

As we move here between our numerous ignorances (whose width and variety, as Housman would have said, are wonderful), we must next confess confusion about the roles of the two named abbots. Cappuyns argued that the existence of two abbots echoed the practice of the *Regula Magistri* whereby a successor abbot could be created in the lifetime of his predecessor if the former holder of the office was near death; then if he survived, the institution would have two abbots.[29] Conversely, it could be supposed that the two officials presided respectively over the Vivarium and the Castellum establishments; but did a hermitage in the hills need an abbot? And why is their flock

---

28. The letter mentioned is a pseudo-Hieronymian martyrology.
29. M. Cappuyns, *RTAM,* 15(1948), 215.

referred to in the singular? Why, finally, does the title of the chapter, supported by all of the manuscripts in one way or another, give the singular "abbatis"? We simply do not know the answers to these questions; the fact of the names of two abbots flatly defeats us.

The last bit of evidence to be gathered from the *Institutiones* is that the name of Cassian appears where Benedict's does not. This pattern recurs at one important point in the *Expositio Psalmorum,* where Cassiodorus follows Cassian and diverges from Benedict on the advisability of using the first line of Psalm 69, "Deus, in adiutorium meum intende," as an ejaculation preparatory to undertaking any monastic activity. Writing at Constantinople fifteen or twenty years after Benedict founded Monte Cassino, Cassiodorus said that "Cassian (who is not always to be trusted, however), discussing this verse's use in his tenth *Collatio,* thought so highly of it that he directed that monks begin every task with a triple recitation of it" (*Ex. Ps.* 69.48–52).

More substantial possible indications of Cassiodorian monastic practice come from the evidence for the canonical hours observed at the Vivarium. Both of the *testimonia* for this, however, come from the *Expositio Psalmorum;* one passage seems to have been corrupted, moreover, by later hands attempting to increase the parallel to Benedictine practice *(Ex. Ps.,* praef. lines 77–85). The one clearly authentic reference has been shown to agree more closely with a pseudo-Augustinian rule (which may have been one of the sources used by Benedict) than with Benedict himself (*Ex. Ps.* 118.3045–3048). Specifically, the hour of prime (mention of which was clearly an interpolation in the passage in the preface) is not mentioned, but compline is already in its place.

On these unsatisfactory and somewhat discordant notes we come to the end of our tether. A review is in order. There is no hard evidence that Cassiodorus had ever even heard of Benedict. There is no evidence that he knew the *Regula Benedicti.* Although there may be enough evidence to link the manuscript tradition of the *Regula Magistri* with Cassiodorus, there is no credible evidence that it played any significant role in his community. There are apparent analogies in Cassiodorian practice with various elements of the monastic culture common at the time and with Christian monasticism of the preceding centuries in general. Cassian is the only monastic author specifically recommended by name for the monks to read. The only picture we are capable of drawing on this basis, I hold, is of an independent foundation guided benevolently and liberally.

After our earlier discussion of the position of Benedictine monasticism in the western tradition, we can see that Cassiodorus' enterprise, understood in this way, was indeed more liberal than Benedict's. If there was less regulation and authoritarian government, there was more concern for the niceties of the spiritual life. Less austere and more genial (on the seashore rather than a mountaintop), the abbey of the Vivarium (with the "secreta suavia"—on a mountaintop—of the Castellum for the most ascetically minded) was perhaps a little too urbane, too gentle to survive beyond the enthusiasm and self-discipline of the first generation of monks. We noted already that Benedict's more tightly disciplined style of monasticism was the one that proved to have the staying power and the inbuilt tendency to self-reform that let it survive and flourish for centuries.

We said earlier that Cassiodorus does not seem to have left a *Regula* for his monks to follow, but everything we have said in this chapter undercuts that statement to some extent. For the book that Cassiodorus did write about his monastery, with its admonitions to seek the heights of monastic spirituality and the discipline of intellectual activity, the *Institutiones,* we must now examine. It seems to have taken the place of a formal *Regula;* it is clearly the founder's apologia for his enterprise and his exhortation and guide for those to come after him. Its form and content tell us most of what we could want to know about the life of the monastery of the Vivarium and the way its founder approached the monastic ideal.

If, in fact, we consider the *Institutiones* as a substitute for a formal monastic rule, some of its characteristics come into plainer light. There is certainly every reason to believe that the work was intended for no wider audience than the monks at the Vivarium. On the very first page of the preface, Cassiodorus addresses his audience familiarly: "*Caritas* inspires me to prepare this introductory volume for you, with the Lord's help, to serve in place of a live teacher [*ad vicem magistri*]" (*Inst.*, praef. 1). If, as Lehmann demonstrated with considerable certainty, the *Institutiones* was first written about 562, this motive becomes even clearer.[30] Cassiodorus was at that time by our best calculations about seventy-five years old, nearing the end of his first decade at Squillace with his monks. Certainly in his own lifetime and in the formative years of the institution especially, Cassiodorus himself would function as the director of studies for this school of Christian learning. But with encroaching old age he would be of a mind to put down his plan to study in the form of a bibliographic guide, to serve "ad vicem magistri" when he had died. Thus it is that the last chapters of the first book of the *Institutiones* are addressed to members of the community, first reminding them of the happy situation of the monastery, praising the work of the scribes and physicians (the two most important supporting specialist groups within the community), then directing a *commonitio* to the abbots and community, and concluding the introduction to the Christian intellectual life with exhortations to seek the heights of the Christian spiritual life of monasticism. Just in the same way, the second book of the *Institutiones,* dedicated to the exposition of the secular arts and disciplines necessary to the Christian scholar, ends in a six-page conclusion that puts the secular sciences back into perspective and recommends readings like the Apocalypse of St. John and the *De videndo Deo* of Augustine.

30. P. Lehmann, in his *Erforschung des Mittelalters* (1959), 2.41–47, dated the *Institutiones* (in first draft) as closely as possible. He showed for the first time that the *terminus post quem* had to come after the visit to Constantinople, then demonstrated that the paschal *computus,* discussed below, clearly dated to 562, is not mentioned in the *Inst.*, even though all four surviving copies of the work are bound in MSS with *Inst.* 2.

There are, of course, many other marks of the audience that the author of the *Institutiones* had in mind; there are specific sections on the contents of the numerous manuscript collections made at the Vivarium and even distinct references to the location of specific books in the cabinets of the monastery's library. In every way, then, this treatise is a handbook of a very practical nature written with a specific audience in mind.

Empirically, then, this work is a handbook for the Christian scholar. But what kind of book is it in formal terms, and how does it achieve its numerous ends? The title itself, howbeit obscured by the manuscript tradition, shows the way. Mynors rightly preferred shorter forms, placing only *Institutiones* on the title page of his edition.[31] Beyond that, the choices offered by the manuscripts are numerous but closely similar; the clearest distinction is always between the contents of the first book (always described with the adjective *divinae*) and the second (almost always *saeculares,* but occasionally *humanae*), reflecting the different contents of the books. Just what the noun for the contents may be is uncertain, but again similar terms occur: *litterae, lectiones, res.*[32] The sense of *institutio* here clearly has to do with education, in the way that Lactantius (whom Cassiodorus may not have known) and Calvin used the word in their *Divinae institutiones* and *Institutio christianae religionis,* respectively. The direct sources of the title may have been twofold; the first was Cassian's *De institutis cenobiorum,* which Cassiodorus knew and recommended to his monks, and which, if it were the source, would add to the character of Cassiodorus' work as something functioning in place of a monastic rule. The second source, even closer at hand, was the *Instituta divinae legis* of Junillus, which, as we have seen, Cassiodorus recommended to his monks, and whose author he probably knew personally. In either case, however, it is to be noted that Cassian and Junillus used the simpler form *instituta;* Cassian used it to denote a work

31. Mynors' introduction, lii–liiii, summarizes the evidence on titles lucidly.

32. While I find *litterarum* more Cassiodorian, no dogmatism is in order; but note Augustine's phrase, "litterae saeculares," *De musica* 6.1.1, a work present at the Vivarium (*Inst.* 2.5.10).

concerned chiefly with monastic discipline, while Junillus used it for one providing guidance in exegetical practice. Cassiodorus wrote a book with both purposes in mind and used the slightly more sesquipedalian word, perhaps only out of a pardonable literary vanity and a preference for longer words.

If the title and certain obvious statements indicate that the two books of the work were meant to be a unified whole, there is much in the respective books, both in tone and content, to belie that assumption.[33] In the first place, Book I is far more personal in tone and far more devoted to specific discussions of practical questions than is Book II; furthermore, it is bibliographical in content, attempting to show the beginning student where to go to begin his course of studies in Christian learning. Book II, by considerable contrast, is far more austere in outline (divided rigidly into seven chapters on the seven components of trivium and quadrivium), and is in fact an attempt to teach a certain amount of material of substance, as well as to provide a propaedeutic for further studies in the subjects covered. We are again face to face with Cassiodorus' theory of the subordination of the secular disciplines to sacred science. Far from being the avid humanist student of secular learning that he is often made out to be, Cassiodorus is here in fact only following the tradition set forth by Augustine's influential *De doctrina christiana,* which urged the acquisition of necessary skills from the secular *doctores* in order to facilitate the accurate interpretation of scripture. Not only is Cassiodorus far from original in the treatment he gives of the secular subjects, he is far from enthusiastic about their study. Note the negative phrasing he uses in describing their worth: "It is not irrelevant to discuss briefly in the following book the rudiments of secular educa-

---

33. See all of *Inst.* 1.27 and the first words of the second book. Books I and II were very early divided from one another for practical purposes, with only three surviving manuscripts containing the authentic tradition of both books together. The tradition has by no means been settled; what we know is best summarized in Mynors' introduction, with later contributions by E. K. Rand, *Speculum,* 13(1938), 443–447; Courcelle, *Revue des études anciennes,* 44(1942), 65–86; and van de Vyver, *Rev. Ben.,* 53(1941), 59–88.

tion, the *artes* and *disciplinae,* as a refresher for those who have already studied them and as a brief compendium for those who cannot read more widely in those subjects. Knowledge of these things, as the *patres* saw, is clearly useful and not to be shunned, since you find them sprinkled throughout the Bible, that fount of universal and perfect wisdom" (*Inst.* 1.27.1). The whole tone of the conclusion at the end of Book II echoes this restrained advice to use the secular studies but not to delight in them too much for their own sake. There is a similarity in his language here, where he speaks of "rejecting and condemning the vanities of this world," and studying the scriptures in such a way "so that what men are seen to have sought on account of earthly praise, we might helpfully refer to heavenly *mysteria,* converting all things to the glory of the Creator. And so, as blessed Augustine and the other learned *patres* said, secular writings ought not be rejected" (*Inst.* 2, concl. 3). Thus, in both places, the emphasis is on the strictly negative formula that secular studies are not to be scorned, not to be fled from.

Thus the *Institutiones* establishes the theoretical principles and guidelines for the kind of study that we saw Cassiodorus himself practicing in the *Expositio Psalmorum.* It is clear that the unified theory that he propounded there about the scriptural origin of the secular sciences dominates the conception of this work.[34] It is no accident, therefore, that the first book is an annotated bibliography of the study of scripture and religious subjects, while the second book is designed chiefly as a textbook in itself.

With this in mind, we are better able to appreciate the internal order of the first book. It begins, as the Christian student's work begins, with the Bible. Cassiodorus expended considerable effort in establishing in his library accurate texts of *Sacra Scriptura.* These included one gigantic edition in nine volumes of a Vulgate text written *per cola et commata,* clearly the chief treasure of the Vivarium library; its traces are seen today in the *codex Amiatinus,* a close descendant of the Cassiodorian edition,

34. The theory is repeated clearly at *Inst.,* praef. 6.

perhaps even including a quaternion of pages from the original archetype. Also influencing the *Amiatinus* was the *codex grandior,* a non-Vulgate text in one large volume. Finally, another text, "minutiore manu," called a pandect, provided a copy of the entire Bible in one volume containing the Vulgate of Jerome.[35]

The order of the first book of the *Institutiones* follows the nine biblical volumes in order, introducing the patristic texts that explain each section of scripture. Thus the first volume of the large edition, containing the Octateuch, is presented with a long list of subsidiary texts; these include no fewer than fifteen works treating in some way the book of Genesis (the most popular subject, I venture, of all patristic exegesis). The list gives an instructive glimpse of the breadth, and occasionally the shallowness, of Cassiodorus' library. There is Basil's *Hexaemeron* (probably in the translation of Eustathius), bound together

35. This summary follows Courcelle, *LLW,* 377. But B. Fischer, *Biblische Zeitschrift,* n.F. 6(1962), 57–79 (summarized in B. Fischer, *Settimane,* 10[1963], 557–561), argued that the nine-volume set used the Vetus Latina text; that the *codex grandior* used Jerome's revised Hexapla in the Old Testament, possibly Jerome's version of the Gospels (but there is no evidence on this point), and the Vetus Latina again for the rest of the New Testament; and that the Amiatinus got its format from the *codex grandior* but its text from other locally available sources. Fischer was followed in this by R. Loewe, *Cambridge History of the Bible,* (1966–1969), 2.116. —In the Amiatinus there is transmitted a miniature that has been thought by many scholars to represent Cassiodorus himself in his library (it purports to be the scribe Ezra); certainly the books in the picture represent the biblical library of the Vivarium very precisely. The picture, considerably enlarged, is most accessible in D. T. Rice, *The Dark Ages* (1965), 243, and has been printed often elsewhere; but none of the color reproductions show very legibly the gold lettering on the nine scriptural volumes in the *armarium;* arranged as they are in the picture (and as can be deciphered if one knows what to look for), they exactly match Cassiodorus' arrangement:

Oct. lib.	Reg.
Hist.	Psalm. lib.
Salomon	Proph.
Evang. IIII	Epist. Ap. XXI
Acta Apost./Apoca.	

With the Amiatinus there is also transmitted a prologue to the whole of scripture that is now assumed to be from Cassiodorus' pen; the text is printed at *PLS* 4.1387–1390.

with Augustine's *De Genesi contra Manichaeos*. Ambrose's *Hexameron* (which, as we've already seen, Cassiodorus knew and used in the earliest days of his political career) is mentioned next, with no mention of the parallels between that work and Basil's, with which it would more appropriately have been bound. There is much more Augustine to be had, understandably, since Augustine wrote prolifically on Genesis. There is his *De Genesi ad litteram* in twelve books, the *Contra Faustum* in thirty-three books, and the *Contra inimicum legis et prophetarum* in two books. Cassiodorus is among the first, though not the last, to point out the last three books of the *Confessiones* as a Genesis commentary; he does not say, however, that he has had those books separated from the whole for juxtaposition with other works on Genesis. Then Cassiodorus praises the *Quaestiones in Heptateuchum* of Augustine, as well as the *Locutiones in Heptateuchum* (which he calls the *De modis locutionum*). The collection of Augustine on Genesis is incomplete, however, since Cassiodorus confesses that he has heard of—but not been able to find—seven sermons of Augustine on the seven days of creation; he seems not to have heard of the *De Genesi ad litteram imperfectus liber*.

The list does not stop with Augustine, however; there are seven books of Ambrose, *De patriarchis,* mentioned for what they offer on Genesis and the other books of the Octateuch. Then there are mentioned the works of Jerome on *Hebraicae quaestiones* and *Hebraeorum nomina,* both of which Cassiodorus recommends highly (and we have seen how he made frequent use especially of the latter in the *Expositio Psalmorum*). Prosper's *Liber de promissionibus* is next on the list, completing the collection of works by Latin authors.

What remains in this chapter is a lengthy discussion of the works and authority of Origen. The Vivarium had three codices of his homilies, covering all the Octateuch except Ruth.[36]

36. Note that to fill out the available material on the Octateuch, Cassiodorus commissioned an original work: *Inst.* 1.1.9. In the case of other books of scripture, notably in the codex of Old Testament historical books, Cassiodorus had occasion to make up pseudo-commentaries (*florilegia* of scattered fragments of patristic works) where none existed before.

Cassiodorus' defense of Origen freely admits the difficulties with that author, balancing Jerome's praise against Pope Vigilius' condemnation and adding other authorities. Cassiodorus quotes what he calls the conclusive dictum already proverbial in his day concerning Origen: "Where he's good, there's none better; but where he's bad, none worse" (*Inst.* 1.1.8). To get around the problems of Origen's heterodoxy, Cassiodorus devised a technique for guiding his monks without mangling his copy of the manuscript: "So in reading the works of Origen, I have marked passages which contradict the teaching of the *patres* with the sign *achresimon*—'unusable'—so that he will not deceive those who heed the warning of that sign" (*Inst.* 1.1.8). This affectation of a scholiastic term in the margin, Cassiodorus is sure, will suffice to warn his monks away from doctrinal error. This is the first place in the *Institutiones* where Cassiodorus mentions precautions of this sort taken to sanitize a doctrinally suspect author. It is perhaps a sign of the underlying respect in which Origen was held (and the relative innocuousness of his errors; Cassian and Pelagius erred on grace and free will, hotter topics than the eternity of creation and *apocatastasis*) that Cassiodorus thinks it sufficient to mark off doubtful passages without going to the trouble of preparing an expurgated edition.[37]

Cassiodorus' practice of introducing the first volume of scripture with its supporting library is repeated in treating the remainder of the Bible. The Old Testament is divided into one volume of historical books, one of prophets, one of sapiential literature (entitled "De Salomone"), one of "Agiographi" (i.e., Esther, Tobias, Maccabees, etc.), and of course the Psalter, with respect to which Cassiodorus offers not only his own introductory commentary, but also Hilary, Ambrose, Jerome, and as much of Augustine (apparently only comments on twenty Psalms) as he has been able to acquire for the Vivarium. There are then three volumes of the New Testament, one of Gospels (with the fewest commentaries associated with it of any of the volumes), one of Epistles, and one of the Acts of the Apostles

---

37. After only a cursory survey: "quantum transiens invenire praevalui" (*Inst.* 1.1.8); cf. *Inst.* 1.8.1 and 1.27.2.

bound together with the Apocalypse. In nine chapters, then, Cassiodorus goes through the contents of his exegetical library.

This only furnishes, as it were, the raw materials for the study of scripture. The practical guidance must now grow more fundamental. Unfortunately, the first chapter with which Cassiodorus began that instruction is the apparent victim of a textual defect that confuses (though it does not destroy) the order of Cassiodorus' suggestions. Briefly, the chapter advises the student to begin with certain elementary guidebooks (Augustine, Tyconius, Adrian, Eucherius, and Junillus—whose short treatises Cassiodorus had bound together in a *codex introductorius*[38]), to proceed by studying existing commentaries on scripture, then *catholici magistri* treating individual theological problems, then various occasional writings of the *patres* (including letters and sermons), and finally to consult the elders of the monastic community.

There is much more to the first book of the *Institutiones,* however. After the first nine chapters on the books of the Bible and the tenth on methodology, there follow numerous chapters of technical information. The first chapter lists the four major synods of the church that are to be accepted as authoritative; the three chapters that follow this listing of the synods (and index the text of their decrees in the library) are actually concordance tables, showing the different listings of the authoritative books of scripture according to different authorities— Jerome, Augustine, and the Septuagint (*Inst.* 1.12–14). This measure enabled students to find their way from one text of scripture to another, a matter that was particularly important since Cassiodorus' own arrangement of the nine-volume set was idiosyncratic and grouped the books according to their contents, in slight violation of the other usual orders. Chapter 14, indeed, concludes with a summary of the codices available at the Vivarium. From this it is a logical step to turn to the subject of correct copying of texts and the precautions to be taken therein: "Sub qua cautela relegi debeat caelestis auctoritas" (*Inst.* 1.15).

---

38. *Inst.* 2, concl.; printed in the apparatus criticus by Mynors, p. 163.

The chapter on accurate transcription is concerned chiefly with preventing eager scribes from altering the inspired words of scripture in the name of grammatical and stylistic rules. Where the text of scripture is not at risk, Cassiodorus encourages the emendation of texts according to the rules of secular *magistri,* but the text of scripture must always be checked against good and ancient exemplars (a principle curiously similar to that with which Richard Bentley planned to edit the New Testament twelve and a half centuries later).

The remainder of the first book of the *Institutiones* is a sequence in no clearly defined order of chapters on other matters of bibliographical importance for the monks of the Vivarium. There is a general chapter, for example, "de virtute scripturae divinae," which repeats some earlier material (e.g., it recommends Augustine's *De doctrina christiana* again) and offers general principles for the study of scripture. A separate chapter is set aside for Christian historians, chiefly making mention of works available at the Vivarium. Then comes a series of chapters naming and praising those doctors of the church whom Cassiodorus esteemed most highly: Hilary of Poitiers, Cyprian, Ambrose, Jerome, Augustine, and his own contemporaries, Eugippius and Dionysius (*Inst.* 1.17–23). We are, of course, most intrigued by his choice of contemporary writers to praise; mention has often been made of the presumed early friendship between Cassiodorus and Dionysius Exiguus, perhaps beginning when the latter was teacher and the former pupil. The choice of Eugippius was at least in part based on comparative geographical proximity (Eugippius wrote from a monastery near Naples), and in part on a similarity of purpose in monastic intellectual enterprise. Cassiodorus, however, seems to have a more personal reason for mentioning him, claiming a relationship to the Proba to whom Eugippius' Augustine anthology was dedicated (*Inst.* 1.23.1).[39]

After a short chapter exhorting the monks to make the study

---

39. M. van den Hout, reviewing Besselaar's *Cassiodorus Senator en zijn Variae* in *AJP,* 69(1948), 233–235, showed at least the tenuousness of the evidence linking Proba to Symmachus; this had been used in the past to demonstrate Cassiodorus' kinship with Boethius and Symmachus.

of scripture the goal of all their intellectual work ("Let us not let an excess of curiosity deflect us toward empty speculations" [*Inst.* 1.24.1]), we get a scattered sequence of chapters on subjects not strictly religious. In fact, had Cassiodorus been of a different mind, these chapters could well have been relegated to the second book on secular studies; they treat cosmographers (like Ptolemy), agronomists (Gargilius Martial and Columella), orthographers, and Greek physicians (*Inst.* 1.25, 1.28, 1.31). There is, moreover, the chapter on the site of the Vivarium and the recommendation for readings on monasticism, chiefly from Cassian, and a chapter "de schematibus ac disciplinis," which introduces and justifies the second book to follow (*Inst.* 1.27, 1.29). Finally, there are the two chapters of *commonitio* to the abbots and community and of prayer in conclusion.

To understand the peculiar difference in structure and style between the first and second books of the *Institutiones,* however, it is necessary to look closely at the chapter in Book I that introduces the second book. It comes in the middle of the sequence of miscellaneous chapters on the auxiliary sciences that monks should study if they are able; it justifies attention to the secular studies by pointing out how useful they are in understanding scripture and how, of course, they got their start from scripture itself. Then Cassiodorus states his particular purpose in composing Book II: "Let us accept the burden of antiquity, collecting in our second book the things they wrote of more extensively in many volumes . . . ; thus what they have furtively carried off will be restored to the service of accurate understanding" (*Inst.* 1.27.2). Book II, therefore, is a kind of extended gloss on this single chapter of Book I, taken out and expanded so that the subject could be treated at an appropriate length without spoiling the structure of the first book.

In this way, Book I of the *Institutiones* is a theoretically complete work, covering everything about divine and secular learning that the student needs to know. But it has been necessary for Cassiodorus to provide a text of the seven *artes* and *disciplinae* of a sort that will reduce those studies to the appropriate state of subservience to scriptural ones, a state they have long avoided in the hands of their secular practitioners.[40] It is true, therefore, that Cassiodorus introduces the study of what we would call "humanities" to his monastery; but he does so only in order to take command of those subjects once and for all, to make them truly a branch of "divinity," to subordinate them to higher things.

It is inevitable, therefore, that the second book should be of vastly less interest to us than the first. In it Cassiodorus is merely repeating what he has been told by the authors he excerpts.[41] It is in many ways difficult for us to appreciate just how so schematic and abstract a treatise could have been of real use to students; I think it must be thought of in connection with Cassiodorus' true *magnum opus,* the *Expositio Psalmorum.* The only students for whom the second book of the *Institutiones* was written were themselves monks. In Cassiodorus' monastery they would have been educated in the *opus Dei,* the divine office, by means of that very Cassiodorian commentary, full of allusions to all the devices of secular learning. For them, then, this second book of the *Institutiones* would be a valuable companion text, taking the material scattered at random according to the disposition of the text in the *Expositio* and presenting it in a unified whole in one short book. Thus the excessive schematization of the presentation would be precisely its virtue; for the student who came from the *Expositio* with his head buzzing with arcane bits of rhetorical and scientific information, the straightforward style of the *Institutiones,* showing the elements of these sciences in their necessary relationships to one another, would provide just the organizational information to enable the student to make sense of what he had learned. Hence, the longest section of the second book is on dialectic, sorting out all

40. *Inst.* 2.3.20 distinguishes between *ars* and *disciplina.* H.-I. Marrou, *ALMA,* 9(1934), 5–25, says Cassiodorus is the only author to insist upon the distinction.

41. See Courcelle's chapters on Cassiodorus, in *LLW,* 330–409, for the most extensive inquiry after the sources of the second book. For an earlier sketch, see L. M. Capelli, *Rendiconti del Reale Istituto Lombardo,* Ser. 2, 31(1898), 1549–1557.

the syllogisms and categories that had been noted in passing throughout the Psalter; after that, rhetoric and arithmetic got the most extended attention.[42]

Thus the *Expositio* and the *Institutiones* provide together all the practice and the theory, respectively, that a monastic scholar needed for introduction to the life of Christian intellectual culture. Having read through the commentary, he would know the monk's book, the Psalter, as well as could be expected, having learned well the techniques of exposition as practiced by Cassiodorus; the *Institutiones* gave theoretical order to the techniques of exposition as well as comprehensive and orderly bibliographical material on the further study of all of scripture, with all the ancillary material that was at the student's disposal in the Vivarium. On this basis the intellectual and cultural enterprise of the Vivarium takes on new unity, in harmony with the monastic enterprise that lay at the base of all life there; we can now see more clearly the kind of education that Cassiodorus had had in mind as far back as the days at Rome when he and Agapetus were conspiring together.

It can also now be seen in what way the two works we have discussed, the *Expositio Psalmorum* and the *Institutiones,* were the centerpieces of Cassiodorus' own intellectual labors through the 540's and 550's. When he had completed these works, in his seventy-fifth year or thereabouts, he could be to some degree confident that he had provided for his monks and for the study of Christian culture. How much success was actually visited upon this endeavor we will attempt to discuss in the next chapter. In the meantime it must not be neglected that there were many other works published for the monks at the Vivarium, spinoffs from the central purposes of the enterprise.

42. It is just possible that the student went the other way. Perhaps the second book was originally a set of lecture notes on the secular sciences from which Cassiodorus taught; as he grew older, he set them down this way, whether for following teachers or for independent study. (This would answer, moreover, Courcelle's objection that Cassiodorus did not use all the works at his command for his treatment of the trivium and quadrivium; teachers are always slow to revise their lecture notes.) Then students would approach the *Expositio Psalmorum* to see theory put into practice.

These works divide themselves into two interacting categories. There were, first of all, numerous works that Cassiodorus had translated from the Greek for the use of his monks; and there were the manuscript collections that he made of numerous works of the Greek and Latin fathers for various purposes. We have already seen that throughout the first book of the *Institutiones* he was mentioning the compilation of manuscript editions of groups of commentaries on individual sections of the Bible.[43] In this regard the *Institutiones* are as much a record of the program of works intended to be compiled as of the work already done; for frequently Cassiodorus mentioned works that he had been unable to get but for which he urged his followers to be vigilant.

The question of translations raises the arguable question of the state of knowledge of Greek at the Vivarium.[44] Despite efforts to prove that Squillace was in a Greek-speaking vicinity and drew its monks from among native Greek speakers, the evidence seems to be that the bulk of the people for whom and with whom Cassiodorus was working neither spoke nor read the Greek language. We know the names of only three individuals (Bellator, Mutianus, and Epiphanius) who worked for Cassiodorus in translating Greek into Latin. Cassiodorus himself seems never to have done any translating.

The chief products of the Greek translators at the Vivarium were three: the Latin version of the homilies of Chrysostom on Hebrews, which had a considerable medieval vogue; the Latin Josephus, a best-seller for centuries; and the *Historia ecclesiastica tripartita.* The other translations included chiefly commentaries on books of scripture for which Latin treatments were not available, but also the work of Gaudentius on music.

Of these works, the only one to show any trace of originality was the *Historia tripartita,* and even it was a borrowed idea.

43. Courcelle, *LLW,* 372–375, gives a careful list of the manuscript *corpora* known to have been compiled at the Vivarium.

44. G. Rohlfs, *Griechen und Romanen in Unteritalien* (1924), 79–82; but cf. F. Blatt, *Classica et Mediaevalia,* 1(1938), 217–242. On the general loss of Greek in the west, see Courcelle, *LLW,* passim, and M. R. P. McGuire, *Classical Folia,* 13.2(1959), 3–25.

Designed to fill up the period from the end of Eusebius' ecclesiastical history (which was present at Squillace in Rufinus' translation), the *Historia tripartita* translated and conflated passages from the three Greek ecclesiastical historians, Socrates, Sozomen, and Theodoret of Cyrrhus, covering the period from the conversion of Constantine down to the year 429, when the narrative of Socrates ends. There is a preface that is obviously by Cassiodorus, but it is also clear that the bulk of the work was done by Epiphanius.[45] There has been a certain amount of scholarly gloating over the translation errors in this work;[46] but a more balanced view shows that it is comparatively accurate for works of that genre and period.[47]

If we assume that Cassiodorus' knowledge of Greek was relatively slight, we will find support in the *Historia tripartita;* Epiphanius had in hand the tripartite history of Theodore the Lector (completed around 530, in Greek), which he followed in selecting passages from the three historians down through the middle of the second book. From there on he had a free hand in the selection and translation of passages, which he seems to have exercised judiciously.[48] A glance at the contents will show, for example, that the compiler largely followed the narrative of Socrates, the best of the three from an historical point of view. The whole project is thus one that Cassiodorus inspired (possibly bringing a manuscript—perhaps a partial one—from Constantinople for the purpose) but that he put almost entirely into the hands of Epiphanius.[49] The Latin of the

45. See most recently R. Hanslik, *Philologus,* 115(1971), 107–113.

46. See S. Lundström, *Übersetzungstechnische Untersuchungen auf dem Gebiete der christlichen Latinität* (1955), and *Zur Historia Tripartita des Cassiodor* (1952).

47. The moderate view is in M. L. W. Laistner, *Harvard Theological Review,* 41(1948), 51–67, esp. 54–56.

48. See also L. Szymanski, *The Translation Procedure of Epiphanius-Cassiodorus in the Historia Tripartita* (1963).

49. M. J. Suelzer, *The Clausulae in Cassiodorus* (1944), showed that the clausulae of the *Hist. trip.* depart from the Cassiodorian pattern widely; cf. esp. p. 14 (although the numbers on that page do not quite match her own charts, where the difference is not so dramatic, though still great).

Historia is good, albeit sounding as much like a translation as it in fact was.[50]

We know of one other original work compiled at the Vivarium at this period: the *computus* that was keyed to the year 562 and designed to explain the Christian calendar. The work is of slightly greater interest than the usual such treatise (although it is very short and simple), because it is the first document from the medieval world that uses the Dionysian system of reckoning dates *anno Domini*. The little treatise was generally ascribed to Cassiodorus in the past (it is transmitted with his work: see below), then denied by Mommsen on the grounds that at that time (1861, in his first edition of the *Chronica*) he thought Cassiodorus must have been dead by 562. Paul Lehmann, however, showed with clarity and vigor that the probability favors a Vivarian origin for the work, in the time of Cassiodorus, for three reasons: that Cassiodorus lived well past 562; that he knew and admired Dionysius Exiguus, the author of the new reckoning, and had just the sort of curiosity about natural history to be intrigued by such a system; and that all four manuscript versions of the *computus* appear in codices bound with Book II of the *Institutiones,* three of them immediately following the end of the authentically Cassiodorian work.[51] The treatise itself is of merely antiquarian interest now, with its rules for determining the year A.D. when the indiction is known and vice versa, as well as rules for determining the arcane numbers of *epactae, adiectiones solis,* the year of the 19-year *circulus,* and the date of the next bissextile day, as well as complex rules for determining the date of Easter and simpler ones for the day of the week.

50. See F. A. Bieter, *The Syntax of the Cases and Prepositions in Cassiodorus' Historia Ecclesiastica Tripartita* (1938); S. Lundström, *ALMA,* 23(1953), 19–34; and L. Szymanski, *The Syntax of the Nominal Forms of the Verb in the Historia Ecclesiastica Tripartita* . . . (1955). The Latin Josephus shows some of the same features; see the introduction to the edition by F. Blatt. On translation errors in the Josephus, see F. Blatt, *Classica et Mediaevalia,* 1(1938), 217–242; and H. Janne, *Byzantion,* 11(1936), 225–227.

51. P. Lehmann, in his *Erforschung des Mittelalters* (1959), 2.51–52, includes the only critical edition.

The last major surviving work produced by the Vivarium enterprise is the only one that shows the continuation of Cassiodorus' work after the master left off. This is the commentary on the Epistles, originally written by Pelagius the heresiarch, revised by Cassiodorus and his school, and now associated with the works of Primasius of Hadrumetum.[52] Cassiodorus knew the work under the name of Gelasius and saw the need to expunge heretical ideas from it (*Inst.* 1.8.1). He himself only managed to get through the part of the commentary that treated Romans, leaving the rest for his monks to expurgate. (Note that this work was so infected as to need a completely revised edition and could not make do, as did Origen and Cassian, with marginal warning notes.) Examples can be adduced of the use of the *Rules* of Tyconius the Donatist in the revision of the commentary on Second Thessalonians and of the use of Eucherius' *Instructiones* in several cases (but never in revising the commentary on Romans); both authors had been recommended by Cassiodorus (cf. *Inst.* 1.10.1). What is more, this later revision gives us a glimpse of the level of intellectual activity at the Vivarium when Cassiodorus himself was not directly involved; where Cassiodorus had relentlessly purged the Pelagian poison on his own authority, his monks had recourse to the most elementary of the scriptural handbooks that Cassiodorus had recommended to them.

For special reasons, the last two works of Cassiodorian authorship have been reserved for consideration in our next chapter. But the picture drawn so far of intellectual activity at the Vivarium is completely consistent with that painted by the *In-*

52. H. Zimmer, *Pelagius in Irland* (1901), thought that pseudo–Primasius was pure Pelagius. C. H. Turner, reviewing Zimmer in *JThS*, 4(1903), 132–141, identified the anti-Pelagian tendencies of the work; it remained for A. Souter to identify pseudo–Primasius with the Cassiodorian revision and to study this at length; see most conveniently his first article, *PBA*, 2(1905–1906), 409–439; the text of pseudo–Primasius appears in *PL* 68, and Souter's restoration and discussion of Pelagius' version appear in *Texts and Studies*, 9(1922–1931). Souter prepared an edition of the expurgated text for *CSEL*, but it has not appeared (A. Souter, *A Glossary of Later Latin* [1949], vi).

stitutiones. It can be clearly seen how ecclesiastical history, translations of commentaries on scripture, and preparation of doctrinally orthodox editions of other commentaries are all elements in the process of studying scripture that Cassiodorus set up.

Not every work in the Vivarium library was produced there, of course. Our last consideration in examining the intellectual enterprise at Squillace must be the question of the copying of manuscripts preserved there. For centuries, the general assumption of scholars has generally been that Cassiodorus was instrumental in establishing the practice of manuscript copying in monasteries and that particularly he was somehow responsible for the preservation of manuscripts of ancient secular classics.[53] We must be blunt: there is no evidence for either assumption. We know that Cassiodorus showed his monks how to copy manuscripts, but they were busied chiefly with scriptural manuscripts and ancillary handbooks and textbooks. It is not, however, surprising that a monastery would be engaged in copying manuscripts of works it needed; even Benedictine monasticism at its inception needed books for distribution to the monks at the beginning of Lent (*Reg. Ben.* 48). Moreover, there is no convincing palaeographical evidence that any surviving manuscripts of pagan classics passed through the Vivarium. Even more damaging is the realization that it cannot be demonstrated that the library at the Vivarium contained so much as a single manuscript of Vergil.[54] In fact, the secular authors whom Cas-

53. R. Beer's pernicious hypothesis, that the classical codices of Bobbio had been transported there from the Vivarium, was a pillar of this theory; see his *Bemerkungen über den ältesten Handschriftenbestand des Klosters Bobbio* (1911). The demolition of this theory is easily accessible, as in Lowe, *CLA,* 4(1947), xxvi–xxvii, and H. Bloch, *Speculum,* 25(1950), 277–287.

54. Cassiodorus' quotations from classical authors in the second book of the *Institutiones* are only through the medium of other rhetorical and dialectical textbooks. (A point seriously misunderstood by R. R. Bolgar, *The Classical Heritage and Its Beneficiaries* [1954], 110, who thought that Cassiodorus meant for his monks to read the classical poets and orators in the original.) Mynors' index to the *Institutiones* shows how bereft the Vivarium library was of classical authors.

siodorus can be shown to have known and used at the Vivarium are only those who can be made use of in some way in the study of scripture. Thus there are grammarians present, but not poets or classical historians.[55]

One is justified in asking, then, what this entire enterprise of students, copyists, and translators added up to. The picture is a simpler one than scholars have ever been willing to admit; it can best be drawn by examining more closely the mind and heart of Cassiodorus at this period.

First, we must rid ourselves of the notion that the retirement to Squillace was a romantic flight to a monastic refuge, that Cassiodorus was taking ancient culture and walling it up inside the monastery with him. In fact, Cassiodorus seems not to have cared one way or the other what happened to secular culture, for he did not admit its theoretical right to exist. Obsessed with his new idea of a Christian culture that rose above and absorbed all previous intellectual culture, he was seeking only the best environment in which to pursue that goal. The decision to work at the Vivarium, on the farthest shore of Italy, was mostly coincidence. The land was there, and we have already seen that the monastery may well have already been there before the idea of locating the school there germinated. Cassiodorus' first choice for a site for his school had been Rome itself; but after the collapse of those efforts and Cassiodorus' departure from Italy, the movement of this man's heart into the monastic life began and quickened. The whole period at Constantinople can only be understood as constituting the time when Cassiodorus the statesman disappears from the stage of history to be replaced by Cassiodorus the monk. Moreover, he had no grandiose conception of himself any longer, if ever he had had one before, nor did he deserve one. He was one man, attempting in his old age to found a school where men might come to a greater knowledge of the things their faith spoke of. To this all his efforts were bent.

---

55. For the limits of Cassiodorus' demonstrable knowledge of poetry, see M. Bacherler, *Bayerische Blätter für das Gymnasialschulwesen,* 59(1923), 215–219.

Second, we must discount all our notions that Cassiodorus saw a great mission for his institution in some way reaching out to all of Europe. There is no credible evidence that he ever looked beyond the boundaries of his estates except to see if he could pick up a copy of an elusive manuscript. The works produced there were narrowly limited to local use; even the *Expositio Psalmorum,* written in metropolitan Constantinople, was later revised in places to include references to specific works in the library at Squillace.[56] We will discuss in the next chapter the largely coincidental way in which Cassiodorus came to have some impact on later developments. But apart from the very remote possibility that the Vivarium would become a source of teachers for other schools (although there is no evidence for this in the texts), or that students would come from afar to study the methods there (again, no evidence), there is every reason to believe that the self-sufficient Christian life of monasticism was all that Cassiodorus really cared for. That this included scholastic activity was implied in Cassiodorus' understanding of monasticism and the faith he professed; in Cassiodorus, monastic and intellectual activity is fused directly in a way that would be duplicated partially, and independently, throughout medieval monastic Europe.[57] We need not look to Cassiodorus, in fact, as the fountainhead of this development; indeed, the love of learning and the desire for God were passions that, when the former was adequately subordinated to the latter, came naturally to the monastic life. In the beginning, one had monks singing the Psalter and reading scripture, doing the *opus Dei.* That the monastic quest for God took on intellectual forms reflects, not the influence of one inventor, but the nature

56. The passages bracketed in Adriaen's edition of the Psalm commentary as additions after Cassiodorus' return to Squillace are taken from suggestions in van de Vyver, *Speculum,* 6(1931), 271 ff.; van de Vyver, *Rev. Ben.*, 53(1941), 79; and Cappuyns, *DHGE,* 11(1949), 1401. These are only, however, to be taken as provisional suggestions; we are always in danger of reading too much biographical information into these passages.

57. See G. Bardy, *SE,* 5(1953), 86–104; and Jean Leclercq's masterly *The Love of Learning and the Desire for God* (1961).

of man himself. It would be astonishing if these men had abided in their cloisters meditating on the Word and not become scholars.

Thus the Vivarium was for Cassiodorus something more than psychotherapy, as one scholar put it,[58] but also something less than an evangelical mission to rescue Europe from intellectual disorder. The real quest of Cassiodorus at Squillace was the soul's search for God through faith; in this he was atypical only in the intelligence and resourcefulness, not to mention the bureaucrat's talent for organization, that he brought to the task.

58. G. Ludwig, *Cassiodor* (1967), 41.

7

Old Age and Afterlives

BECAUSE the whole span of Cassiodorus' activity in his monastery presents itself to us in one image in the *Institutiones,* it is easy, too easy, to think of that period as homogeneous. For that reason it is particularly valuable to separate the study of his activity there into two parts, following natural lines offered by the evidence. There are two particular pieces of evidence, one a text, the other the history of a text, that show us the progress of Cassiodorus' work.

To begin with, Cassiodorus gave a clear list of works written after his retirement in the preface to the *De orthographia:* "[1] After the Psalm commentary, to which I gave my first attention at the time of my conversion, [2] and after the *Institutiones,* . . . [3] and after the commentary on Romans, from which I removed the blots of Pelagian heresy, leaving the rest for others to expurgate, [4] and after the volume in which I gathered the *Artes* of Donatus with his *Commenta,* a work on etymologies, and another book of Sacerdos on *schemata,* for the benefit of the less sophisticated brethen [*simplices fratres*], [5] and after the book of *tituli* of Scripture . . . , [6] and after the volume of *Complexiones,* [7] I have come to treat my old friends the orthographers in the ninety-third year of my life" (*De orth.* 144.1–16). It will quickly be seen that in the preceding chapter we have really only examined Cassiodorus' career through the production of the first three of these seven works: the *Expositio Psalmorum,* the *Institutiones,* and the expurgation of the commentary on Romans. We have already put a *terminus ante quem* for the first draft of the *Institutiones,* embodying most of the educational program and the collection of manuscripts, at 562, almost a decade after Cassiodorus' return to Squillace. Thus the remaining four works are the fruits of almost two decades of presumably less intense work by the aging Cassiodorus.

Here the textual history of the *Institutiones* comes into play, albeit with arguable significance. The evidence on the question makes only one thing certain: that Cassiodorus himself did put a hand to revising his own work, including new material (mentioning, e.g., the *De orthographia*), and correcting obvious errors in the first edition (such as calling a Priscian a Greek, a slip rectified when Cassiodorus had obtained a codex of his work in Latin). The further difficulty, however, is that the original edition survived (apparently) and was itself the basis for successive interpolated editions by other hands of the second book particularly, which includes further information on the seven liberal arts. There is some possibility, then, that a copy of the *Institutiones* in its first draft left the Vivarium and began to receive accretions. Thus there survive copies of the entire work (revised by Cassiodorus, uninterpolated), copies of Book II (also revised and uninterpolated), and numerous additional copies of Book II (not revised by Cassiodorus, interpolated by persons unknown in two stages).[1]

This new information is not decisive, but it throws light on the subject from a new angle, putting better relief on the contours of the later years of Cassiodorus' career. Returning to the *Complexiones* and to the *De orthographia,* we can examine the quality, as well as the quantity, of the later works. What is most noteworthy is the decline in originality; of the last four works named, three are mere compilations, including a codex of grammatical texts, a handbook of chapter headings from the Bible for ready reference, and the *De orthographia* itself. Only the *Complexiones* shows any meager originality on Cassiodorus' part. Far from surprising us, this should confirm what we can surmise about Cassiodorus' life at this period. He had by and large completed the establishment of his library, with a few

1. I follow the stemma given by A. van de Vyver, *Rev. Ben.*, 53(1941), 59–88, against the more unwieldy version of P. Courcelle, *Revue des études anciennes,* 44(1942), 65-86. The raw material for the history of the text is lucidly presented in Mynors' edition.

lacunae remaining, and prepared the major textbooks for the training of young monk-scholars. By this time Cassiodorus was in his mid-seventies, full of years and for the most part ready to rest in the contemplation of divine things. While he did not cease literary activity entirely, there were yet no gaps that he alone could fill; for he had not the vigor to undertake any major labors of commentary on other books of scripture, the more so because of his earlier diligence in preparing codices containing comments gathered from many sources where integral works did not exist. There was then a last major textbook to be put together on grammar (matching the ones already mentioned in the *Institutiones* on rhetoric and dialectic) and the handbook of chapter headings, perhaps something of an old man's pastime, something to keep the pen moving while he read through the whole corpus of scripture over several months.

There is no particular reason why either of those works should have survived; what did survive from this period were the *Complexiones* and the purely functional *De orthographia*.

Turning to the *Complexiones* from the *Expositio Psalmorum*, we see how much Cassiodorus' approach to writing scriptural commentary had changed from his active days at Constantinople (when he was in his fifties) to the last years at Squillace (for the preface to the *De orthographia* seems to say that the *Complexiones* was being written just at the time of that work, in other words, at some time around the turn of Cassiodorus' tenth decade, c. 575). The single surviving manuscript, discovered in 1712 by Scipio Maffei with his trove of Verona manuscripts, goes back itself to the sixth century, but apparently to a northern writing center otherwise unidentifiable.[2] Maffei was excited by the work because he thought it provided independent authority for textual readings in the Latin Bible, since Cas-

2. Lowe, *CLA*, 4.496, says of Verona XXXIX(37), that it is "Uncial, saec. 6–7; written in Italy and apparently in the North." On Maffei's discovery and publication of the *Complexiones,* see Maffei's own remarks at the beginning and end of his edition and also W. Telfer, *Harvard Theological Review*, 36(1943), 169–246, esp. 229–230.

siodorus clearly did not follow the Vulgate. In particular, Maffei leapt to point out that Cassiodorus already knew the trinitarian interpolation at I John 5.7–8, and took that as proof that the reading is valid (it is not).

The difference between this work and the *Expositio Psalmorum* is not merely in the scale, but also in the purpose and the style. In the preface, Cassiodorus put forth this cryptic explanation of his work: "*Breves* of the Apostles, which we can more accurately call *complexiones,* embrace various things summarily, showing what things are treated there, striking a balance between diffuse description and excessive (omissive) brevity" (*PL* 70.1321–1322). What Cassiodorus then promised was a brief narration, summarizing the *intentiones* of the sacred authors, not discussing every word of the text. "This is the difference between *breves* and *complexiones:* that *breves* are an analytical index of what follows, while *complexiones* give a consecutive narration of the same things" (*PL* 70.1322). This seems to mean that Cassiodorus is not intending to provide a set of canons to accompany a text of scripture, but rather an independent work capable of being read on its own.

The purpose of the work, then, is to introduce the reader to the non-evangelical books of the New Testament: "For reasons of brevity I omit mention of some doctrinal disputes, the purpose being to introduce the reader to the text, not to tell him all there is to know" (*PL* 70.1382A).

The procedure by which this introduction is achieved is formal and simple to a much greater degree than that of the *Expositio Psalmorum.* The scripture was divided up arbitrarily into numbered sections, which are the units of commentary.[3] The numbered sections each begin with a scriptural lemma, the first words of that section of the text. Explanation follows very literally, very directly; what is given is scarcely more than a paraphrase. The actual words of the lemma need not be the subject of the explanation (cf. ad Rom. 9.1 [*PL* 70.1327B]), nor

3. An examination of Maffei's facsimile of a text page reveals these sections are so numbered in the sixth-century manuscript; the numbers may well have been keyed to the master copy of the text at the Vivarium.

is every word of the passage considered (cf. ad Rom. 1.18–24
[*PL* 70.1323A], where Romans 1.20, a popular text in the middle ages but one neglected in the *Expositio Psalmorum,* is passed
over in silence). Throughout the work the purpose of the
comments is to clarify and to simplify, with frequent references
to parallel texts of scripture, especially the Psalter.

Insofar as this work fits the categories of early medieval
exegesis, it is resolutely literal. There is virtually no allegorical
interpretation, not even of individual figures; thus the mention
of Noah in I Peter 3.17 is ignored. On the other hand, no part
of the text is considered worthy of outright neglect; on I Peter
5.8, Cassiodorus summarizes the contents of the author's personal greetings and commendation of the letter's bearer. The
closest he comes to allegory is on Apocalypse 3.1, where he
reads a phrase thus: "and in shining vestments, that is, a purified conscience" (*PL* 70.1408A). Nor is there digression, nor
anything not explicitly called for by the text.

As described so far, then, this is a work almost without
interest except as a guide to the original text itself, perhaps intended as a way of finding explicit references to particular contents of the books of scripture covered. But in this apparent
desert, the one visible theological preoccupation stands out all
the sharper. The work is filled, even overflowing, with repeated
and fervent insistences on the entirety and unity of the Holy
Trinity. Most commonly, these take the form of gratuitous as-
sertions, when one member of the trinity is mentioned, that the
naming of the one implies automatically all three. This is a pro-
nounced habit particularly in the Pauline epistles, where the
first verse of every letter, offering greetings in the name of
God, is elucidated by reference to all three members of the
Trinity. At the beginning of II Corinthians, for example, Cassiodorus describes Paul as "seeking that peace and grace be
granted them by God our Father and the Lord Jesus Christ:
these two are named, but the Holy Spirit is recalled often, for
the simple mention of one member of the Trinity embraces all
three completely" (*PL* 70.1339A–B). On Ephesians, he describes Paul as hoping "that they might have grace and peace

from the Father and Christ the Lord; where the religious spirit senses the allusion to the Holy Spirit" (*PL* 70.1345D). More explicitly, on the opening of I Thessalonians: "Nor does it matter that he omits mention of the Holy Spirit; for whether he mentions one or, as just now, two persons of the Trinity, he means the whole Trinity to be understood" (*PL* 70.1349C). This same admonition is repeated over and over again throughout the commentary. For example, the triple prepositional phrases of Romans 11.36 excite the remark: "Veritably he proclaims the work of the Holy Trinity to be incomprehensible; for *ex ipso,* namely from the Father, and *per ipsum,* namely through the Son, and *in ipso,* namely in the Holy Spirit, all things exist; and to show the unity indivisible in them he adds, 'glory to them forever' " (*PL* 70.1329A).

What is remarkable and valuable about this penchant of the nonagenarian scholar for insisting on the unity and coequality of the members of the Trinity is that it is not (apparently) directed at any particular heretical tendency of the age; where the Trinitarian features of the *Expositio Psalmorum* showed Cassiodorus very much bound up in the controversies that raged around him in Constantinople, this habit in the *Complexiones* is merely the repetitiousness of an old man who is also a patient teacher, insistently drumming the central dogma of the Christian faith into his students' ears and eyes. A lifetime spent in the company of heretics and controversialists disagreeing violently among themselves about the Trinity had left Cassiodorus acutely conscious of the necessity of inculcating proper doctrine in the inexperienced, to avoid prolongation and repetition of the controversies that had rent the church for centuries. The enemies of the truth had receded in the distance from Squillace, but the need to teach and preserve the true interpretation lived on. It is particularly noteworthy that Cassiodorus shows no sign of contact with Lombard Arianism, with lingering disagreement in Italy over the Three Chapters edict, or with any contemporary eastern arguments. The isolation of the Vivarium was complete.

We have seen, therefore, that the originality of Cassiodorus' last independent work of scholarship is not very great after all. In his old age he was still preparing textbooks, but with none of the resourcefulness that he showed when doing the *Expositio Psalmorum*.[4] Apart from witnessing the progress of Cassiodorus the man into grave old age, however, we should also notice that there was still a demand for this kind of work in his community. Not all of his monks, however many had stayed on through twenty years and however many new ones had entered, were capable of advancing to the level of their teacher, and the ones for whom he was writing were still relatively unadvanced in their own studies.

If this strikes us as being the case with the *Complexiones*, it forcibly speaks to us on every page of the *De orthographia*. The very need for the textbook clearly shows us something of the state of affairs inside the Vivarium around 580. For comparison, we should first recall that Cassiodorus had already had something to say about the subject of correct spelling, in the *Institutiones;* in the chapter on copying manuscripts, after the careful instructions to observe the idioms of scripture, there follows about a page of orthographic instructions (*Inst.* 1.15). The instructions are simple and very much to the point; they enjoin, for example, careful observation of the use of *b* and *v, n* and *m,* and *-e* and *-ae* endings. Some of what he advised was exotic as well, as his insistence that *narratio* be spelled with one *r* out of deference to its derivation (and he has his etymology right for once) from *gnarus*—not even the manuscripts of that particular passage obey him on that point. But in general at that stage, Cassiodorus was addressing serious problems faced by the best scribes of the period; his advice reflects not any local weakness of scribes but a general difficulty in the contemporary Latin culture.

If we date that state of affairs to around 560, we can see how much things had changed by the time Cassiodorus came to write the *De orthographia*. We see first that the idea for the work

4. Traces of the old habits break through, as ad Rom. 8.24 (*PL* 70.1326C): "Hoc argumentum dicitur climax, id est gradatio, quod etiam in subsequentibus frequenter assumit."

came from someone else (as Cassiodorus always claimed except, significantly, for the *Institutiones*): "When I was working on my *Complexiones* of the Apostles, monks suddenly began to clamor, 'What use is it to us to know the thoughts of the ancients, or even your own, if we have no idea [*omnimodis ignoremus*] how to write them down? Neither can we read aloud things written in indecipherable script'" (*De orth.* 143.1–6). The picture conjured up is striking and sufficiently unflattering to Cassiodorus and his enterprise to make us think there is truth in it. Consider the situation: Cassiodorus, in his tenth decade of life, the most senior and most revered member of the community, even if loved as much for his knowledge as for his sanctity, is approached by his monks to set down on paper a last volume of ideas for their benefit: a spelling book.

Now consider the implications: For this spelling book they came to Cassiodorus himself, already preoccupied with the *Complexiones* and surely slowed by age, instead of approaching any other member of the monastic community. Are we to assume that he was the only one who retained the confident ability to handle even so rudimentary a subject in a professional fashion? I fear that we are, for when we look at the contents of the work we see that it is but a digest of other texts, all of which must have been readily present. Thus we are to presume that no one in the community had the minimal ability to do the relatively mechanical task of compilation, and more, that the brothers who needed this service could not make use of the original works themselves, but positively needed to have the digest made. If any reader of the *Institutiones* has come away with a glamorous notion of the lofty intellectual life of the ordinary monks at the Vivarium, this state of affairs will be enough to disillusion him and more. How dismal a failure was the whole enterprise if, almost thirty years after the founder's arrival from Constantinople, there was still more need for a spelling book than anything else?

When we turn to the work, we find our fears confirmed. It is no particular surprise that the old, old man has not written an original tract, nor that he has abridged material sometimes carelessly and ineffectively. His sources are a handful of Roman grammarians going back to the first century A.D., including L. Annaeus Cornutus Neptitanus (from the age of Nero, not otherwise known), Curtius Valerianus (of whom nothing is known), Papirianus (also known to Priscian), Adamantius Martyrius (whose work survives separately for comparison with Cassiodorus' treatment), Eutychis (also surviving), Caesellius Vindex (quoted only twice, known to and quoted by Aulus Gellius), and finally Priscian himself.[5] Cassiodorus' task was to abridge these authors' works, following certain observable principles.

Particularly where we can compare Adamantius Martyrius on the same page of Keil's edition, we can see that Cassiodorus followed his source closely, with some few liberties. He abbreviated a number of the examples given, but above all he simplified. For example, Adamantius said, "Greek usage vindicates *Bacchus* and *baccar*" (Adam. 172.4–5),[6] the meaning of which could be elusive; Cassiodorus gives the rule to be followed very simply: "for *Bacchus* and *Baccha* and *baccar* are written with a *b*" (*De orth.* 172.4–5). Later there is a complicated hypothetical case that does not in fact occur in Latin; Cassiodorus omits it entirely (Adam. 187.10–13). In other places, he reverses procedure to insert explanations and examples where Adamantius may be opaque.[7] A little later, Cassiodorus

---

5. H. Keil, in his introduction to his edition of the *De orth.*, *Grammatici Latini* (1880), 7.129–142, summarizes what we know of the sources.

6. Adamantius is cited by page and line from *Gram. Lat.* 7, where Keil printed Adamantius in parallel on the same pages with Cassiodorus' excerpts, thus resulting in duplicate page and line numbers as I cite them here.

7. Cassiodorus (*De orth.* 195.1–5): "bibo quoque propter discretionem a vita per v, a potu per b scribendum est; et abeo, id est discedo, obeo circumeo, subeo succedo ac similia praepositionum gratia per b arbitror scribenda, etiam deponentia b mutam in scriptura tenere usus et consuetudo antiquitus tradidit." Adamantius (195.2–4): "bibo quoque propter discretionem, et abeo obeo subeo ac similia praepositionum gratia, arbitror enim deponens b mutam in scriptura tenere usus et consuetudo antiquitus tradidit." Adamantius used *arbitror* as an example of the use of the letter *b*, while Cassiodorus misunderstood and rewrote the sentence to give it a place of its own in the syntax.

gives the example, "ut amo amabo, voco vocabo, doceo docebo," where Adamantius has only "ut amabo docebo" to illustrate the future (*De orth.* 198.11; Adam. 198.6).

If Cassiodorus digested the different prescriptions and etymologies of his sources, he was not always able to sort them out. The two following dicta from different sources occur scarcely ten pages apart. Following Cornutus he said, "There are those who write *quotidie* with a *co-*: *cotidie;* they would give up that error if they knew *quotidie* is derived from *quot diebus,* that is, 'on all days' " (*De orth.* 149.6–8). Following Papirian: "*Cotidie* is spoken and written with *co-*, not with a *quo-*, since it is derived not from *quoto die,* but from *continenti die*" (*De orth.* 158.18–19). Only the alert reader, not the aged Cassiodorus, notes any contradiction here.

To recount the vicissitudes of a spelling book is a tedious chore and happily ended. What emerges from even the briefest glance, however, is that the whole purpose of the work was different from Cassiodorus' earlier brief essay in orthographic instruction in the *Institutiones.* Then the purpose had been to warn against the most common errors; now the need was to lay down the most basic rules for every contingency. In the earlier case, Cassiodorus seems to have envisaged giving advice to inexperienced but competent scribes; here he is offering the rudiments to scribes with very little competence at all. It is impossible to refrain from what seems the obvious conclusion: that the intellectual level of achievement at the Vivarium, as judged from competence in reading and writing Latin texts, had fallen off so far (or perhaps had never risen above a level that Cassiodorus had originally overestimated) as to give a very poor showing for the members of the community. One sturdy argument from silence stands forth to support this hypothesis: we never hear of any work written, or any students taught, by any member of the community of the Vivarium not under the immediate supervision and initiative of Cassiodorus himself. If the expurgation of the Pelagian commentary extended in time past the founder's death, it is the only work we know of that did so, and we have already seen the decline in intellectual acuity and

accuracy from the portions revised by Cassiodorus to the remaining sections. After thirty years of Cassiodorus instructing
the monks in the sciences of scriptural interpretation, not one of
Cassiodorus' students ever had a career independent of the master. This Socrates had neither a Plato nor a Xenophon (for that
matter, this Anselm had no Eadmer); the intellectual history of
the Vivarium ends with Cassiodorus' death. Moreover, as we
shall see, the history of the community at the most rudimentary
level is wrapped in mystery and rapidly comes to an end; the
works preserved there disseminated to Europe, but through
means we can only surmise. After Cassiodorus, there is silence
at Squillace.

If Cassiodorus was being besought for a spelling book in his
ninety-third year, he must have had some inkling that his experiment had failed on the level of worldly success; he does not
speak of this, nor is he concerned by it visibly, nor, on the level
of contemplation, should he have been. It is possible that one
factor in our ignorance of the fate of the Vivarium may not be
the fault of the inhabitants, but of the broader sweep of history.
Throughout the Vivarium years, there is something missing
from the life of Cassiodorus that we have always seen there
before: an awareness of wider geographical horizons. For a man
who had been a statesman in the highest circles of power, who
had traveled the Mediterranean himself and sent others on mis-
sions around the known world, the horizons from Squillace
were suddenly very close and very narrow indeed. There is
some mention of seeking out manuscripts from a distance, but
this may or may not ever have been successful. Instead we see
Cassiodorus isolated and alone at Squillace, out of touch with
the political and theological events of the day, with only the
companions of his self-imposed exile to write to and for. When
he came to mention ecclesiastical writers of his own age, he
named only Dionysius and Eugippius, both some decades dead.
On the rest of the history of the second half of the sixth century
in Italy, Cassiodorus is silent. (Out there in the wider world, by
around 575–580, Justinian was a decade and more dead, the
Lombards were in control of the plains of northern Italy, and

Gregory was on his way to Constantinople as papal apocrisiarius.)

This isolation in turn is an accident of history and a by-product of the remoteness of Cassiodorus' hideaway. The farthest tip of the Calabrian peninsula is unique in having been spared the ravages of the sixth century's wars. When Roman and Gothic forces raged up and down, they always clung to the west coast, seeking the straits of Messina. Years later, when the Lombards entered Italy in the late 560's, they never quite got as far as Squillace. The toe of Italy had passed quietly back into Byzantine hands while Cassiodorus was away in the north and then in Constantinople, and it remained Byzantine until the Normans came in 1060. The actual fate of Cassiodorus' monastery is murky, as we have said. Gregory the Great mentioned the establishment in two letters, one arbitrating a dispute with the bishop of Squillace as late as 598; but after that there is silence.[8] As discussed in the last chapter, we surmise that Basilian monks took over some of the remnants of the institution, and we saw how Cassiodorus himself might have been an object of their veneration (to judge by the Greek graffiti on his sarcophagus). The *patria* of the man who had run all of Italy for the Ostrogoths, the site of his last and proudest achievement, is reduced to merely another gaggle of monks looking no farther than the next cloister.

What is remarkable about Cassiodorus in his old age, however, is that in his last work, the *De orthographia,* there appeared personal touches and signs of the individual spirit behind the literary *persona* with which we have for so long dealt, to an even greater degree than in the *Institutiones.* We have already quoted his proud, quiet passage listing the works he had written since his retirement and taking up the request of his monks to provide them with one more textbook. He saw that this was the task of a true "modern," receiving and preserving some of the heritage of antiquity: "It is our intention to weave

---

8. Greg. Mag., *Ep.* 8.32 (*MGH, Epp.* 2.35), mentioning "monasterium Castelliense"; and *Ep.* 8.30 (*MGH, Epp.* 2.32), arranging ordination of a priest for the community, also dated to 598. See H. Thiele, *Studien und Mitteilungen zur Geschichte des Benediktiner-Ordens und seiner Zweige,* 50(1932), 378–419.

into one fabric and assign to proper usage whatever the ancients have handed down to modern custom. But the things which were only customary in the past it is best to abandon with hesitation, lest extra care be taken beyond what is needed nowadays" (*De orth.* 145.14–18).[9] This very nearly summarizes the entire enterprise of Cassiodorus' years in retirement, discarding what is useless of the ancient, preserving into the new age the useful treasures of olden days.

Cassiodorus was never, as we have seen, the most original of writers, always preferring another man's carefully chosen words to his own composition. So too at the end of his preface, when he wished to say a few words of general advice, he had recourse to another writer's words: "But before beginning our treatise on orthography, we have decided to cite the preface of Phocas, the writer on *artes,* since it seems to fit our whole endeavor [*cuncto operi nostro*] as if we had written it ourselves" (*De orth.* 146.20–22). Note how he insists that these verses are so much of his sense that they are as good as his own.

Ars mea multorum es, quos saecula prisca tulerunt;
    sed nova te brevitas asserit esse meam.
omnia cum veterum sint explorata libellis,
    multa loqui breviter sit novitatis opus.
te relegat iuvenis, quem garrula pagina terret,
    aut siquem paucis seria nosse iuvat;
te longinqua petens comitem sibi ferre viator
    ne dubitet, parvo pondere multa vehens;
te siquis scripsisse volet, non ulla queretur
    damna nec ingrati triste laboris onus.
est quod quisque petat: numquam censura diserti
    hoc contemnet opus, si modo livor abest.

(*De orth.* 146.13–24)[10]

9. Cassiodorus is the first writer to use the word *modernus* regularly (in works as early as the *Variae*); cf. W. Freund, *Modernus und andere Zeitbegriffe des Mittelalters* (1957), 27–40.

10. "You belong to many, my book, whom past ages have brought forth, but new brevity claims you as my own. When all the sayings of the ancients have

This elegy is good as an epitaph for Cassiodorus himself and shows us more clearly than anything else how he envisioned his own work. There can be no question that his was an age for the abbreviator; the second book of the *Institutiones,* prepared as an ancilla to the more important first book and as a propaedeutic to the *Expositio Psalmorum,* itself became a prime source of handbook knowledge of the liberal arts, revised and interpolated as the opportunity came. We see here, too, antiquity's prolixity reduced into a shorter, simpler, modern compass; and there is the plea that the work not be scorned by learned men simply because it is brief, since it directly serves a useful human purpose.

Those are not quite the last words of a personal nature from Cassiodorus, however. There is a conclusion at the end of the *De orthographia,* a final *envoi.* It would not be a work of Cassiodorus, one feels, if the number twelve were not a distinguishing feature, and certainly this is no exception. There have been twelve chapters of excerpts, which the conclusion explains once again: "For if, as we know, twelve hours make a day, twelve months complete the year and its seasons, twelve signs of the zodiac hem in the plains of heaven in a solid ring, then it ought to be enough that we have excerpted twelve volumes of orthographical writings to set out the rules for correct spelling" (*De orth.* 209.22–27). Then there is a last, more personal paragraph of direct address: "Farewell, brethren; deign to remember me in your prayers. I have written this brief guide to spelling, and I have prepared copious instructions on the interpretation of scripture. Just as I have sought to separate you from the ranks of the unlearned, so may the heavenly power

---

been mined from their books, there is need of a fresh approach to say much in a brief space. Let the young man whom wordy pages terrify study you instead, or anyone who likes to find out important things in few words; let the traveler starting a long journey not hesitate to take you along, carrying a lot without being weighed down; if anyone wishes to copy you, he won't be able to complain of the trouble or the burden of doing so. This is what everyone wants: the censure of the scholar will never berate this work, if only envy is withheld."

not allow us to be mixed with evil men in community of punishment" (*De orth.* 209.28–210.5). There can be no doubt that
this conclusion refers to the spelling book just completed.
There is not, to be sure, any mention of secular sciences here;
Cassiodorus' achievement, the thing on which he stakes his
hope of heaven, is the material he has prepared *copiosissime* (contrasted neatly with the *brevitas* of the work at hand) for the
understanding of holy scripture.

And that is that. Completed in the ninety-third year of his
life, somewhere around 580, the *De orthographia* is the last thing
Cassiodorus ever wrote, excepting minor modifications to the
Institutiones. When did Cassiodorus die? There are no legends of
his having been taken off into the hills around Squillace to return again at the onset of the next dark age, but neither is there
any evidence to tell us of the scholar's death and the monk's
entry into the next life. We only know that he survived into his
ninety-third year, but not how much longer; our conclusion in
Chapter 1 was that his birth was somewhere between 484 and
490, so we see him surviving until at least 576 and perhaps as
late as 582 by the time of the *De orthographia.* As with Cassiodorus' birth, his death enfolds us in ignorance.

We have already alluded to the speedy disappearance of his
monastery from the stage of history, perhaps within about two
decades of his death. Cassiodorus himself suffered one injustice
at the hands of fate, perhaps as a result of the speedy dissolution
of his monastery: he never achieved recognition as a saint. In
large part this is the result of there never having been an organized *cultus* and, more pertinently, the result of Cassiodorus'
having neglected to leave behind a hagiographer prepared to
state his case. If one looks into the *Acta Sanctorum,* however,
one will find the name Cassiodorus listed, on the authority of a
late martyrology, under March 17, a day already associated
with a saint of the century of Cassiodorus' birth. But this is at
best legend. The most interesting survival of Cassiodorus'
name in hagiographical history turns Cassiodorus into two
martyrs of a group of four assigned to the age of the Antonines
and recorded in *Acta Sanctorum* on September 14 under the

names Senator, Viator, Cassiodorus, and Dominata. Hippolyte Delahaye published the story of this text, which he dated to the eighth to eleventh centuries, discounting all historical authenticity except to note that the name of our subject must have been embraced by legend at some time in the early middle ages.[11]

As we saw in the last chapter, there has come to light in this century evidence of a debatable nature that may indicate the rudiments of a *cultus* directed toward the founder of the Vivarium: the graffiti on the sarcophagus from San Martino di Copanello at Squillace. Written in Greek, their clear import is to appeal to the coffin's occupant as a holy spirit and intercessor.[12] Even this, however, would not be enough to establish a formal case for canonization. What recognition Cassiodorus has received in the afterlife will have to be confined to the land that eye has not seen; for what it is worth, Dante did not recall seeing him there.

There is a more mundane kind of afterlife that writers of books are given to suffer here below in the material world. In the past the survival and transmission of Cassiodorus' works in the middle ages has been a favorite pastime for scholars, especially palaeographers. This study does not pretend to present original research on the subject for many reasons, the most substantial of which is the simplest: the topic is of less pressing interest than we have, in the past, wanted it to be.

The vulgate opinion of Cassiodorus has it that he is the veritable savior of western civilization,[13] and even that he was a pagan at heart secretly using the monastic system to preserve

11. H. Delahaye, *Mélanges Paul Fabre* (1902), 40–50; cf. p. 49, placing the work "parmi les romans les plus absurdes qui deshonorent la littérature hagiographique." Another manuscript with a litany containing the same names is noted by M. Coens, *Analecta Bollandiana,* 59(1941), 272–298.

12. G. Jacopi, ΠΕΠΡΑΓΜΕΝΑ ΤΟΥ Θ′ ΔΙΕΘΝΟΤΣ ΒΥΖΑΝΤΙΝΟΛΟΓΙΚΟΥ ΣΤΝΕΔΡΙΟΤ (1955), 1.204.

13. J. Hammer, *Bulletin of the Polish Institute of Arts and Sciences in America,* 3(1944–1945), 369–384, is a popularizing lecture along this line.

for future generations the fruits of ancient culture.[14] Moreover, just at the point when scholarship found itself in a position to assess this claim, there arose the theory that the manuscripts of the Vivarium had been transported to Bobbio, providing a nucleus library around which the Irish additions brought by Columbanus were built. While that theory, now totally exploded, clung to a tenuous existence, the moment of crisis passed and Cassiodorian scholars with the range and depth of learning to attack the broader assumption had passed from the scene or come to work no longer on Cassiodorus. In the last decades, there has been a gradual tendency in the most specialized studies to recognize the nature of Cassiodorus' contribution and influence for what it was, but old misconceptions die hard.[15]

Cassiodorus' influence on medieval culture was, to be blunt, insignificant. When we assess his contribution we can say, for example, that he was found useful without going beyond that to insist that his utility had any particular influence on the recipients of his intellectual legacy. Likewise we can find that he was a respected author without making the further leap to deducing that he was influential. These things need to be kept in mind as we glance briefly at the history of Cassiodorus' legacy since his death.

We lack direct evidence for the earliest history of the dissemination of the Vivarium's manuscripts. The only sixth-century manuscript surviving of any of Cassiodorus' own works, that of the *Complexiones,* already comes from a northern

14. See G. Slaughter, *Calabria: The First Italy* (1939), who dedicates a chapter to Cassiodorus, "the Last of the Romans." Slaughter may have been led astray by the baseless claim of F. Schneider, that Cassiodorus was not "im Ernste" about religion (*Rom und Romgedanke im Mittelalter* [1926], 92, in an essay held in too high esteem for too long).

15. Courcelle, *LLW*, 401: "It appears then, contrary to the hitherto held view, that Cassiodorus' influence was more weighty for the preservation of Christian literature than for that of the profane writers." See also R. Schlieben, *Cassiodors Psalmenexegese* (1970), 248: "Überhaupt ist Cassiodors Einfluss auf das Mittelalter eher überschätzt worden. . . . Cassiodor passt nicht so gut ins frühe Mittelalter, wie man oft gemeint hat."

scriptorium and offers no information except that the dissemination began early; on the other hand, of this particular work
no other copy survives anywhere, implying that this one case
may be irregular to begin with. There is one surviving manuscript that seems to be a product of the Vivarium itself (MS
Leningrad Q.v.I.6–10); this codex, with several characteristic
Cassiodorian features, is only a collection, however, of works
of a pseudo-Rufinus, Fulgentius, Origen, and Jerome, and its
post-Vivarian history is obscure.[16]

An hypothesis has grown up in this century which argues
that the contents of the Vivarium were at some point around
the end of the sixth century transferred to the library of the
Lateran at Rome.[17] The idea is attractive, since it hearkens back to
the original effort to found a school of Christian learning in Rome
(for the contents of Agapetus' library were probably also taken
over by the Lateran). On the other hand, such conscious design
seems to imply that Cassiodorus himself had something to do
with the decision to transfer, even if only as a deathbed instruction to his monks to give up all they had strived for in the intellectual sphere and send the library to Rome. Another hypothesis, with benefits and disadvantages of its own, might be
that Cassiodorus had a copy of each of the important manuscripts of his library made to be sent to Rome as a present to a
reigning pontiff. This runs into the particular obstacle that not
only the works of Cassiodorus and his colleagues themselves
but also the particular codices of compilations of other authors'
works seem to find themselves represented among the survivors
(to judge by later manuscripts). Moreover, we do know that
at least one of the great biblical manuscripts, or a copy of one,
went eventually to England. At that point we must ask
whether there was such a surplus of personnel and materials at

16. Courcelle, *LLW*, 387, approves tacitly, and Lowe, *CLA*, 11.1614, finds
"seemingly cogent" the arguments for Vivarian origin (and possible Cassiodorian autograph on a part) set forth by O. Dobiache-Rojdestvensky, *Speculum*,
5(1930), 21–48.

17. Courcelle, *LLW*, 361–375, on the Lateran theory; for further evidence,
A. Ceresa-Gastaldo, *Giornale Italiano di Filologia*, 22.3 (1970), 39–46.

the Vivarium to allow for the conception of so substantial a program of production of gift copies; then we must add the query whether Cassiodorus would have prepared such a gift without making a slightly revised edition of the *Institutiones* (with a new preface and cosmetic modifications elsewhere) to accompany the library as an index.

On balance, then, our ignorance will go so far as to allow us to say that it seems that Cassiodorus' library made its way to Rome, and thence to the world, not long after his death. The circumstances are opaque to us.

Of Cassiodorus' own works the early fate is no less obscure. We saw that the second book of the *Institutiones* in its interpolated versions may have derived from a copy of the first edition prepared by Cassiodorus and unrevised later. All this is obscure to us as well, raising the question whether a copy left the Vivarium before the revised edition was prepared or whether the original edition was kept uncorrected (most of the changes were very minor) side by side with the revision. Compared with his other works, however, the *Institutiones* tells a simple and clear tale of its origins; for we know nothing of the early history of the others until they begin receiving mention in the works of other authors and are copied in manuscripts that survive.[18]

Of the medieval fate of the Vivarium works themselves rather more is known. Of course, the *Gothic History* perished completely, and the *Complexiones* survived in only one manuscript. All of Cassiodorus' other works were more fortunate, with the historical translations (Josephus and the *Historia tripartita*) being the most widely successful, while of his own original works, the second book of the *Institutiones* and the Psalm commentary had the widest vogue. Let us now examine the fate of each work in sequence.[19]

18. E.g., earliest MSS: *Inst.*, 8th century; *De an.*, 9th; *Var.*, 11th.

19. For information in the following paragraphs dealing with the knowledge of Cassiodorus in England, I use without footnoting in each case, J. D. A. Ogilvy, *Books Known to the English, 597–1066* (1967), 106—108, a model catalogue of its kind. I further make frequent use of entries from M. Manitius,

1. Variae. Apparently not known in England before the Normans, this work survives in manuscripts that are all comparatively late and mostly contain only portions of the entire work.[20] Two manuscripts of the last four books survive from the eleventh century, with the bulk from the twelfth through fourteenth centuries.[21] Of the three surviving manuscripts of the entire work, two are fourteenth-century, one fifteenth. One surmises that the work became more popular in the later middle ages when Europe rediscovered political thought as a subject distinct from ethics and saw in the *Variae* a handbook of examples of moral Christian political action.[22] This is certainly the impulse that drove Marsilius of Padua to open his *Defensor Pacis* with a quotation on the benefits of the tranquility of civil regimes taken from the first letter of the *Variae* (Theoderic's appeal to Anastasius to reaffirm their peaceful relations in 508). Manitius' manuscript catalogues show that copies are indicated only beginning in the twelfth century. Today over a hundred manuscripts are known.

2. Chronica. The only mention in Manitius' catalogues is ninth-century and German. The work, obviously, was not especially important, since it was abbreviated, derivative, and ended with the sixth century. One surmises that it remained useful for a time, however, wherever other historical calendars

---

Handschriften antiker Autoren im Mittelalterlichen Bibliothekskatalogen (1935), s.v. Cassiodorus and Josephus. Finally, I take note of references to Cassiodorus in medieval authors from Garet's list, printed in *PL* 69, from J. J. van den Besselaar, *Cassiodorus Senator en zijn Variae* (1945), from L. W. Jones's introduction to his translation of the *Inst.*, pp. 49–59, from occasional notices by myself and colleagues, and from other sources as noted specifically below.

20. See the discussion of MSS in Mommsen's preface to *MGH.AA.*XII, lxviii–cx.

21. L. W. Jones, *op. cit.*, 55, on 12th-century quotations from the *Variae;* all of Jones's conclusions have to be checked against his emendatory article in *Speculum,* 22(1947), 254–256.

22. Cf. W. Ullmann, *The Individual and Society in the Middle Ages* (1966), 119, on the distinction between political and ethical theory transmitted by Aristotle.

of this sort were lacking. Ranulphus Higden only quotes Cassiodorus indirectly, but his entry for him mentions the *Chronica:* "There flourished also Cassiodorus Senator, who expounded the Psalter and published a chronicle [*chronicam*] of emperors and pontiffs."[23]

3. *Ordo generis Cassiodororum.* As discussed in Appendix I, this survived only in connection with two relatively early copies of the *Institutiones,* from which the individual paragraphs have occasionally been borrowed as they appear in other manuscripts. The information that the fragment contains, particularly the crucial affirmation of Boethian authorship of theological tractates, was forgotten.

4. *De anima.* One hundred and eighteen manuscripts survive independently or with unrelated works (including the *Institutiones*), another fifty bound with the *Variae,* which Cassiodorus tells us was the original disposition of the manuscript. Mentions in medieval catalogues are fewer but come as early as the tenth century;[24] the work was specifically cited by Rabanus Maurus and Hincmar of Rheims and used in the *De anima* of Aelred of Rievaulx, then quoted later by Albertus Magnus and Johannes Pecham. Representing a typical prescholastic view of the soul, it had its small place in late controversies; short and attractive, it was useful as a devotional tract. It was unknown in England before the Normans.

5. *Expositio Psalmorum.* This was the most successful of Cassiodorus' own works. It was known in continental catalogues of every century and used frequently as early as Bede and Alcuin, who spoke of the work highly; Alcuin listed it in the York library. The utility of the work was obvious, since it was the only complete Psalm commentary from the patristic era except for Augustine's much bulkier and less well-organized col-

---

23. P. Lehmann, *Erforschung des Mittelalters* (1959), 2.39; the mention of pontiffs in Higden's citation may indicate that he did not look too closely at the *Chronica* itself.

24. J. W. Halporn, introduction to the *De anima, CCSL* 96.516–527.

lection of sermons; and Cassiodorus' express purpose had been
to produce a more useful work than Augustine's. The passage
from Ranulphus Higden cited above shows the priority of mention of this work.[25] Adriaen collected *testimonia* to this work
from Bede and Paul the Deacon (in the eighth century); Alcuin,
Theodulf of Orleans, Amalarius, Hildemar, Gottschalk, Hincmar of Rheims, Prudentius of Troyes, Angelome, and Not-
ker Balbulus (in the ninth century); Flodoard of Rheims (in
the tenth century); Berno of Reichenau, Bruno of Würzburg,
and Durandus of Troarn (in the eleventh century); and Abelard
and the Decretals of Gratian (in the twelfth century). The
work's popularity faded only with that of its style of exegesis
and the rise of the great *Glossa ordinaria.*[26]

6. *Institutiones.* At a very early date, the two books were dis-
sociated from each other in most copies. The first book, with
its specific references to the library of the Vivarium, was less
universally useful and had much less broad distribution. The
second book was a handy introduction to the liberal arts and
spread far and wide (influencing Rabanus Maurus' *De institutione clericorum*); it was also interpolated frequently, however, and used by authors of other textbooks as much as it was
used directly itself. Alcuin's *De rhetorica* is an example of the
later trend, more interesting because by that time the first book
of the *Institutiones* had not, to our knowledge, reached England.
The difficulties in using Book I, however, were not insur-
mountable, and it found itself used, and modified, in many
ways. A short eighth-century abstract of Italian origins, for
example, interpolated a schedule of readings from scripture
throughout the church year into the last chapter on the books

25. And cf. Paul the Deacon, *Hist. Langobard.* 1.25 (quoted by Mommsen,
*MGH.AA.*XII, vii): "Huius temporibus Cassiodorus apud urbem Romam tam
saeculari quam divina scientia claruit, qui inter cetera quae nobiliter scripsit
psalmorum praecipue occulta potentissime reseravit. hic primitus consul, deinde
senator, ad postremum vero monachus extitit."

26. Some scraps of evidence for its influence can be gleaned from B. Bischoff, *SE*, 6(1954), 189–281.

of the Bible.[27] Some later monasteries seem to have used it as a loose guide in establishing and organizing their own libraries.[28] In the later middle ages, the first book was taken occasionally for a *"De viris illustribus"* and passed on under such a title.[29]

7. *De orthographia.* Spelling books were always popular, and there are a variety of catalogue citations from the eleventh to the fourteenth centuries. This particular work may have been known to Bede, and was definitely known to Alcuin.[30]

To the catalogue of Cassiodorus' own works, the most important additions to be made are the Latin Josephus and the *Historia tripartita,* published in Latin at the Vivarium, and the *Instituta* of Junillus, in whose transmission the Vivarium played a crucial part.

1. *Josephus.* Not yet published in a full modern edition, the Latin version of the *Antiquitates* gave the medieval scripture

27. MS Vercelli Biblioteca Capitolare CLXXXIII (Lowe, *CLA,* 4.469); containing on folios 99v to 102v the abstract entitled "Notitia librorum catholicorum doctorum, qui in divinis voluminibus expositionem fecerunt; Cassiodori Senatoris." Lowe assigns it to northern Italy, probably Vercelli, early eighth century; semicursive script. A page of this curious work can be read by the eagle-eyed in P. Liebaert and F. Ehrle, eds., *Specimina codicum latinorum vaticanorum,* ed. 2(1932), no. 9, showing 102r; the work is described in A. Reifferscheid, *Bibliotheca patrum latinorum italica* (1865–1871), 2.203. The abstract is wholly functional, with chunks of Cassiodorus' rhetoric omitted and the schedule of pericopes set out very baldly.

28. W. Milde, *Der Bibliothekskatalog des Klosters Murbach aus dem 9. Jahrhundert* (1968).

29. Lehmann, *Erforschung des Mittelalters* (1959), 2.40; cf. 2.66, on Cassiodorus' influence: "Nicht einmal von den Iren und Angelsachsen des 7./8. Jahrhunderts ist es mir gewiss, ob sie die ganzen Inhalt der *Institutiones* gekannt haben. Und als dann im karolingischen Zeitalter das genannte Werk weiterer Kreisen bekannt wurde und der Sinn für die Studien wuchs, selbst da sah man in den *Institutiones* mehr eine Wissensquelle als dass man aus ihnen die Richtlinien ernster wissenschaftlicher Arbeit entnahm."

30. There also circulated a treatise, "De oratione et octo partibus orationis" (*PL* 70.1219–1240) attributed to Cassiodorus; it may even be genuine, as M. Cappuyns, *DHGE,* 11(1949), 1374, argued.

student priceless background information about the historical context of the New Testament. By an examination of relative numbers of citations in Manitius' report of medieval library catalogues, this appears in fact to be the single most often copied historical work of the middle ages, followed most closely by Sallust, more distantly by writers like Orosius, Prosper of Aquitaine, and Paul the Deacon. There are 171 manuscripts of the Latin Josephus listed by the most recent editor, including a fragmentary sixth-century papyrus in Milan, perhaps a close relative of the original. Bede knew and used Cassiodorus' translation.[31]

2. *Historia tripartita.* Cassiodorus' abridgment of the ecclesiastical historians was less popular by far than either Josephus, Eusebius, or Orosius. Nevertheless, preserving the story of an important century of church history, it retained a vigorous antiquarian interest and its survival was assured. Boniface and Alcuin quoted the work, and all six surviving ninth-century manuscripts are in continental monasteries with close English connections, perhaps indicating a crucial role for Alcuin in its distribution. A specific check of its appearance in medieval catalogues is available, showing it in seven from the ninth century, two from the tenth, nine from the eleventh, thirteen from the twelfth, seven from the thirteenth, and six each from the fourteenth and fifteenth centuries.[32] The earliest reference to the work, however, is contemporary with Cassiodorus: Liberatus of Carthage used the work in his *Breviarium* (dated 560–566). Gregory the Great knew the work in 597, only to reproach its indulgence toward the authors of the Three Chapters.[33] A competitor appeared in the ninth century in the form of a *Chronographia tripartita* translated into Latin by Anastasius Bibliothecarius, but this work spread much less rapidly and widely.[34] A medieval translation by one Leopold Stainreuter of

31. G. Bardy, *Revue d'histoire ecclésiastique,* 43(1948), 179–191.

32. M. L. W. Laistner, *Harvard Theological Review,* 41(1948), 51–67, esp. 63–64.

33. Greg. Mag., *Ep.* 7.31 (*MGH, Epp.* 1.478–481).

34. H. de Lubac, *Exégèse Médiévale* (1959–1964), 1.270.

Vienna has recently been edited, showing a vernacular interest in Cassiodorus' compilation.[35]

3. Junillus. That Cassiodorus was instrumental in the transmission of Junillus' *Instituta* to the western world can be easily demonstrated; in the *Institutiones* Cassiodorus gave Eucherius and Junillus as the last two authors (in that order) of the five whose works were included in his *codex introductorius* (*Inst.* 1.10.1). In three manuscripts of the seventh to ninth centuries, that is precisely the order in which those two authors appear one after the other.[36] Since, moreover, the *Instituta* was written c. 542 and apparently returned to Italy with Cassiodorus ten years later, it is already probable that the Vivarium marked the work's entry into the west. It was a popular treatise, containing as it did a brief introduction to the Antiochene style of scriptural exegesis.[37]

But the transmission of Junillus contains a significant blunder that was not uninfluential in later medieval literature. The original work was a dialogue between a teacher asking questions and his pupils answering; writing in Constantinople, Junillus used a device from the Greek alphabet to indicate this, using the Greek capital letter delta (for διδάσκαλος to indi-

35. Edited by Christine Boot, Diss., University of Texas at Austin, 1968 (*DA* 29A.560).

36. MS St. Gall Stiftsbibliothek 908 (Lowe, *CLA,* 7.965) contains Junillus and the *Formulae* of Eucherius (fragm.), both in the primary script of twenty-four palimpsest folios that have been recut and written on in the opposite direction so as to be fragmentary at all times. Primary script is north Italian pre-Carolingian minuscule, dated to saec. 7–8 *(CLA),* saec. 6 (H. Kihn, *Theodor von Mopsuestia und Junilius als Exegeten* [1880]), saec. 8 (Lindsay, *Notae Latinae* [1915], 485). That manuscript was not listed by M. L. W. Laistner, *Harvard Theological Review,* 40(1947), 19–32; in his catalogue there, pp. 24–26, I find: Karlsruhe Augiensis 111, fragments of Eucherius and fragments of Book I of Junillus on folios 66v to 72v (early ninth century, from Reichenau); and Valenciennes 95, Eucherius and Junillus (ninth century, from St. Amand). (And concerning the Augiensis, recall that the *Ordo generis* is preserved in full in Augiensis 106, perhaps indicating a common Vivarian descent.)

37. M. L. W. Laistner, *Harvard Theological Review,* 40(1947), 19–32, showed MSS from before the ninth century from locations as diverse as southern England, northern France, and northern Italy.

cate the teacher's questions and a Greek capital mu (for μαϑηταί) for the students' responses. But in the manuscripts of Junillus this system has gotten confused. They give the following text in the preface: "Lest any confusion should arise, as so often does through scribal negligence, I have designated the teacher [*magister*] with a Greek letter M and his students [*discipuli*] with a Δ, so that all error may be avoided by the use of foreign characters not used in writing Latin" (*PL* 68.17). The vulgate text says shortly afterwards that the work gives the text of the dialogue in true-to-life fashion, where "everything is simply and clearly written as if with students asking questions and the teacher answering them" (*ibid.*). The scribes have taken the Greek letter M to apply to the Latin word beginning with the same letter and have reversed the application of the two Greek letters; in their versions the dialogue takes place between inquisitive students and an answering teacher, a press conference style rather than the catechism that the work was originally intended to be.[38]

The confusion that exists in the Junillus manuscripts sprang, one doubts not, from the copying of the work by Latin-trained scribes, presumably away from Constantinople, to whom the allusion to the Greek words for "teacher" and "students" did not occur.[39] My purpose in rehearsing this history is to suggest

38. The proof is in the MSS. In the first passage quoted, one MS, and a good one, reverses the letters, giving the delta to the teacher, the mu to the students. In the second passage, two different ancient MSS, closely related (and not including the one with the first variant), give the text as "magistro interrogante" and "discipulis respondentibus." Finally, in the text of all MSS of the dialogue itself, the questions are asked by "D" and answered by "M," except that one of the two manuscripts which kept the roles straight in the second passage further recognized the inconsistency and went all the way through reversing the initials. Through this haze of variants, the original use as given in the text above is visible; it was first descried by A. Rahlfs, *Nachrichten von der Gesellschaft der Wissenschaften zu Göttingen* (1891), 242–246, who rightly labeled the dialogue a catechism.

39. For this curious breakdown in transmission between Latin and Greek authors, see L. Traube, *Vorlesungen und Abhandlungen* (1911), 2.99–100. The confusion influenced the form of later literary dialogues, including Eriugena's *Periphyseon* (9th century). G. Pasquali, *Storia della tradizione e critica del testo* (2nd

that, given Cassiodorus' crucial role in the transmission of Junillus, it is worth asking whether he and his monks were to blame, at least partially, for the confusion. There are two possibilities: either they reversed the delta and mu in the introduction and rewrote the other passage into "discipulis interrogantibus" and "magistro respondente," thus setting the tradition reversed only by a few isolated and presumably early scribes who knew a little Greek; or they copied the original manuscript slavishly, never thinking that the apparent contradiction between the initials and words would be puzzling to Latin readers, in which case the three surviving accurate or half-accurate readings would be direct survivals and the vast majority of corrupted manuscripts would be the result of an easy and natural corruption. On balance, the latter is more likely, with Cassiodorus meriting at least some blame for not recognizing the likely confusion and taking steps to produce a version that would be immediately intelligible to a Latin audience. (Reversing the letters both in the preface *and* all the way through in the dialogue would have sufficed, as one scribe tried to do later.) In either case, the history of Junillus' text shows Cassiodorus' enterprise at its best and worst, preserving a mildly influential work otherwise unknown in the west, but not thinking through adequately the circumstances of its transmission to insure an accurate tradition.

In addition to these specific traces of individual works, there is of course a variety of other information about the uses to which Cassiodorus was put in the middle ages. Lehmann has shown that he was known to and drawn upon by Isidore for his *Etymologiae,* for example.[40] In the confusion of medieval at-

---

ed., 1962), 147–148, touched on the issue and barely missed seeing the whole Cassiodorus connection. The *Tusculan Disputations* of Cicero suffer a related contamination: see M. Pohlenz, *Hermes,* 46(1911), 627–629.

40. Lehmann, *Erforschung des Mittelalters* (1959), 2.66–79, traces the fortunes of the *Institutiones* and prints a text from a medieval compendium comprising the heart of Book I, including Chapters 1–9, 16, 17, 19, 22, 23, 24, 25, 30, and 28 (in that order).

tributions of authorship, we find the curious product of a commentary on the Psalms attributed to Bede; in that work each comment on a given Psalm is preceded by a shorter *explanatio* depending heavily, sometimes word for word, on Cassiodorus.[41] Another pseudo-Bedan work on music consists of only twenty-nine definitions of technical terms, twenty-five wholly from Cassiodorus, and two more partly from him and partly from Arnobius and Jerome.[42] Similarly there is a phony letter on clausulae attributed to Cicero confected out of Martianus Capella and Cassiodorus.[43] Finally there are little traces up and down the middle ages of the survival of various Vivarian influences, as in the case of Cluny, where we know Mutianus' version of Chrysostom on Hebrews was included in the annual round of reading in the refectory.[44]

The picture of Cassiodorian survivals in the medieval period is thus set out before us like a mosaic whose pattern momentarily eludes us. What emerges from the welter of detail is a realization of the importance of the distinction that I suggested we carry into this examination. There can be no question that Cassiodorus was a respected author, not quite of the rank of a Father of the Church, but yet approved and appreciated by all who mention his name; and their number is considerable. There can further be no question that much of what Cassiodorus did was of great utility to medieval scribes and readers. The situation for which he prepared his own works at the Vivarium and designed the program of compilations and translations was very much the paradigm case of the medieval center of intellectual activity: the monastic school of scripture and spirituality. Thus the works he put together for his monks were of considerable use to monks up and down Europe. Further, it is important that Cassiodorus, a guide to the monastic

41. M. L. W. Laistner, *Speculum,* 5(1930), 217–221, esp. 219. See also B. Fischer, *Festschrift Bernhard Bischoff* (1971), 90–110; and P. Salmon, *Les "tituli psalmorum" des manuscrits latines* (1959), 151–186.

42. M. L. W. Laistner, *Speculum,* 5(1930), 221.

43. F. Di Capua, *Il Mondo Classico,* 9(1939), 211–218.

44. Joan Evans, *Monastic Life at Cluny, 910–1157* (1968), 98.

intellectual life, began to fade from view in the twelfth and later centuries, when the center of intellectual life was shifted to the universities and thus changed into something radically new. It is in this period that Cassiodorus' major surviving work from his own secular career, the *Variae,* began to come into its own. The final judgment of the middle ages, however, was respectful but, coming from a Renaissance humanist who resembled Cassiodorus in more ways than one, not enthusiastic: "I readily number Cassiodorus among the happy and distinguished—a man of such high rank and such good fortune, so learned and so pious; but I cannot altogether approve his embracing all the sciences, both sacred and profane, in his writings."[45]

But was Cassiodorus influential? Have we seen anything to indicate that his ideas themselves had any greater life in the middle ages, that his educational scheme itself took root and thrived? We have not. As constituted, Cassiodorus' works lend themselves to being used, but do not succeed in passing on theological or educational ideas.[46] For example, the Cassiodorian notion of the harmony of scripture and secular learning very nearly died with the author.

There is another level at which Cassiodorus has often been presumed to have been an influential figure: in the model he gave of the monastic intellectual life, by the example of the Vivarian enterprise. Unfortunately, the evidence is lacking to

45. Erasmus, *Ep.* 2143, quoted by Mynors on p. 87 of his edition of the *Inst.*

46. For Cassiodorus' reputation in medieval eyes as a librarian, Lehmann, *Erforschung des Mittelalters* (1959), 2.81–83, printed the following poem from MS St. Gall 199, possibly by Peter of Pisa:

> Cassio- libripotens titulaverat ordine -dorus
> quae docili patres sanxerunt dogmata sensu,
> dicta notans vatum divino famine farsa
> summaque praelibans cumulum confecit opimum,
> historicosque viros, claro sermone nitentes,
> prudenter calamo perstrinxerat atque notavit
> septena priscos pollentes arte magistros.
> Insuper in summum redi⟨g⟩ens geminosque libellos
> picturis, numeris, titulis ciclisque rotundis
> egregia forma discentibus ipse reliquit.

support this hypothesis (one might almost call it rather a vain hope), and the balance of probability weighs against it. In order for Cassiodorus to be important in this regard, the success of the first book of the *Institutiones* would have to be more noticeable; for that work to fall into disregard for centuries indicates that such was not the case. We know too well now that the Vivarium was not the only monastery copying manuscripts in the sixth century, and we have seen in this study that the scope and nature of Cassiodorus' enterprise itself is nowhere so ambitious as has been suggested in the past. In particular, apart from a faint hint that we may owe the survival of Cato's *De re rustica* to Cassiodorus, his long-presumed importance in the history of the transmission of classical manuscripts has almost disappeared in the light of close scrutiny.[47] Where his works did appear and become most useful, apparently reaching the continent anew from England with Alcuin, they followed upon a revival of interest in monastic intellectual activity and cannot be shown to have instigated it in any way. In fact, it is still more probable that it is with Cassiodorus that we see the beginning of the period of *neglect* of secular classics; into his own century the senatorial aristocracy had been patronizing the copying of the most pagan of classics, but after Cassiodorus and the decision to concentrate on *litterae divinae,* the practice virtually disappeared until the Carolingian revival.[48]

But we can see how Cassiodorus won his reputation. The superficial reader of the *Institutiones* would notice that there was apparently equal treatment of secular and sacred science (in Migne and earlier editions, the two books were printed as separate works, the second almost as long as the first, owing to the interpolations) and would find a chapter in the first book devoted to the science of copying manuscripts. That chapter in particular would warm the hearts of palaeographers and textual critics wishing later medieval scribes had been so well-

47. For the suggestion on the survival of Cato, see E. Norden, *Die antike Kunstprosa* (3rd ed., 1898), 664.

48. Note how proportionately few classical texts are preserved in the MSS indexed in *CLA*.

instructed; those factors combined in minds desirous of finding a little classical humanism in the long gap between the last pagan aristocrats and the Carolingian Renaissance, and the monster of that Cassiodorus who could be called "a pagan at heart" was born. [49]

Happily the modern fate of Cassiodorus has not been marred completely by those who would make of him what he was not. He broke into print irregularly through the first centuries after Gutenberg, finding an editor for his complete works in the rather undistinguished Maurist Johannes Garet, who gave the complete works (lacking only the then-undiscovered *Complexiones*) to the light of day at Rouen in 1679. [50] This is the version that survives in *Patrologia Latina*. The nineteenth and twentieth centuries have been kinder, however, with a wide variety of eminent scholars doing serious, if piecemeal, work on his texts. [51] Because of the fragmentation of Cassiodorian studies into separate departments for church historians, theologians, Roman historians, palaeographers, etc., the immediate benefit was that scholars of considerable eminence from different fields would be moved to the study of the one author. The only problem is that Cassiodorus has thus had to wait so long to be treated as a unity.

The real landmarks of modern Cassiodorus scholarship mark a proud record of scholarly advance. Two German dissertations just over a century ago, one by A. Franz and the other by A. Thorbecke, performed the useful service of setting forth the state of knowledge at that time in convenient form. [52] Not long after, while Mommsen had been editing the *Chronica,* Holder's

49. There is now a journal of European origin entitled *Vivarium* that seeks to honor Cassiodorus by dedicating itself to the study of the secular side of medieval culture; that was an ignorant choice of title.

50. The 1679 edition is considerably rarer than the reprint made in 1729 at Venice.

51. Cassiodorus has not, to be sure, held much of a place in the literary imagination of modern man. Jordanes found a place in the libraries of the Abbé Faria (in A. Dumas, *Le Comte de Monte-Cristo*) and des Esseintes (J. K. Huysmans, *À Rebours*).

52. Works noted in this paragraph are listed by authors in the Bibliography.

happy discovery of the *Ordo generis* and its publication with a commentary by Hermann Usener offered new stimuli to look at Cassiodorus. Mommsen, by default, became the editor of the *Variae* for the *Monumenta Germaniae Historica,* having just done the *Getica,* but his edition shows no trace of haste or carelessness; what is more, it is graced with an index by Ludwig Traube that is a model of its kind and the starting place for all serious study of the *Variae.* For several decades, scholars were digesting this new mass of material; Lehmann's "Cassiodorstudien" and van de Vyver's first article were fruits of this rumination. Then in the 1930's, apparently unbeknownst to each other, two young scholars undertook work on Cassiodorus and the *Institutiones.* Pierre Courcelle was intending an edition of the work when he was forestalled by the remarkable edition published by R. A. B. Mynors. This edition was limited in its intention, providing a text of considerable critical authority for the use of scholars, without pretending to a final determination of the history of the text and its interpolations or providing a commentary on the many problems the text raised. Courcelle's work went not for naught, as we have seen repeatedly in the notes to this study.[53] His early article on the site of the Vivarium was followed by the magisterial study of Greek influence in the west in the fifth and sixth centuries, which includes the most careful study of the survival of Cassiodorian manuscript materials. Since that time there has been a new scattering of work, some missing the mark but stimulating much helpful discussion in so doing, such as Cappuyns' identification of Cassiodorus as the author of the *Regula Magistri* and Momigliano's hypothesis about the origins of the *Getica.* With the establishment of the Corpus Christianorum project, the means were at last at hand to bring the remaining works into modern editions. Adriaen's edition of the *Expositio Psalmorum* is scarcely more than a redaction of Garet's original edition, and plagued by typographical errors at that; a critical edition is in preparation

---

53. For Courcelle's intended edition, see É. Michon, *Comptes-rendus de l'Académie des inscriptions et belles-lettres* (1937), 214.

by J. W. Halporn for the Vienna Corpus. The new volume of Corpus Christianorum containing the *Variae* and the *De anima* is a more useful contribution, though the *Variae* there is plagued by misprints and sorely misses Traube's index. The only remaining work from Cassiodorus' pen without a critical edition is the *Complexiones;*[54] but that is the work least desperate for a new edition, since it survives in one undamaged uncial manuscript ably published by Maffei.

54. There is an edition by P. Donelin that covers approximately half of the work in his dissertation at the Catholic University of America in 1970. This edition restores MS readings eighty times against Maffei, emends further thirty times, and includes an index of linguistic and stylistic matters. The work should be brought to a conclusion.

Epilogue

THE history of Cassiodorus was only a small part of a much larger story, of course. By the categories that we are taught in textbooks, his life formed a part of the transition from antiquity to the middle ages, or—in the more melodramatic formulation—the "Decline and Fall of the Roman Empire." But what is striking at the conclusion of a minute examination of Cassiodorus' life and works is just how useless and inapplicable the larger categories are for our purposes. Only at a distance does the world seem simple enough to fit into such comfortable slots; viewed up close, as always, all sense of grand pattern disappears and we are left with a complex network of men and events, of purposes and cross-purposes, an inextricable tangle of success and failure.

Cassiodorus himself comes through the often stiff and artificial prose of his works as a man intent on backing carefully into the future. His concerns seem always to connect the past with the present: the Roman empire with the Ostrogothic kingdom, traditional forms of rhetorical education with the need for religious indoctrination. But for a man so dull and pedantic in his personal style, he was at the same time a great seizer of opportunities and someone who, all unwilling, was on the side of change and innovation.

For example, if the Ostrogoths had settled their dynastic problems and been left to their own devices by Justinian, Italy as a whole might have survived into the middle ages as a considerably more unified and politically viable nation than it in fact did. In such an alternate version of history, Cassiodorus would appear as an important figure in the adaptation of Roman culture to barbarian rule (and Theoderic might be credited with having presided at the birth of modern Europe).

In his monastic career, Cassiodorus showed the same characteristics. He was never, one feels, a charismatic leader, but an organizer. Had his school of Christian studies at Rome survived, he might indeed almost deserve the reputation that he has wrongly attained as the savior of western civilization. But his impact on medieval culture was less dramatic than that. He was in the main a purveyor of textbooks to posterity.

Cassiodorus was more a doer than a thinker. By most common criteria, he was in fact a failure in most of what he did. The Ostrogothic kingdom for which he labored so long and faithfully was itself only a fading memory long before Cassiodorus himself ever left this world. His school at Rome was fated to a particularly brief existence, while his monastery at Squillace scarcely survived its entrepreneur.

Nevertheless, Cassiodorus was never simply a politician and an administrator. In the course of his life he came to care very deeply about his religion and the way in which it was studied and taught. And if his schemes did not achieve success, by the kinds of standards historians commonly use, Cassiodorus nevertheless must have felt some considerable satisfaction in reflecting on the course of his life (this is palpable in the preface to the *De orthographia,* as we saw). What he had done, he had done well and faithfully to the best of his abilities. Contingent historical events over which he had no control would to a large extent minimize the influence that Cassiodorus would have on the world at large. But in the end, as Tertullian said, no man is born for another who is destined to die for himself. Cassiodorus might himself have been pleased with greater "success," but at the same time he could have rendered, I venture, a pretty fair account of the way he had succeeded in the end in conducting his own life. By definition, the view from the monastery is meant to be directed towards a heavenly, not an earthly, city. In some ninety-odd years of life, Cassiodorus had become proficient in the ways of both cities, a remarkable achievement in any age.

Appendix I

The *Ordo generis Cassiodororum*

THE text here presented was discovered by Alfred Holder in the course of a study of Reichenau manuscripts. He turned it over to Hermann Usener, who published it in pamphlet form with a commentary in 1877.[1] It has been reprinted frequently since, with each editor lending his hand to the task of emending the crucial passages.[2] In the intervening century, other copies of the fragment have come to light, all apparently derived from the first copy discovered; but there is one possibly improved reading in one of the other manuscripts.

The original discovery was made in Karlsruhe Augiensis 106, dating from the tenth century, containing a good copy of one of the interpolated versions of the second book of the *Institutiones*. Mynors quoted Bischoff to the effect that the script is typical of northern France. The other principal copy is Reims 975, another tenth-century copy of the same interpolated version of the second book of the *Institutiones*, where, however, only the last paragraph of the *Ordo generis*, pertaining to Cassiodorus himself, has been preserved; it has not been formally collated with the other copy, but Cappuyns reported one variant reading of significance that it contains.[3] Finally, it has been

---

1. Hermann Usener, *Anecdoton Holderi* (1877).

2. I have seen editions in the prefaces to Mommsen's editions of Jordanes and of the *Variae;* in C. Cipolla, *Memorie della Reale Accademia delle Scienze di Torino,* Ser. 2, 43(1893), 99–134; in J. J. van den Besselaar, *Cassiodorus Senator en zijn Variae* (1945), 206 (where he makes certain unfortunate silent emendations that only serve to obscure important points); and at the beginning of Fridh's introduction to his edition of the *Variae.*

3. The MSS are described by Mynors in the introduction to his edition of the *Inst.,* pp. xxxii–xxxiii. Cappuyns' discussion of the *Ordo generis* with his suggested readings occurs in *DHGE,* 11(1949), 1367–1368.

reported that certain later manuscripts with connections to Reichenau transmit the paragraph dealing with Symmachus; one manuscript even conflates the *Ordo generis* paragraph with a narrative of the martyrdom of Boethius and Symmachus.[4]

Because any substantive emendations involve decisions about the dating of the text and the chronology of Cassiodorus' career, I will give the text of the fragment following the manuscript as closely as possible, giving in my text only the unanimously accepted corrections (with readings of Aug. 106 in the apparatus). A commentary on the various difficulties follows.

1. Text

Excerpta ex libello Cassiodori Senatoris
monachi servi dei ex patricio, ex consule
ordinario quaestore et magistro officiorum,
quem scripsit ad Rufium Petronium Nicomachum
5   ex consule ordinario patricium et magistrum
officiorum. ordo generis Cassiodororum: qui
scriptores extiterint ex eorum progenie vel
†ex quibus eruditis†.

    Symmachus patricius et consul ordinarius,
10   vir philosophus, qui antiqui Catonis fuit
novellus imitator, sed virtutes veterum
sanctissima religione transcendit. dixit
sententiam pro allecticiis in senatu, parentesque
suos imitatus historiam quoque Romanam septem
15   libris edidit.

    Boethius dignitatibus summis excelluit.
utraque lingua peritissimus orator fuit. qui
regem Theodorichum in senatu pro consulatu
filiorum luculenta oratione laudavit. scripsit
20   librum de sancta trinitate et capita quaedam

---

4. G. Schepss, *Neues Archiv*, 11(1886), 123–140. One such manuscript is St. Gall 845, cited in P. Courcelle, *La Consolation de Philosophie dans la tradition littéraire* (1967), 275. Others are Einsiedeln 179 and Metz 377; readings from all three are cited in the edition given by Cipolla, *op cit.*, 133–134; the only one of interest (but undoubtedly only a scribal correction) is "imitatur" for "imitatus" in line 14 (in Einsiedeln and Metz, but not St. Gall).

dogmatica et librum contra Nestorium. condidit
et carmen bucolicum. sed in opere artis logicae
id est dialecticae transferendo ac mathematicis
disciplinis talis fuit ut antiquos auctores aut
25   aequiperaret aut vinceret.
        Cassiodorus Senator vir eruditissimus et multis
dignitatibus pollens. iuvenis adeo, dum patris
Cassiodori patricii et praefecti praetorii
consiliarius fieret et laudes Theodorichi regis
30   Gothorum facundissime recitasset, ab eo quaestor
est factus, patricius et consul ordinarius,
postmodum dehinc magister officiorum; et
†praefuisset† formulas dictionum, quas in duodecim
libris ordinavit et Variarum titulum superposuit.
35   scripsit praecipiente Theodoricho rege historiam
Gothicam, originem eorum et loca mores XII
libris annuntians.

1 *Excepta* (et Mommsen); *casiodori*   2 *& cōs*
5 *& cons ordinarium*   6 *offociorū; casiodorūq*
13 *proalecticiis*   16 *Botius*   20 *cap̄*
22 *bocholicum; loicae*   24 *fuit* (bis scriptum,
priore loco erasum)   25 *eq. perar&*
28 *praecorii* (apud Usener), *praecarii* (apud Fridh)
29 *consilianus fier& laudes*   32 *offociorum* (corr.
a manu prima)   36 *& loca mores in libris* (et Mommsen)

2. Commentary

2–3. *monachi servi . . . officiorum.* The original text of the
work from which this is excerpted dates, at the latest, from the
years at Constantinople. It is therefore to be assumed that the
first sentence is the work of a later copyist, identifying what he
is about to excerpt. Mommsen deleted these two lines, as
though the rest of the sentence could be Cassiodorus' own
words.

2. *ex patricio.* This is not formally correct; the patriciate was
an honorary title held for life.

4–5. *Rufium Petronium Nicomachum ex consule.* Usener stigmatized this phrase for omitting the usual late Roman designator of rank (in this case, *V.I.* for *Vir Illustris*); but it is significant that such designators are omitted for all the figures of this fragment. A monastic copyist (implied by the mention of monasticity in line 2) might easily omit them.

8. †*ex quibus eruditis*†. Usener replaced *quibus* with *civibus;* Mommsen began (in the preface to his edition of Jordanes) with *vel qui eruditi;* in his edition of the *Variae* he allowed the manuscript reading to stand, voicing a suspicion that some verb like *profecerint* had dropped out after *eruditis.* Mynors, quoted by Momigliano, *PBA,* 41(1955), 231, offered *claruerit* after *eruditis,* with an understood subject like *genus* or *progenies.* Finally, Cappuyns, in his discussion of the *Ordo generis* cited above, offered the simplest emendation: *eruditi sunt* (but he probably should have said *sint*). The point at issue is a vital one, unfortunately, for a clear reading of the text would make it clear just what relationship Cassiodorus was claiming existed between himself and the two figures described. On balance, the most obvious readings of the text seem to downgrade the probability of strict blood or marriage relationship between Cassiodorus and the others; but the whole gist of the document as preserved seems to be to list individuals who *are* related to the Cassiodori. Since, further, the fragment preserved is only an excerpt from some presumably longer work, the difficulties presented are insoluble; we can only balance probabilities and possibilities. (And recall that the title, *Ordo generis Cassiodororum,* does not go back demonstrably further than the excerptor, who may have misunderstood the purport of the work himself.)

11. *imitator.* Note that the same idea is repeated fifteen words later, 14 *imitatus.*

13–14. *parentesque suos imitatus.* An allusion to the *Annales* of Virius Nicomachus Flavianus (A.D. c. 334–394), recorded in *CIL* 6.1783 (cf. J. Matthews, *Western Aristocracies and Imperial Court, A.D. 364–425* [1975], 231).

16–25. This is, of course, the text that radically increased the difficulty of arguing that Boethius the Christian was not the same individual as Boethius the philosopher (cf. especially V.

Schurr, *Die Trinitätslehre des Boethius im Lichte der "skythischen Kontroversen"* [1935]). But note that no mention of the *Consolatio philosophiae* is made. (The *carmen bucolicum* probably refers to the earlier literary activity mentioned in the first lines of the *Consolatio*.)

28. Notice that the usual formula *praefectus praetorio* is here altered by the substitution of the genitive *praetorii* (restored by Usener). Again a monastic scribe unaccustomed to the terminology of chanceries is indicated.

29. The *et* is another of Usener's restorations, and a likely one. Note here and in line 26 the superlatives applied to Cassiodorus in this paragraph; the description of the putative author of the fragment is every bit as impersonal and eulogistic as those of the other two subjects.

31. *patricius.* If we knew when Cassiodorus received this title, whether early in life like Boethius or late like his own father, it would help to date the *Ordo generis*.

33. †*praefuisset*†. Usener was happy to delete everything from *et* (end of line 32) through *superposuit* (line 34). Mommsen emended *praefuisset* to run "praefectus praetorio. suggessit formulas...." B. Hasenstab, *Studien zur Variensammlung des Cassiodorus Senator* (1883), 3, suggested "praefectus praetorio fuit et formulas dictionum in duodecim libris...." Fridh gives "praefectus praetorio. composuit et formulas...." He does not seem to know, however, the suggestion made by Cappuyns, who apparently found in Reims 975 the single word *praefectus* already in the text for *praefuisset*; but Cappuyns' report of the reading (*DHGE*, 11[1949], 1368) is clumsily presented in such a way as to make only further hash of an already jumbled sentence.

The only unavoidable problem with the text is the at least unclassical use of *praefuisset*, which (1) does not ordinarily take the accusative direct object, and (2) is in the subjunctive in an apparently independent clause where we would expect the indicative.

A hitherto unnoticed solution runs this way: In the first lines of the *Ordo generis*, Cassiodorus' *cursus* is only carried as far as his tenure as *magister officiorum*. In the last paragraph the only justification for seeing an allusion to the period of his prefecture lies in the relative clause beginning "quas in duodecim libris" (referring to the *Variae* and thus to the end of the prefecture) and in the appearance on the same part of the page of the letters *praef-* in *praefuisset*. If we assume, however, that the simplest reading of the evidence is the correct one, namely that the text before us dates in its original form to some time towards the end of Cassiodorus' term as *magister officiorum* (or at least to before his appointment as prefect), then the words put in Athalaric's mouth in *Var.* 9.25.7–8 take on considerable significance: "Erat solus ad universa sufficiens: ipsum dictatio publica, ipsum consilia nostra poscebant, et labore huius actum est, ne laboraret imperium. Repperimus eum quidem magistrum, sed implevit nobis quaestoris officium. . . ." This is documentary evidence for the view, canvassed at length and generally approved in Chapter 1 above, that the documents in *Var.* 5–10 from after Cassiodorus' formal term as quaestor were things written above and beyond the call of duty, that Cassiodorus' proficiency as a ghostwriter was so remarkable that he was called upon to perform what were technically quaestorial functions long after he had risen higher in the ranks. In that regard his superintendence of the preparation of the *formulae dictionum* might well be a matter of remark and a sign of the regard in which he was held by his superiors.

In that light, *praefuisset* is not so bad a reading after all. The first difficulty mentioned above can be overcome by concluding either that the Latinity of the author or scribe of our text had weakened to the point of accepting an accusative direct object after forms of *praesum* (on analogy from *praeficio*?) or that some other verb is intended for this site (and that would be related to the mistaken subjunctive) or that, indeed, *formulas* has assimilated the *-as* ending from *quas* after having originally been in fact *formulis*. The second difficulty, the subjunctive, is easier to resolve. In the first place, it seems to echo the earlier subjunctives in the paragraph, especially *recitasset* three lines earlier; and second, if the text originally contained a verb from a different root that the scribe was mistakenly attempting to correct, the incorrect form given here could echo as well the shape of the original word. What such another verb might be, I am not sure, but I note that it could as easily have begun with *pro-* as with *prae-*. (But might not the simplest emendation of all, to *praefuit formulis,* yet be the best?)

With all this out of the way, Cappuyns' new reading of *praefectus* for *praefuisset* merits treatment along with the relative clause beginning *quas in duodecim libris.* If we assume an initial date for this work of c. 527–533, it is clear that the actual excerpt represented here comes from a later period, probably (as other indications have shown) from some time in Cassiodorus' monastic career. Thus the clause describing the *Variae* would be the interpolation, obviously suggested by the pre-existing mention of the *formulae dictionum.* As for the altered *praefectus,* perhaps the scribe of Reims 975 was simply quicker (by a millennium or so) to emend than Hasenstab, Mommsen, or Fridh.

A final note on the date of the making of the excerpt: as indicated in Chapter 6 above, following A. van de Vyver, *Rev. Ben.,* 53(1941), 59–88, the interpolated versions of the second book of the *Institutiones* with which this fragment survives derive from the earliest edition of the complete *Institutiones* prepared in 562. Apparently a copy of at least the second book had left the Vivarium before Cassiodorus could make his own later revisions on it, thus probably in Cassiodorus' own lifetime; if that assumption is true, then the *Ordo generis* may well have been placed on the manuscript which left the Vivarium to identify the author of the *Institutiones.* But we cannot be certain that this did not take place until after Cassiodorus' death.

36. *loca mores XII libris.* Usener's restoration of this passage ("loca moresque XII libris") was dropped by Mommsen but partly accepted by Fridh (who drops the *-que* but retains the *XII*). I accept Fridh's reading; I am as sensitive as Usener to the greater elegance and correctness added by the enclitic *-que* but find no reason to depart from the manuscript. The *XII* seems to me an important correction for two reasons. First, Cassiodorus' passion for writing works in twelve books, chapters, etc.,

seems to me so strong that he would mention it here as well, especially if the reference just before to the *Variae* is by Cassiodorus himself. Even if that passage is an interpolation, however, the form of that interpolation may well have been further conditioned by the surrounding text, including this precise point. Second, the paragraph on Symmachus makes it very clear, at just this parallel point in the last line, that his Roman history contained seven books; the formality of the whole piece and the impersonality of the descriptions indicates to me that the parallelism would be carried out, even by an interpolating excerptor.

Appendix II

Cassiodorus' Name

THE Syrian origin of the name Cassiodorus was demonstrated by A. J. Letronne.[1] He identified the connection with the cult of Zeus Cassius, centered on Mount Cassius between Antioch and the sea, across the Orontes from Seleucia.[2] Fridh asserts that the cult continued at Seleucia and near Pelusium even into the sixth century.[3] It was attended by the apostate Julian while he resided at Antioch.[4] The name itself appears in Greek inscriptions three times (twice in the genitive, Κασιο-δώρου; once in the nominative, Κασσιοδώρος);[5] these inscriptions are the best evidence for the accepted spelling of the name ending in -rus. Scholars before Mommsen's edition of the *Variae* usually accepted Cassiodorius, for the oldest manuscript of any of Cassiodorus' works dates from the late sixth century and gives the genitive very clearly as *Cassiodorii*.[6] But that testimony is apparently only secondhand. M. J. Cappuyns had an ingenious solution to accommodate all the evidence, arguing that the name was Cassiodorus through three and a half generations known to us (MSS of the *Variae* are unanimous in using -rus), but that in his pedantic old age Cassiodorus Senator

1. *Mémoires de l'Académie des inscriptions et belles-lettres,* 19.1(1851), 63.
2. G. Downey, *Ancient Antioch* (1963), 30, 97, treats epochs in the cultivation of this deity.
3. *CCSL* 96, vi.
4. Julian, *Misopogon* 361D–362B; Ammianus 22.14.4–5.
5. *IG* 4.136a = *CIG* 2, add. 2322b(32); *IG* 3.2.2325; *CIG* 3.4466. All three are reprinted in J. J. van den Besselaar, *Cassiodorus Senator en zijn Variae* (1945), 205, but he erroneously gives the double sigma to all three.
6. MS Verona XXXIX(37); Lowe, *CLA* 4.496, dated the MS to late sixth century, northern Italy.

added the iota for etymological elegance.[7] This is a quaint thesis but altogether unlikely.

It should finally be noted that Cassiodorus' known relative at Constantinople, Heliodorus, bears a name ending in a similar -dorus.

7. M. J. Cappuyns, *DHGE,* 11(1949), 1350.

Appendix III

The Amals and Their Royal Kin

THE following table is based on a similar table by T. Hodgkin, corrected and supplemented with Mommsen's editions of the *Getica* and *Variae,* and with N. Wagner, *Getica* (1967), 51–56. I have throughout this work used forms of German names as faithful to the originals as Latin spelling allows, even where this results in slight variations from traditional English spellings.

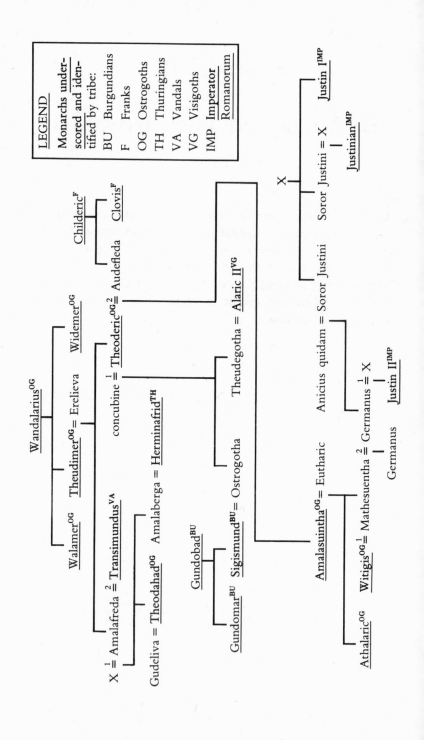

Appendix IV

Momigliano's Hypothesis

In an attractive article that has received wide attention, Arnaldo Momigliano has argued that Cassiodorus himself must have been involved in revising the *Gothic History* down to the marriage of Germanus and Mathesuentha in 550, else there would not be any emphasis on the connections of Germanus with the Anicii.[1] This is a seductive argument, but one for which there is in the end just too little support. First, we do not even know for sure whether Cassiodorus was claiming in the *Ordo generis* actual kinship with Boethius and Symmachus; second, we do not know that he thought of that relationship as going through the *gens Anicia*;[2] third, there is no other evidence for Cassiodorus' involvement in Gothic politics after his retirement from the praetorian prefecture over a decade before the putative date of a Cassiodorian final revision of the *Gothic History*; and finally, it has been shown that there is more than adequate room on the imperial family tree of Constantinople for an Anician parent for Germanus himself.[3]

1. A. Momigliano, *PBA,* 41(1955), 207–245, esp. 216–220; he has repeated many of these contentions, with no new evidence, in his *Secondo contributo alla storia degli studi classici* (1964), 231–253; and now treats his hypothesis as a proven fact, as at *Annali della Scuola Normale Superiore di Pisa, Classe di Lettere e Filosofia,* 3.2(1973), 397–418.

2. Neither in the *Ordo generis* nor in the *Variae* are Boethius and Symmachus called Anicii; the only Anicius called by that name anywhere in Cassiodorus' own works is one Maximus (*Var.* 10.11.2, 10.11.3), a luminary of low wattage, honored with a meaningless office on the occasion of his marriage to a minor Gothic princess: a union of Amal and Anicius about which Cassiodorus makes little fuss.

3. N. Wagner, *Getica* (1967), 51–56, provides a crucial demonstration of the possibility—which is all that is needed to offset Momigliano's contrary possibility; see the tentative genealogy given in the preceding appendix.

Cassiodorus' love of literary formalities should also be recalled, as one symptom of which the *Gothic History* is only one
of many Cassiodorian works composed in twelve units; it is
not likely that Cassiodorus would have broken up that formal
pattern with additions and deletions after the fact, for his literary fastidiousness and vanity were simply too great.[4] Finally, it
must be recalled that the purpose of the *Gothic History* was not
that of a modern historical narrative, to record events fully,
fairly, and accurately, it was merely another species of panegyric, an attempt to provide a legitimate, honorable history
of flattering antiquity for newcomers on the Roman scene.
If Cassiodorus is to be imagined as adding to the original work
as time went on, we must also assume that he gave up the
original purpose of the work entirely for a newer motive that is
nowhere acknowledged. Furthermore, the quality of the information recorded after Theoderic's death in the abridgement is
simply so sketchy (as opposed to the usual ancient practice of
becoming more prolix as the author approached his own times)
that it is far likelier that the last two chapters are a hasty addition, not an abridgment of a fuller chronicle.

4. The twelve-part pattern was broken by Jordanes, but see Chapter 2, note
24, above, for speculation on traces of the pattern. Note that the division of the
Edictum Athalarici (*Var.* 9.18) into twelve *capitula* is native with Cassiodorus
(*Var.* 9.19.2).

Bibliography

THIS list aspires to survey the specialist literature on Cassiodorus along with the most important related works found useful in the present study. Hence it is not a comprehensive register of all works cited in this study, but it does include for the sake of completeness a small number of items that I have not seen (mostly unobtainable in American libraries) and a somewhat larger number of items not noticed in the footnotes for reasons of space or pertinence. Editions of Cassiodorus' works listed earlier in the Abbreviations are not repeated here. Asterisks indicate special studies worthy of particular attention.

Aeberg, Nils. *Die Goten und Langobarden in Italien*. Uppsala, 1923. (Arbeten Utgifna med Understöd af Wilhelm Ekmans Universitetsfond, Uppsala, 29.)

Alberdingk Thijm, P. P. M. *Iets over M. A. Cassiodorus Senator en zijne eeuw*. Amsterdam, 1857.

Alfonsi, L. "Cassiodoro e le sue *Institutiones*." *Klearchos*, 6(1964), 6–20.

Altaner, Berthold. "Altlateinische Übersetzungen von Schriften des Athanasios von Alexandreia." *Byzantinische Zeitschrift*, 41(1941), 45–59.

———. "Beiträge zur Geschichte des altlateinischen Übersetzungen von Väterhandschriften." *Historisches Jahrbuch*, 61(1941), 208–226.

———. "Der Einfluss und das Fortleben der griechischen Literatur im Abendland vom Ende des 4. bis in die zweite Hälfte des 6. Jahrhunderts." *Theologische Revue*, 48(1952), 41–50.

Amatucci, Aurelio-Giuseppe. "D'un luogo di Cassiodoro che si riferisce al *De re rustica* di Columella." *Bollettino di filologia classica*, 2(1895–1896), 21–23.

Amelli, Ambrogio. *Cassiodoro e la Volgata*. Grottaferrata, 1917.

——. "Cassiodoro e San Benedetto." *Rivista storica benedettina*, 11(1920), 168–172.

Andersson, Theodore M. "Cassiodorus and the Gothic Legend of Ermanaric." *Euphorion*, 57(1963), 28–43.

Ashworth, Henry. "The Psalter Collects of Pseudo-Jerome and Cassiodorus." *Bulletin of the John Rylands Library*, 45(1962–1963), 287–304.

Aubert, Marcel. "L'église du monastère de Cassiodore, en Calabre." *Bulletin monumental*, 98(1939), 231–232; reprinted in *Revue archéologique*, 14(1939), 208.

Bacherler, Michael. "Cassiod. *inst. saec.* im Bambergensis und bei Garet-Migne." *Philologische Wochenschrift*, 42(1922), 1217–1223.

——. "Cassiodors Dichterkenntnis und Dichterzitate." *Bayerische Blätter für das Gymnasialschulwesen*, 59(1923), 215–219.

Baehrens, W. A. *Überlieferung und Textgeschichte der lateinisch erhaltenen Origeneshomilien zum Alten Testament*. Leipzig, 1916. (Texte und Untersuchungen, 42.1.)

Bardy, Gustave. "Cassiodore et la fin du monde ancienne." *Année theologique*, 6(1945), 383–425.

——. *L'église et les derniers Romains*. Paris, 1948.

——. "Les origines des écoles monastiques en Occident." *SE*, 5(1953), 86–104.

——. "Le souvenir de Josèphe chez les Pères." *Revue d'histoire ecclésiastique*, 43(1948), 179–191.

——. "Sur les anciennes traductions latines de saint Athanase." *Recherches de science religieuse*, 34(1947), 239–242.

Basabe, Enrique. "La conservación de los clásicos." *Helmantica*, 3(1952), 381–419.

Baudi di Vesme, Carlo. "Frammenti di orazioni panegiriche di Magno Aurelio Cassiodoro." *Memorie della Reale Accademia delle Scienze di Torino* (Scienze morali, storiche, e filologiche), Ser. 2, 8(1846), 169–212.

Beer, Rudolf. *Bermerkungen über den ältesten Handschriftenbestand des Klosters Bobbio*. (Anzeiger der kaiserlicher Akademie der

Wissenschaften zu Wien, philosophisch-historischen Klasse, 48[1911], Heft 11.)

Bergmüller, Ludwig. *Einige Bemerkungen zur Latinität des Jordanes.* Programm, Augsburg, 1903.

Berza, M. " *'Causidicus'* dans les textes latins du moyen âge." *Revue historique du sud-est européen,* 23(1946), 183–195.

Bessel, W. "Ueber *'defloratis prosperitatibus'* beim Cassiodor." *Forschungen zur Deutschen Geschichte,* 1(1862), 639–643.

Besselaar, Joseph J. van den. "Cassiodoro Senador e la cultura retórica de sua época." *Revista de Letras,* 1(1960), 11–52.

*————. *Cassiodorus Senator en zijn Variae: De Hoveling, De Diplomatieke Oorkonden der Variae, De Rhetor.* Nijmegen, 1945. (See the review by M. van den Hout, *AJP,* 69[1948], 233–235.)

————. *Cassiodorus Senator, Leven en Weerken van een Staatsman en Monnik uit de Zesde Eeuw.* Harlem-Amsterdam, n.d. [1950]. (For a general audience.)

Bianchi, Dante. "Note sui *Getica* di Giordane e le loro clausule." *Aevum,* 30(1956), 239–246.

Bieter, Frederic A. *The Syntax of the Cases and Prepositions in Cassiodorus' Historica Ecclesiastica Tripartita.* Washington, D.C., 1938. (*SMRL,* 6.)

Bischoff, Bernhard. "Vier angebliche Freunde Cassiodors." *Studien und Mitteilungen zur Geschichte des Benediktiner-Ordens und seiner Zweige,* 55(1937), 100–101.

————. "Wendepunkte in der Geschichte der lateinischen Exegese im Frühmittelalter." *SE,* 6(1954), 189–281. Reprinted in Bischoff's *Mittelalterliche Studien* (Stuttgart, 1967), 1.205–273.

Blatt, Franz. *The Latin Josephus.* Volume I: Introduction and Text, the *Antiquities:* Books I–V. Aarhus, 1958. (Acta Jutlandica: Aarsskrift for Aarhus Universitet, 30, 1; Humanistik Serie 44.) (See the important review by J. A. Willis, *JRS,* 51[1961], 272.)

————. "Remarques sur l'histoire des traductions latines." *Classica et Mediaevalia,* 1(1938), 217–242.

Blum, Hans. "Über den Codex Amiatinus und Cassiodors Bibliothek in Vivarium." *Zentralblatt für Bibliothekswesen*, 64(1950), 52–57.

Bradley, Dennis R. "The Composition of the *Getica*." *Eranos*, 64(1966), 67–79.

Bruyne, Donatien de. "Cassiodore et l'Amiatinus." *Rev. Ben.*, 39(1927), 261–266.

———. *Préfaces de la Bible latine*. Namur, 1920.

Bulhart, V. "Textkritisches VI." *Rev. Ben.*, 70(1960), 639–641.

———. "Zur *Historia Tripartita*." *ALMA*, 24(1953), 5–17.

Burns, Thomas S. *Transformations in Ostrogothic Social Structure*. Dissertation, University of Michigan, 1974. Abstract in *DA*, 35A.4355.

Bury, J. B. *History of the Later Roman Empire from the Death of Theodosius I to the Death of Justinian I*. Reprint, New York, 1958.

Cameron, Alan. "The End of the Ancient Universities." *Cahiers d'histoire mondiale*, 10(1967), 653–673.

Capelli, Luigi Mario. "I fonti delle '*Institutiones humanarum rerum*' di Cassiodoro." *Rendiconti del Reale Istituto Lombardo*, Ser. 2, 31(1898), 1549–1557.

Cappuyns, Maïeul J. "L'auteur de la *Regula Magistri*: Cassiodore." *RTAM*, 15(1948), 209–268.

*———. "Cassiodore." In M. Baudrillart et al., *DHGE*, 11(1949), 1349–1408. (The best short survey.)

Carcopino, Jérôme. *Souvenirs de sept ans, 1937–1944*. Paris, 1953.

Cazzaniga, Ignazio. "Spigolature critiche III: Osservazioni ad alcuni passi di Cassiodoro-Epifanio." *La Parola del Passato*, 11(1956), 110–115.

———. "Varia Graeco-Latina — III." *Rendiconti dell'Istituto Lombardo* (Classe di Lettere, Scienze morali e storiche), 75(1941–1942), 349–366.

Ceresa-Gastaldo, Aldo. "Contenuto e metodo dell' *Expositio psalmorum* di Cassiodoro." *Vetera Christianorum*, 5(1968), 61–71.

———. "Da Vivario a Roma: Appunti per la storia del codice Vaticano Latino 5704." *Giornale Italiano di Filologia*, 22.3(1970), 39–46.

————. "La tradizione virgiliana nell'esegesi biblica di Cassiodoro." *Rivista di Studi Classici,* 16(1968), 304–309.

Chapman, John. "Cassiodorus and the Echternach Gospels." *Rev. Ben.,* 28(1911), 283–295.

————. "The Codex Amiatinus and Cassiodorus." *Rev. Ben.,* 37(1925), 139–150; 39(1927), 12–32.

————. "The Codex Amiatinus Once More." *Rev. Ben.,* 40(1928), 130–134.

————. *Notes on the Early History of the Vulgate Gospels.* Oxford, 1908.

————. *Saint Benedict and the Sixth Century.* London, 1929.

Charlier, Célestin. "Cassiodore, Pélage et les Origines de la Vulgate Paulinienne." *Studiorum Paulinorum Congressus Internationalis Catholicus, 1961 (= Analecta Biblica,* 17–18), 2.461–470.

Chastagnol, André. *Le sénat romain sous le règne d'Odoacre: Recherches sur l'épigraphie du Colisée au Ve siècle.* Bonn, 1966. (*Antiquitas,* Reihe 3, Band 3.)

Chatelain, Émile. "Palimpsestes de Turin, IV. Fragments des Panégyriques de Cassiodore." *Revue de philologie,* n.s. 27(1903), 45–48.

Church, R. W. "Cassiodorus." *Miscellaneous Essays.* London, 1888.

Ciampi, Ignazio. *I Cassiodori nel V e nel VI secolo.* Rome, 1877.

Cipolla, Carlo. "Considerazioni sulle *Getica* di Jordanes e sulle loro relazioni colla *Historia Getarum* di Cassiodorio Senatore." *Memorie della Reale Accademia delle Scienze di Torino* (Classe di Scienze morali, storiche, e filologiche), Ser. 2, 43(1893), 99–134.

————. "Richerche di Scipione Maffei intorno alle testo delle *Variae* di Cassiodoro." *Rendiconti della Reale Accademia dei Lincei* (Classe di Scienze morali, storiche e filologiche), Ser. 5, 16(1907), 393–400.

Coens, Maurice. "Anciennes litanies de saints." *Analecta Bollandiana,* 59(1941), 272–298.

Corssen, P. "Die Bibeln des Cassiodorius und der Codex Amiatinus." *Jahrbücher für protestantische Theologie,* 9(1883), 619–633.

Courcelle, Pierre. "De la *Regula Magistri* au Corpus Vivarien des *'Chroniques.'* " *Revue des études anciennes,* 56(1954), 424–428.

———. "Histoire d'un brouillon cassiodorien." *Revue des études anciennes,* 44(1942), 65–86.

———. *Histoire littéraire des grandes invasions germaniques.* 3rd ed., Paris, 1964.

*———. *Late Latin Writers and Their Greek Sources.* Cambridge, Mass., 1969. (Translated by H. E. Wedeck from *Les lettres grecques en Occident de Macrobe à Cassiodore;* 2nd ed., Paris, 1948.)

———. "Nouvelles recherches sur le monastère de Cassiodore." *Actes du Vᵉ congrès international d'archéologie chrétienne* (Rome, 1957), 511–528.

*———. "Le site du monastère de Cassiodore." *MEFR,* 55(1938), 259–307.

Courtès, Jean-M. "Figures et tropes dans le Psautier de Cassiodore." *Revue des études latines,* 42(1964), 361–375.

Crocco, A. "Il *liber de anima* di Cassiodoro." *Sapienza,* 25(1972), 133–168.

*Curtius, Ernst Robert. *European Literature and the Latin Middle Ages.* New York, 1953. (Translated by W. R. Trask from *Europäische Literatur und lateinisches Mittelalter;* Bern, 1948.)

Dahn, Felix. "Ueber Cassiodor. Variarum XII.g.: Paschasio praefecto annonae Senator Praefectus Praetorio." *Bausteine: gesammelte kleine Schriften* (Berlin, 1880), 2.275–289.

Delahaye, Hippolyte. "Saint Cassiodore." *Mélanges Paul Fabre: Études d'histoire du moyen âge* (Paris, 1902), 40–50. Reprinted in his *Mélanges d'hagiographie grecque et latine* (Brussels, 1966 = Subsidia Hagiographica, 42).

Della Valle, Giuseppina. *"Moenia."* *Rendiconti della Accademia di Archeologia, Lettere e Belle Arti di Napoli,* n.s. 33(1958), 167–176.

Di Capua, F. "Cassiodoro. *De institutione divinarum litterarum."* *Bollettino di Filologia Classica,* 19(1912), 89–90.

———. "Una pseudoepistola di Cicerone *De numerosa oratione* e le irregolarità ritmiche del latino biblico." *Il Mondo Classico,* 9(1939), 211–218.

Dobiache-Rojdestvensky, Olga. "Le Codex Q.v.I.6–10 de la Bibliothèque Publique de Leningrad." *Speculum,* 5(1930), 21–48.

Donelin, Paul F. *Cassiodori Senatoris Complexiones in Epistulis Sancti Pauli.* Dissertation, the Catholic University of America, 1970. Abstract in *DA,* 32A.916.

Dubuat-Nancay, Louis Gabriel. "Abhandlung von dem Leben des Cassiodors." *Abhandlungen der Churfürstlich bayerischen Akademie der Wissenschaften zu München,* 1(1763), 79–96.

Duchesne, Louis. *L'église au VIe siècle.* Paris, 1925.

Duckett, Eleanor Shipley. *The Gateway to the Middle Ages.* New York, 1938.

Durand, V. *Quid scripserit de anima M.A. Cassiodorus.* Toulouse, 1851.

Eberle, Josef. "Dank an Cassiodor." *Lateinische Nächte* (Stuttgart, 1966), 186–202.

Ennis, Mary Gratia. *The Vocabulary of the Institutiones of Cassiodorus.* Washington, D.C., 1939. (*SMRL,* 9.)

Ensslin, Wilhelm. "Aus Theoderichs Kanzlei." *Würzburg Jahrbücher für die Altertumswissenschaft,* 2(1947), 75–85.

————. "Beweise der Romverbundenheit in Theoderichs des Grossen Aussen- und Innenpolitik." *Settimane,* 3(1956), 509–536.

————. *Des Symmachus Historia Romana als Quelle für Jordanes.* Munich, 1949. (Sitzungsberichte der bayerischen Akademie der Wissenschaften, philosophisch-historische Klasse, 1948, Heft 3.)

————. *Theoderich der Grosse.* Munich, 1947. (There is also a 2nd ed., 1959.)

Erdbrügger, Henricus. *Cassiodorus unde etymologias in Psalterii commentario prolatas petivisse putandus sit.* Dissertation, Jena, 1912.

Ermini, Filippo. "La scuola in Roma nel VI secolo." *Archivum Romanicum,* 18(1934), 143–154.

Esposito, Sebastiano. "Cassiodoro, la Bibbia e la Cultura Occidentale." *Divus Thomas,* 61(1958), 193–204.

Feuerlein, Fredericus. *Disputatio circularis de M. A. Cassiodoro.* Altdorf, 1686.

Fiebiger, Otto, and Ludwig Schmidt. *Inschriftensammlung zur Geschichte der Ostgermanen.* Vienna, 1917–1939. (Denkschriften der Akademie der Wissenschaften in Wien, philosophisch-historische Klasse, 60[1917], Abh. 3; 70 [1939], Abh. 3.)

Fischer, Bonifatius. "Bedae de titulis psalmorum liber." *Festschrift Bernhard Bischoff* (Stuttgart, 1971), 90–110.

———. "Bibelausgaben des frühen Mittelalters." *Settimane,* 10(1963), 519–600, with discussion on 703–704.

———. "Codex Amiatinus und Cassidor." *Biblische Zeitschrift,* n.F. 6(1962), 57–79.

Forstner, K. "Schriftfragmente des 8. und früheren 9. Jahrhunderts in Salzburger Bibliotheken." *Scriptorium,* 14(1960), 245–246.

Fortin, Ernest L. *Christianisme et culture philosophique au cinquième siècle: la querelle de l'âme humaine en Occident.* Paris, 1959.

Franceschini, Ezio. "La polemica sull'originalità della Regola di S. Benedetto." *Aevum,* 23(1949), 52–72.

———. "Regula Benedicti, Neoterici Magistri, Regula Magistri." *Liber Floridus: Festschrift Paul Lehmann* (St. Ottilien, 1950), 95–119.

Franz, Adolph M. *M. Aurelius Cassiodorius Senator. Ein Beitrag zur Geschichte der theologischen Literatur.* Breslau, 1872.

Frend, William Hugh Clifford. *The Rise of the Monophysite Movement.* Cambridge (England), 1972.

Freund, Walter. *Modernus und andere Zeitbegriffe des Mittelalters.* Köln and Graz, 1957. (Neue Münstersche Beiträge zur Geschichtsforschung, 4.)

Fridh, Åke J. *Contributions à la critique et à l'interprétation des Variae de Cassiodore.* Göteborg, 1968. (Acta Regiae Societatis Scientiarum et Litterarum Gothoburgensis, Humaniora 4.)

———. *Études critiques et syntaxiques sur les Variae de Cassiodore.* Göteborg, 1950. (Göteborgs Kungl. Vetenskaps- och Vitterhets-Samhälles Handlingar, 6. följden, Ser. A, 4:2.)

*——— .*Terminologie et formules dans les "*Variae*" de Cassiodore:

Études sur le développement du style administratif aux derniers siècles de l'antiquité. Stockholm, 1956. (Studia Graeca et Latina Gothoburgensia, 2.)

Friedrich, J. "Über den kontroversen Fragen im Leben des gotischen Geschichtsschreibers Jordanes." *Sitzungsberichte der philosophisch-philologischen und der historischen Klasse der königlichen bayerischen Akademie der Wissenschaften zu München*, 1907, 379–442.

Fuchs, Siegfried. *Kunst der Ostgotenzeit*. Berlin, 1944.

Galtier, P. "Pénitents et 'Convertis': de la pénitence latine à la pénitence celtique." *Revue d'histoire ecclésiastique*, 33.1(1937), 1–26, 277–305.

Gaudenzi, Augusto. *Gli Editti di Teodorico e di Atalarico e il Diritto Romano nel Regno degli Ostrogoti*. Bologna, 1884.

———. *L'Opera di Cassiodorio a Ravenna*. Bologna, 1887. (Reprinted from *Atti e Memorie della Reale Deputazione di Storia Patria per le Provincie di Romagna*, Ser. 3, 3[1885], 235–334; 4[1886], 426–463.)

Gissing, George R. *By the Ionian Sea*. London, 1901.

Gladysz, B. "Cassiodore et l'organisation des écoles médiévales." *Collectanea theologica*, 17(1936), 51–69.

Goetz, G. "Zu Varro *de lingua latina*." *Berliner Philologische Wochenschrift*, 30(1910), 1367–1368.

Gomoll, Heinz. "Zu Cassiodors Bibliothek und ihren Verhältnis zu Bobbio." *Zentralblatt für Bibliothekswesen*, 53(1936), 185–189.

Gorce, Denys. *La lectio divina des origines du cénobitisme à s. Benoît et Cassiodore*. Paris, 1925. (Not quite what the title promises, but useful nonetheless.)

Grimm, Jacob. "Über Iornandes und die Geten." *Kleinere Schriften* (Berlin, 1866), 3.171–235.

Gross, Julius. "Cassiodorus und die augustinische Erbsündenlehre." *Zeitschrift für Kirchengeschichte*, 69(1958), 299–308.

Hägg, Emil. *Linköpingshandskriften af Cassiodorus' Variae*. Göteborg, 1911.

Hagendahl, Harald. *La prose métrique d'Arnobe. Contributions à la connaissance de la prose littéraire de l'Empire*. Göteborg, 1937.

(Göteborgs Högskolas Årsskrift, 42[1936], 1.) (Covers a wide range of authors.)

*Hahner, Ursula. *Cassiodors Psalmenkommentar: Sprachliche Untersuchungen.* Munich, 1973. (Münchener Beiträge zur Mediävistik und Renaissance-Forschung, 13.) (Technical in form, significant in substance.)

Halporn, James W. "*Ecclesiam adunare* in Cassiodorus." *RTAM,* 28(1961), 333–334.

————. "The Manuscripts of Cassiodorus' *De Anima.*" *Traditio,* 15(1959), 385–387.

Hammer, Jacob. "Cassiodorus, the Saviour of Western Civilization." *Bulletin of the Polish Institute of Arts and Sciences in America,* 3(1944–1945), 369–384.

Hansen, Günther. "Einige Corrigenda zur neuen Cassiodor-Ausgabe." *Theologische Literaturzeitung,* 80(1955), 123–124.

Hanslik, Rudolf. "Epiphanius Scholasticus oder Cassiodor? Zur *historia ecclesiastica tripartita.*" *Philologus,* 115(1971), 107–113.

Hasenstab, B. *De codicibus Cassiodori Variarum Italis.* Munich, 1879.

————. *Studien zur Variensammlung des Cassiodorus Senator.* Programm, Munich, 1883.

Haussleiter, Johannes. "*Contropatio.*" *Archiv für lateinische Lexicographie und Grammatik,* 14(1906), 360.

Heerklotz, Alexander Theodor. *Die Variae des Cassiodorus Senator als kulturgeschichtliche Quelle.* Dissertation, Heidelberg, 1926.

Helbling, L. *Vom Adel des Menschen.* Einsiedeln, 1965. (Sigillum, 26.) (Translation of the *De anima.*)

Hodgkin, Thomas. *Italy and Her Invaders.* Volumes 3 and 4. Oxford, 1885.

*————. *The Letters of Cassiodorus.* London, 1886. (Abridged translation of the *Variae* with introduction and notes.)

Hörle, G. H. *Frühmittelalterliche Mönchs- und Klerikerbildung in Italien.* Freiburg im Breisgau, 1914.

Hofinger, Max. *Cassiodors und Tertullians De Anima.* Dissertation, Vienna, 1970.

Hofmeister, Adolf. "Zur Überlieferung von Cassiodors *Variae.*" *Historische Vierteljahrschrift,* 26(1931), 13–46.

Hoppenbrouwers, H. "*Conversatio:* une étude semasiologique." *Graecitas et Latinitas Christianorum Primaeva,* Supplementa, Fasciculus 1 (Nijmegen, 1964), 47–95.

Houghton, Grace L. *Cassiodorus and Manuscript Illumination at Vivarium.* Dissertation, State University of New York at Binghamton, 1975. Abstract in *DA,* 36A.1136.

Hubrecht, A. V. M. "Cassiodorus Senator en het Monasterium Vivariense." *Hermeneus,* 30(1959), 130–133.

Jacob, Walter. *Die handschriftliche Überlieferung der sogenannten Historia tripartita des Epiphanius-Cassiodor* (ed. R. Hanslik). Berlin, 1954. (Texte und Untersuchungen, Bd. 59 = Ser. 5, Bd. 4.)

Jacopi, G. "Sarcofago (forse di Cassiodoro?) con iscrizioni graffite scoperto a S. Martino di Copanello, sul Golfo di Squillace." ΠΕΠΡΑΓΜΕΝΑ ΤΟΥ Θ′ ΔΙΕΘΝΟΥΣ ΒΥΖΑΝΤΙΝΟΛΟΓΙΚΟΥ ΣΥΝΕΔΡΙΟΥ (Athens, 1955), 1.201–205.

Jäger, A. "Cassiodorus." *Pharus,* 18(1927), 401–417.

Janne, Henri. "Un contresens de Cassiodore: les 'furets' du *Contra Apion.*" *Byzantion,* 11(1936), 225–227.

Janson, Tore. *Latin Prose Prefaces.* Stockholm, 1964. (Studia Latina Stockholmensia, 13.)

Jaspert, B. "*Regula Magistri, Regula Benedicti.* Bibliographie ihrer Erforschung, 1938–1970." *Subsidia Monastica,* 1(1971), 129–171.

Jones, A. H. M. "The Constitutional Position of Odoacer and Theoderic." *JRS,* 52(1962), 126–130; reprinted in his *The Roman Economy* (Oxford, 1974), 365–374.

Jones, Leslie Webber. *Cassiodorus Senator. An Introduction to Divine and Human Readings.* New York, 1946. (A translation of the *Institutiones,* with an introduction and notes whose indebtedness to earlier scholarship should have been more candidly documented.)

———. "Further Notes Concerning Cassiodorus' Influence on Mediaeval Culture." *Speculum,* 22(1947), 254–256.

———. "The Influence of Cassiodorus on the Mediaeval Culture." *Speculum*, 20(1945), 433–442.

———. "Notes on the Style and Vocabulary of Cassiodorus' *Institutiones*." *Classical Philology*, 40(1945), 24–31.

Jungmann, J. A. "Die Abwehr des germanischen Arianismus und der Umbruch der religiösen Kultur im frühen Mittelalter." *Zeitschrift für katholische Theologie*, 69(1947), 36–99.

Kahrstedt, U. "Kloster und Gebeine des Cassiodorus." *Mitteilungen des Deutschen Archäologischen Instituts (Römische Abteilung)*, 66(1959), 204–208.

Kappelmacher, Alfred. "Columella und Palladius bei Cassiodor." *Wiener Studien*, 39(1917), 176–179.

Klauser, Theodor. "Vivarium." *Robert Boehringer: Eine Freundesgabe* (Tübingen, 1957), 337–344.

Knaack, G. "Cassiod. *var*. III.51." *Hermes*, 25(1890), 82–90.

*Knowles, David, "The *Regula Magistri* and the *Rule* of St. Benedict." *Great Historical Enterprises: Problems in Monastic History* (London, 1963), 135–195.

Kremmer, Martin. *De catalogis heurematum*. Dissertation, Leipzig, 1890.

Laistner, M. L. W. "The Mediaeval Organ and a Cassiodorus Glossary Among the Spurious Works of Bede." *Speculum*, 5(1930), 217–221.

———. *Thought and Letters in Western Europe, 500–900 A.D.* 2nd ed. Ithaca, N.Y., 1957.

———. "The Value and Influence of Cassiodorus' Ecclesiastical History." *Harvard Theological Review*, 41(1948), 51–67; reprinted in his *The Intellectual Heritage of the Early Middle Ages* (Ithaca, N.Y., 1957), 22–40.

Lamma, Paolo. "Cultura e vita in Cassiodoro." *Studium*, 43(1947), 234–241.

Lanciani, Rodolfo. *The Destruction of Ancient Rome*. New York, 1899.

Lauterborn, Robert. "Die *Clusurae Augustanae* des Kassiodor als gotische Grenzsperre am Alpenrhein." *Germania*, 10(1926), 63–67.

Lecce, M. "La vita economica dell'Italia durante la dominazione dei Goti nelle *Variae* di Cassiodoro." *Economia e Storia,* 3(1956), 354–408.

Lechler, G. *Die Erlasse Theoderichs in Cassiodors Varien, Buch I–V.* Programm, Heilbronn, 1888.

Leclercq, Henri. "Cassiodore." *DACL,* 2(1910), 2357–2365.

———. "Vivarium." *DACL,* 15(1953), 3133–3140.

Leclercq, Jean. *The Love of Learning and the Desire for God.* Translated by C. Misrahi. New York, 1961.

Lécrivain, Charles. "Remarques sur les formules du *curator* et du *defensor civitatis* dans Cassiodore." *MEFR,* 4(1884), 133–138.

Lehmann, Paul. "Cassiodorstudien." *Philologus,* 71(1912), 278–299; 72(1913), 503–517; 73(1914), 253–273; 74(1918), 351–358; reprinted in his *Erforschung des Mittelalters* (Stuttgart, 1959), 2.38–108.

Lejay, Paul. "Bobbio et la bibliothèque de Cassiodore." *Bulletin d'ancienne littérature et d'archéologie chrétiennes,* 3(1913), 259–265.

Lenormant, François. *La Grande-Grèce: paysages et histoire.* Paris, 1881–1884.

Leroy-Molinghen, Alice. "De quelques traductions latines littérales ou fautives." *Latomus,* 4(1940–1945), 35–39.

Letronne, Antoine Jean. "Mémoire sur l'utilité qu'on peut retirer de l'étude des noms propres grecs pour l'histoire et l'archéologie." *Mémoires de l'Académie des inscriptions et belles-lettres,* 19.1(1851), 1–139.

Löffler, G. A. *Der Psalmenkommentar des M. Aur. Cassiodor Senator. Die exegetische Bildung des Verfassers und sein Psalmentext.* Freiburg im Breisgau, 1920.

Löwe, Heinz. "Cassiodor." *Romanische Forschungen,* 60(1947), 420–446; reprinted in his *Von Cassiodor zu Dante* (1973).

Loewe, Raphael. "The Medieval History of the Latin Vulgate." *Cambridge History of the Bible* (Cambridge [England], 1966–1969), 2.102–154.

Lohr, M. "Kasjodora klaztor 'Vivarium.'" *Studia Warminskie,* 2(1965), 371–387.

Lowe, Elias Avery. *Codices Latini Antiquiores.* Oxford, 1934–

1971. (See the review of volume 4 by H. Bloch, *Speculum*, 25[1950], 277–287.)

―――. "An Uncial (Palimpsest) Manuscript of Mutianus in the Collection of A. Chester Beatty." *JThS*, 29(1927), 29–33; reprinted in his *Palaeographical Papers, 1907–1965* (Oxford, 1972), 1.233–238.

Lubac, Henri de. *Exégèse Médiévale: les quatre sens de l'écriture*. Paris, 1959–1964.

Lucchesi, E. "Note sur un lieu de Cassiodore faisant allusion aux sept livres d'Ambroise sur les Patriarches." *Vigiliae Christianae*, 30(1976), 307–309.

Ludwig, Günter. *Cassiodor: Über den Ursprung der abendländischen Schule*. Frankfurt-am-Main, 1967.

Lundström, Sven. "*Insertus* statt *insitus*." *ALMA*, 27(1957), 231–234.

―――. "Sprachliche Bemerkungen zur *Historia Tripartita* des Cassiodorus." *ALMA*, 23(1953), 19–34.

―――. *Übersetzungstechnische Untersuchungen auf dem Gebiete der christlichen Latinität*. Lund, 1955. (Lunds Universitets Årsskrift, Ny Följd, 1. Audelningen, Bd. 51, 3.)

―――. *Zur Historia Tripartita des Cassiodor*. Lund, 1952. (Lunds Universitets Årsskrift, Ny Följd, 1. Audelningen, Bd. 49, 1.)

Lusito, N. "Giudizio di Cassiodoro sulla scuola romana del suo tempo." *Euphrosyne*, 6(1973–1974), 155–161.

McGuire, Martin R. P. "The Decline of the Knowledge of Greek in the West from c. 150 to the Death of Cassiodorus." *Classical Folia*, 13.2(1959), 3–25.

MacMullen, Ramsay. "Roman Bureaucratese." *Traditio*, 18(1962), 364–378.

Mair, John R. S. "A Note on Cassiodorus and the Seven Liberal Arts." *JThS*, 26(1975), 419–421.

Manitius, Max. *Handschriften antiker Autoren im mittelalterlichen Bibliothekskatalogen*. Leipzig, 1935. (*Zentralblatt für Bibliothekswesen*, Beiheft 67.)

Marcello, Alessandro. "I vimini flessibili nella lettera di Cassiodoro ai Tribuni Maritimi." *Atti del'Istituto Veneto di Sci-*

enze, Lettere ed Arti (Classe di scienze morali e lettere), 122(1963–1964), 543–549.

Marrou, Henri-Irénée. "Autour de la bibliothèque du pape Agapit." *MEFR*, 48(1931), 124–169.

———. "*Doctrina* et *Disciplina* dans la langue des pères de l'église." *ALMA*, 9(1934), 5–25.

———. *A History of Education in Antiquity.* Translated by G. Lamb. New York, 1964.

———. "La technique de l'édition à l'époque patristique." *Vigiliae Christianae*, 3(1949), 217–224.

Masai, F. "Cassiodore peut-il être l'auteur de la *Regula Magistri?*" *Scriptorium*, 2(1948), 292–296.

Mercati, G. "*Fastucium.*" *Biblica*, 29(1948), 282–283.

Merton, Thomas. *A Prayer of Cassiodorus.* Worcester (England), 1967. (Translation of an excerpt from the *De anima*, with introductory essay.)

Michon, Étienne. "Rapport sur les travaux de l'École Française de Rome durant l'année 1935–1936." *Comptes-rendus de l'Académie des inscriptions et belles-lettres*, 1937, 207–224.

Mierow, Charles C. *Jordanes: The Gothic History.* Princeton, 1915. (Translation of the *Getica*, with introduction.)

Milde, W. *Der Bibliothekskatalog des Klosters Murbach aus dem 9. Jahrhundert. Ausgabe und Untersuchung von Beziehungen zu Cassiodors Institutiones.* Heidelberg, 1968. (*Euphorion*, Beiheft 4.)

Milkau, F. "Zu Cassiodorus." *Von Büchern und Bibliotheken: Festschrift A. Kuhnert* (Berlin, 1928), 38–44.

Minasi, G. *Cassiodoro Senatore nato a Squillace in Calabria nel quinto secolo. Ricerche storico-critiche.* Naples, 1895.

Mohrmann, Christine. "À propos des collectes du psautier." *Vigiliae Christianae*, 6(1952), 1–19; reprinted in her *Études sur le Latin des Chrétiens* (Rome, 1965), 3.245–263.

———. "*Regula Magistri*: À propos de l'édition diplomatique des mss. lat. 12205 et 12634 de Paris." *Vigiliae Christianae*, 8(1954), 239–251; reprinted in her *Études sur le Latin des Chrétiens* (Rome, 1965), 3.399–411.

Momigliano, Arnaldo. "La caduta senza rumore di un impero

nel 476 d.C." *Annali della Scuola Normale Superiore di Pisa, Classe di Lettere e Filosofia,* 3.2(1973), 397–418.

———. "Cassiodorus and Italian Culture of His Time." *PBA,* 41(1955), 207–245; reprinted in his *Secondo contributo alla storia degli studi classici* (Rome, 1964), 191–229; and in his *Studies in Historiography* (London, 1966), 181–210.

———. "Gli Anicii e la storiografia latina del VI sec. d.C." *Secondo contributo alla storia degli studi classici* (Rome, 1964), 231–253.

*Mommsen, Theodor. "Ostgotische Studien." *Gesammelte Schriften* (Berlin, 1910), 6.362–484; originally in *Neues Archiv,* 14(1889), 225–249, 453–544; 15(1890), 181–186.

Moore, Clifford Herschel. "The Oxyrhynchus Epitome of Livy in Relation to Obsequens and Cassiodorus." *AJP,* 25(1904), 241–255.

Morin, Germain. "L'ordre des heures canoniales dans les monastères de Cassiodore." *Rev. Ben.,* 43(1931), 145–152.

———. "Une compilation antiarienne inédite sus le nom de S. Augustin issue de milieu de Cassiodore." *Rev. Ben.,* 31(1914–1919), 237–243.

Mortet, Victor. "Notes sur le texte des *Institutions* de Cassiodore d'après divers manuscrits." *Revue de philologie,* 24(1900), 103–118, 272–281; 27(1903), 65–78, 139–150, 279–287.

Nickstadt, Helmut F. A. *De digressionibus quibus in Variis usus est Cassiodorus.* Dissertation, Marburg, 1921.

Ogilvy, J. D. A. *Books Known to the English, 597–1066.* Cambridge, Mass., 1967.

Olleris, Alexandre. *Cassiodore: Conservateur des livres de l'antiquité latine.* Paris, 1841.

Paschali, G. J. *Untersuchungen zu Cassiodors Institutiones.* Dissertation, Marburg, 1947.

Pfeilschrifter, Georg. *Der Ostgotenkönig Theoderich der Grosse und die katholische Kirche.* Münster, 1896. (Kirchengeschichtliche Studien, 3).

Picotti, Giovan Battista. "Osservazioni su alcuni punti della politica religiosa di Teoderico." *Settimane,* 3(1956), 173–226.

————. "Il *Patricius* nell'ultima età imperiale e nei primi regni barbarici d'Italia." *Archivio storico italiano,* Ser. 7, 9(1928), 3–80.

Piétri, Charles. "Le sénat, le peuple chrétien, et les partis du cirque sous le pape Symmaque (498–514)." *MEFR,* 78(1966), 122–139.

Pluta, Alfons. "Ergänzende Bemerkungen zur Verbindung eines *ut* mit einem Imperativ." *Wiener Studien,* n.F. 2(1968), 218–224.

Punzi, A. G. *L'Italia del secolo VI nelle Variae di Cassiodoro.* Aquila, 1927.

Quacquarelli, A. "L'Epembasi in Cassiodoro (Exp. in Ps.)." *Vetera Christianorum,* 1(1964), 27–33.

Rand, Edward Kennard. *Founders of the Middle Ages.* Cambridge, Mass., 1929.

————. "The New Cassiodorus." *Speculum,* 13(1938), 443–447.

Ranke, Leopold von. "Jordanes." *Weltgeschichte* (Leipzig, 1883), 4.2.313–327.

Reeve, M. D. "Seven Notes." *Classical Review,* 20(1970), 134–136.

Reifferscheid, A. "Mittheilungen aus Handschriften." *Rheinisches Museum,* 23(1868), 127–146.

————. "Die römischen Bibliotheken." *Sitzungsberichte der kaiserliche Akademie der Wissenschaften zu Wien,* 56(1867), 441–556.

*Riché, Pierre. *Éducation et culture dans l'occident barbare, vi^e–viiie siècles.* Paris, 1962. (Patristica Sorbonensia, 4.) (English translation published Columbia, S.C., 1976.)

Riz, J. *De praepositionum in Cassiodori Variis orationumque reliquiis vi atque usu.* Dissertation, Innsbruck, 1920.

Rohlfs, Gerhard. *Griechen und Romanen in Unteritalien.* Geneva, 1924. (Biblioteca dell' *Archivium Romanicum,* ser. 2, vol. 7.)

Rougé, Jean. "Sur un mot de Cassiodore: *Exculcatoriae—Sculcatoriae–Sulcatoriae.*" *Latomus,* 21(1962), 384–390.

*Ruggini, Lellia. *Economia e società nell' "Italia Annonaria": Rapporti fra agricoltura e commercio dal IV al VI secolo d.C.* Milan, 1961. (Fondazione Guglielmo Castelli, Collana, 30).

Russo, F. "Tradizione umanistica in Calabria da Cassiodoro a Telesio." *Archivo storico per la Calabria e la Lucania,* 24(1955), 309–336.

Saint-Marthe, F. D. de. *La vie de Cassiodore.* Paris, 1695.

Salmon, Pierre. *Les "tituli psalmorum" des manuscrits latines.* Rome, 1959. (Collectanea Biblica Latina, XII.)

Salvioli, Giuseppe. "L'Italia agricola nelle lettere di Cassiodoro." *Studi di storia napoletano in onore di Michelangelo Schipa* (Naples, 1926), 1–4.

Schaedel, Ludwig. *Plinius der Jüngere und Cassiodorius Senator.* Darmstadt, 1887.

Schepss, G. "Geschichtliches aus Boethiushandschriften." *Neues Archiv,* 11(1886), 123–140.

Schirren, C. *De ratione quae inter Iordanem et Cassiodorum intercedat commentatio.* Dorpat, 1858.

*Schlieben, Reinhard. *Cassiodors Psalmenexegese. Eine Analyse ihrer Methoden als Beitrag zur Untersuchung der Geschichte der Bibelauslegung der Kirchenväter und der Verbindung christlicher Theologie mit antiker Schulwissenschaft.* Dissertation, Tübingen, 1970.

————. *Christliche Theologie und Philologie in der Spätantike: Die schulwissenschaftliche Methoden der Psalmenexegese Cassiodors.* Berlin, 1974. (Arbeiten zur Kirchengeschichte, 46.) (Abridged version of the dissertation listed above.)

Schmauch, J. *Die eschatalogischen Gedankengänge Cassiodors.* Munich, 1958.

Schmidt, K. W. *Quaestiones de musicis scriptoribus romanis imprimis de Cassiodoro et Isidoro.* Giessen, 1899.

Schmidt, Ludwig. "Cassiodor und Theoderich." *Historisches Jahrbuch,* 47(1927), 727–729.

Schneider, Artur. "Die Erkenntnislehre bei Beginn der Scholastik." *Philosophisches Jahrbuch der Görres-Gesellschaft,* 34(1921), 225–264, 339–369.

Schneider, Fedor. *Rom und Romgedanke im Mittelalter.* Munich, 1926.

*Schubert, Hans von. *Das älteste germanische Christentum oder der sogen. "Arianismus" der Germanen.* Tübingen, 1909.

*Schurr, Viktor. *Die Trinitätslehre des Boethius im Lichte der "skythischen Kontroversen."* Paderborn, 1935. (Forschungen zur christlichen Literatur- und Dogmengeschichte, 18.1.) (Fundamental for the ecclesiastical politics of the Ostrogothic period.)

Schuster, I. "Come finì la biblioteca di Cassiodoro." *La scuola cattolica,* 70(1942), 409–414.

Schwartz, Eduard. *Zu Cassiodor und Prokop.* Munich, 1939. (Sitzungsberichte der bayerischen Akademie der Wissenschaften, philosophisch-historische Abteilung, 1939, Heft 2.)

Siegmund, Albert. *Überlieferung der griechischen christlichen Literatur in der lateinischen Kirche bis zum zwölften Jahrhundert.* Munich, 1949. (Abhandlungen der bayerischen Benediktiner-Akademie, 5.)

Simon, Manfred. "Zur Abhängigkeit spätrömischer Enzyklopädien der *artes liberales* von Varros *Disciplinarum libri.*" *Philologus,* 110(1966), 88–101.

Sinnigen, William G. "Administrative Shifts of Competence Under Theodoric." *Traditio,* 21(1965), 465–467.

Skahill, Bernard Henry. *The Syntax of the Variae of Cassiodorus.* Washington, D.C., 1934. (*SMRL,* 3.)

Slaughter, Gertrude. *Calabria: The First Italy.* Madison, Wisc., 1939.

Soraci, R. *Aspetti di storia economica italiana nell' età di Cassiodoro.* Catania, 1974.

Souter, Alexander. "Cassiodorus's Copy of Eucherius's *Instructiones.*" *JThS,* 14(1913), 69–72.

―――. "Cassiodorus' Library at Vivarium: Some Additions." *JThS,* 41(1940), 46–47.

*―――. "The Commentary of Pelagius on the Epistles of Paul: The Problem of Its Restoration." *PBA,* 2(1905–1906), 409–439.

―――. *The Earliest Latin Commentaries on the Epistles of Saint Paul.* Oxford, 1927.

―――. *Pelagius's Expositions of Thirteen Epistles of St. Paul.* Cambridge (England), 1922–1931. (*Texts and Studies,* 9.)

———. "An Unrecorded Reference to the *Rules* of Tyconius." *JThS,* 11(1910), 152–153.

Sowa, G. *Die Musikanschauung Cassiodors.* Dissertation, Berlin, 1953.

Spengel, L. "Die Subscriptio der *Institutiones* des Cassiodorus im Bamberger codex." *Philologus,* 17(1861), 555–557.

Stangl, Theodor. "Cassiodoriana." *Blätter für das bayerische Gymnasialschulwesen,* 34(1899), 249–283, 545–591.

———. "Cassiodoriana II." *Wochenschrift für klassische Philologie,* 32(1915), 203–214, 228–240.

———. "Ein Fund zu Cassiodorius Senator." *Wochenschrift für klassische Philologie,* 1(1884), 315.

———. "Zu Cassiodorus Senator." *Sitzungsberichte der philosophisch-historischen Classe der kaiserlichen Akademie der Wissenschaften zu Wien,* 114(1887), 405–413.

Stanley, M. *The Monastery of Vivarium and Its Historical Importance.* Unpublished B. Litt. thesis, Oxford, 1939.

*Stein, Ernest. "Deux questeurs de Justinien et l'emploi des langues dans ses novelles." *BARB,* Ser. 5, 23(937), 365–390; reprinted in his *Opera Minora Selecta* (Amsterdam, 1968), 359–384.

*———. "La disparition du sénat de Rome à la fin du VIᵉ siècle." *BARB,* Ser. 5, 25(1939), 308–322; reprinted in his *Opera Minora Selecta,* 386–400.

Stettner, Thomas. "Cassiodors Enzyklopädie eine Quelle Isidors." *Philologus,* 82(1926), 241–242.

———. "Cassiodors Name." *Philologus,* 81(1925), 233–236.

Suelzer, Mary Josephine. *The Clausulae in Cassiodorus.* Washington, D.C., 1944. (*SMRL,* 17.)

Suerbaum, Werner. *Vom antiken zum frühmittelalterlichen Staatsbegriff.* Münster, 1961. (Orbis Antiquus, Heft 16/17.)

Sundwall, Johannes. *Abhandlungen zur Geschichte des ausgehenden Römertums.* Helsinki, 1919. (Öfversigt af Finska Vetenskaps-Societetens Förhandlingar, 70[1917–1918], Afd. B, No. 2; reprinted, New York, 1975.)

Svennung, J. "Zur Cassiodor und Iordanes." *Eranos,* 67(1969), 71–80.

Sybel, Hans von. *De fontibus libri Iordanis de origine actuque Getarum.* Berlin, 1838.

———. "Zu dem Aufsatz: Geten und Gothen." *Allgemeine Zeitschrift für Geschichte,* 7(1847), 288.

Szymanski, L. *The Syntax of the Nominal Forms of the Verb in the Historia Ecclesiastica Tripartita of Cassiodorus-Epiphanius, Book I.* Dissertation, Washington, D.C., 1955.

———. *The Translation Procedure of Epiphanius-Cassiodorus in the Historia Tripartita, Books I and II.* Washington, D.C., 1963. (*SMRL*, 24.)

Tannery, Paul. "*Var.,* III, 52." *Revue de philologie et de littératures anciennes et d'histoire,* n.s., 27(1903), 245–247.

Tanzi, Carlo. "Studio sulla cronologia dei libri '*Variarum*' di Cassiodorio Senatore." *Archeografo Triestino,* n.s., 13(1887), 1–36.

Tea, Eva. "I committenti d'arte a Ravenna nel V e VI secolo." *Studi in onore di Aristide Calderini e Roberto Paribeni* (Milan, 1956), 3.747–751.

Teutsch, L. "Cassiodorus Senator, Gründer der Klosterbibliothek von Vivarium. Ein Beitrag zur Würdigung seiner wissenschaftlich-bibliothekarischen Leistung." *Libri e Rivisti,* 9(1959), 215–239.

Thiele, Hans. "Cassiodor, seine Klostergründung Vivarium und sein Nachwirkung im Mittelalter." *Studien und Mitteilungen zur Geschichte des Benediktiner-Ordens und seiner Zweige,* 50(1932), 378–419.

Thorbecke, August. *Cassiodorus Senator. Ein Beitrag zur Geschichte der Völkerwanderung.* Heidelberg, 1867.

Titz, F. *Cassiodors Stellung zu Theoderich.* Programm, Gablonz a. N., 1901.

Toribios, Anastasio. "O 'Mestre' não pode ser Cassiodoro." *Mensageiro de S. Bento,* 19(1950), 123–126.

Trijia, C. *M.A.Cassiodoro di Calabria.* Rome, 1909.

Tross, Carl Ludwig. *In Cassiodori Variarum libros sex priores symbolae criticae.* Paris, 1853.

———. "Nachricht für den künftigen Bearbeiter der Variarum des Cassiodor." *Archiv,* 6(1838), 485–487.

*Usener, Hermann. *Anecdoton Holderi. Ein Beitrag zur Geschichte Roms in ostgothischer Zeit.* Bonn, 1877. (Festschrift zur Begrüssung der XXXII. Versammlung deutscher Philologen und Schulmänner zu Wiesbaden.)

Vaccari, A. "La Bibbia nell'ambiente di S. Benedetto." *Scritti di erudizione e di filologia* (Rome, 1952), 1.257–281.

———. "Cassiodoro e il pāsûq della Bibbia ebraica." *Biblica,* 40(1959), 309–321.

———. "Una definizione compagna." *Scritti di erudizione e di filologia* (Rome, 1952), 1.142.

Vaccari, Pietro. "Concetto ed ordinamento dello Stato in Italia sotto il governo dei Goti." *Settimane,* 3(1956), 585–594.

Vandenbroucke, François. "Saint Benoît, le Maître et Cassiodore." *RTAM,* 16(1949), 186–226.

———. "Sur les sources de la Règle bénédictine et de la *Regula Magistri.*" *Rev. Ben.,* 62(1952), 216–273.

Vanderhoven, H. "Regle du Maître, statistiques et manuscrits." *Scriptorium,* 3(1949), 246–254.

*van de Vyver, Andrè. "Cassiodore et son oeuvre." *Speculum,* 6(1931), 244–292. (Marks a considerable advance over all earlier work.)

———. "Les étapes de développement philosophique du haut moyen-âge." *Revue belge de philologie et d'histoire,* 8(1929), 425–452.

———. "Les *Institutiones* de Cassiodore et sa fondation à Vivarium." *Rev. Ben.,* 53(1941), 59–88.

Vega, Angel C. "El comentario al Cantar de los Cantares atribuido a Cassiodoro ¿es español?" *Ciudad de Dios,* 154(1942), 143–155.

Viarre, Simone. "À propos de l'origine égyptienne des arts libéraux: Alexandre Neckam et Cassiodore." *Arts Libéraux et Philosophie au Moyen Âge* (Paris, 1969), 583–591. (Proceedings of the Fourth International Congress on Medieval Philosophy, 1967.)

Vismara, Giulio. "Rinvio a fonti di diritto penale ostrogoto nelle *Variae* di Cassiodoro." *Studia et Documenta Historiae et Iuris,* 22(1956), 364–375.

―――. "Romani e Goti di fronte al diritto nel regno ostrogoto." *Settimane,* 3(1956), 409–463.

Vogüé, Adalbert de, ed. *Regula Magistri.* (With concordance by
J. Neufville et al.) Paris, 1964–1965. (*SC* 105–107.)

*Wagner, Norbert. *Getica. Untersuchungen zum Leben des Jor-
danes und zur frühen Geschichte der Goten.* Berlin, 1967.
(Quellen und Forschungen zur Sprach- und Kulturge-
schichte der germanischen Völker, n.F. 22.) (The best
work on Jordanes, not yet widely enough known.)

Weinberger, Wilhelm. "Handschriften von Vivarium." *Miscel-
lanea Francesco Ehrle, scritti di storia e paleografia* (Rome,
1924), 4.75–88.

Weissengruber, Franz. "Cassiodors Stellung innerhalb der
monastischen Profanbildung des Abendlandes." *Wiener
Studien,* 80(1967), 202–250.

―――. *Epiphanius Scholasticus als Übersetzer.* Vienna, 1972. (Sitzungsberichte der Österreichischen Akademie der Wissenschaften, philosophisch-historische Klasse, Bd. 283.)

―――. "Zu Cassiodors Wertung der Grammatik." *Wiener Studien,* 82(1969), 198–210.

Werner, Fritz. *Die Latinität der Getica des Jordanis.* Dissertation,
Halle, 1908.

Wes, M. A. *Das Ende des Kaisertums im Westen des Römischen
Reiches.* The Hague, 1967. (Archeologische Studiën van het
Nederlands Historisch Instituut te Rome, Deel 2.) (See the
review by P. R. L. Brown, *Rivista storica italiana,* 80[1968],
1018–1022; reprinted in his *Religion and Society in the Age of
Saint Augustine* [1972], 227–234.)

White, H. J. "The Codex Amiatinus and Its Birthplace" (with
an appendix by W. Sanday). In his *Studia Biblica* (Oxford,
1890), 2.273–324.

Wilamowitz-Möllendorff, Ulrich von. "Lesefrüchte." *Hermes,*
34(1899), 203–230.

Wilhelmsson, Ingrid. *Studien zu Mutianus dem Chrysostomusüber-
setzer.* Dissertation, Lund, 1944.

Winkelmann, Friedhelm. "Spätantike lateinische Übersetzungen christlicher griechischer Literatur." *Theologische Literaturzeitung,* 92(1967), 229–240.

Witty, Francis J. "Book Terms in the Vivarium Translations." *Classical Folia,* 28(1974), 62–82.

———. *Writing and the Book in Cassiodorus.* Dissertation, the Catholic University of America, 1967. Abstract in *DA,* 28A.2226.

Wölfflin, Eduard. "Zur Latinität des Jordanes." *Archiv für lateinische Lexicographie und Grammatik,* 11(1900), 361–368.

Wrede, Ferdinand. *Über die Sprache der Ostgoten in Italien.* Strassburg, 1891. (Quellen und Forschungen zur Sprach- und Culturgeschichte der germanischen Völker, Heft 68.)

Zahn, Theodor. "Ein Stück aus den *Institutiones divinarum litterarum* des M. Aurelius Cassiodorus." In his *Geschichte des Neutestamentlichen Kanons* (Erlangen, 1888–1890), 2.267–284.

Zeiller, Jacques. "Les églises ariennes de Rome à l'époque de la domination gothique." *MEFR,* 24(1904), 17–33.

———. "Étude sur l'arianisme en Italie à l'époque ostrogothique et à l'époque lombarde." *MEFR,* 25(1905), 127–146.

Zetzel, James E. G. *Latin Textual Criticism in Antiquity.* Dissertation, Harvard University, 1972. Abstract in *HSCP,* 78(1974), 284–287

Zimmer, Heinrich. *Pelagius in Irland.* Berlin, 1901. (See the important review by C. H. Turner, *JThS,* 4[1903], 132–141.)

Zimmermann, F. "Cassiodors Schrift *Über die Seele." Jahrbuch für Philosophie und spekulative Theologie,* 25(1911), 414–449.

Zimmermann, Odo John. *The Late Latin Vocabulary of the Variae of Cassiodorus, with special advertence to the technical terminology of administration.* Washington, D.C., 1944. (*SMRL,* 15.)

Index

Works by Cassiodorus are
alphabetized under the first word
of their Latin titles.

L.D.S.

Design	Hal Hershey
Composition	Typesetting Services of California
Lithography	Thomson-Shore
Binding	Thomson-Shore
Text	VIP Bembo
Display	Photo Typositor Solemnis
Paper	50lb. P & S Offset Vellum Natural